Excel

Revise in a Month

Year 5
NAPLAN*-style
Tests

PASCAL
PRESS

Alan Horsfield & Allyn Jones

Revised in 2020 for the NAPLAN Online tests

Reprinted 2020, 2021, 2022, 2023

ISBN 978 1 74125 208 8

Pascal Press
PO Box 250
Glebe NSW 2037
(02) 9198 1748
www.pascalpress.com.au

Publisher: Vivienne Joannou
Project editors: Fiona Sim, Mark Dixon and Rosemary Peers
Edited by Fiona Sim, Mark Dixon and Rosemary Peers
Answers checked by Peter Little, Dale Little, Elaine Horsfield and Carolyn Lain
Typeset by Precision Typesetting (Barbara Nilsson) and Grizzly Graphics (Leanne Richters)
Cover and page design by DiZign Pty Ltd
Printed by Vivar Printing/Green Giant Press

Reproduction and communication for educational purposes

Reproduction and communication for other purposes

Acknowledgements

Bowden, David and Dibly, Jenny, *Kites*, HBJ, Sydney, 1990
Broome, Eric, *Spooked*, HBJ, Sydney, 1990
Collinson, Rachael, *The Face on Mars*, HBJ, Sydney, 1990
Edwards, Hazel, *Show Off*, HBJ, Sydney, 1990
Horsfield, Alan, *Cadaver Dog*, Lothian Books, Melbourne, 2003
Horsfield, Alan, *The Rats of Wolfe Island*, Lothian Books, Melbourne, 2002
Horsfield, Elaine, 'Rain', unpublished
Horsfield, Elaine, 'Stray Dog', unpublished
Horsfield, Elaine, 'Washing the Car', from *Kids' Stuff*, Peranga Post Publishers, Peranga (Qld), 2005
Jones, Stephen, *What a Waste!*, HBJ, Sydney, 1990
Madsen, Chris and Cooke, Julie, *Unusual Pets*, Henderson Publishing Ltd, Woodbridge (England), 1992
O'Connor, Pamela, *The Incredible Experience of Megan Kingsley*, Sydney, 1990
Ruffles, John, 'As The Wind Blows', from *The Bondi View* Community Newspaper, vol. 4, issue 22, September 2004
Small, Mary, *Night of the Muttonbirds*, HBJ, Sydney, 1992

NAPLAN is a trademark of Australian Curriculum, Assessment and Reporting Authority (ACARA).

Disclaimer

Notice of liability

Contents

NAPLAN and NAPLAN Online

WHAT IS NAPLAN?

- NAPLAN stands for National Assessment Program—Literacy and Numeracy.
- It is conducted every year in March and the tests are taken by students in Years 3, 5, 7 and 9.
- The tests cover Literacy—Reading, Writing, Conventions of Language (spelling, grammar and punctuation)—and Numeracy.

WHAT IS NAPLAN ONLINE?

Introduction

- In the past all NAPLAN tests were paper tests.
- From 2022 all students have taken the NAPLAN tests online.
- This means students complete the NAPLAN tests on a computer or tablet.

Tailored test design

- With NAPLAN paper tests, all students in each year level took exactly the same tests.
- In the NAPLAN Online tests this isn't the case; instead, every student takes a tailor-made test based on their ability.
- Please visit the official ACARA site for a detailed explanation of the tailored test process used in NAPLAN Online and also for general information about the tests: https://nap.edu.au/online-assessment.
- These tailor-made tests mean broadly, therefore, that a student who is at a standard level of achievement takes a test mostly comprised of questions of a standard level; a student who is at an intermediate level of achievement takes a test mostly comprised of questions of an intermediate level; and a student who is at an advanced level of achievement takes a test mostly comprised of questions of an advanced level.

Different question types

- Because of the digital format, NAPLAN Online contains more question types than in the paper tests. In the paper tests there are only multiple-choice and short-answer question types. In NAPLAN Online, however, there are also other question types. For example, students might be asked to drag text across a screen, measure a figure with an online ruler or listen to an audio recording of a sentence and then spell a word they hear.
- Please refer to the next page to see some examples of these additional question types that are found in NAPLAN Online and how they compare to questions in this book. As you will see, the content tested is exactly the same but the questions are presented differently.

NAPLAN Online question types

Additional NAPLAN Online question types	Equivalent questions in this book
Matching shapes and statements Here are four angles. Match the angles with the type of angle. <table><tr><td>Right angle</td><td>Obtuse angle</td><td>Acute angle</td><td>Reflex angle</td></tr><tr><td></td><td></td><td></td><td></td></tr></table>	Here are four angles. Which angle is the obtuse angle? A B C D
Online ruler Parvati lays her eraser and her pencil next to each other. Use the online ruler to measure the length of the pencil. What is the length of the pencil? [ ] cm	Parvati lays her eraser and her pencil along her ruler. What is the length of the pencil? [ ] cm
Text entry We _____ the bell when we were a block from school. Click on the play button to listen to the missing word. ⏸ 🔊 ————●———— 0.08 / 0.09 Type the correct spelling of the word in the box.	Please ask your parent or teacher to read to you the spelling words on page 202. Write the correct spelling of each word in the box. <table><tr><th>Word</th><th>Example</th></tr><tr><td>26. heard</td><td>We heard the bell when we were a block from school.</td></tr></table>
Drag and drop Drag these events to show the order in which they happened in the text. Use the tab to read the text. 1 Kingy and the narrator set off across the lagoon in a boat. 2 3 4 5 Kingy and the narrator arrived at a village with thatched roofs. Kingy and the narrator waited by the road in the shade of a tree. Kingy and the narrator set off across the lagoon in a boat. The bus let passengers off at Buka Buka turn-off. A bus arrived in a cloud of dust.	Write the numbers 1 to 5 in the boxes to show the order of events in the text. [ ] Kingy and the narrator arrived at a village with thatched roofs. [ ] Kingy and the narrator waited by the road in the shade of a tree. [1] Kingy and the narrator set off across the lagoon in a boat. [ ] The bus let passengers off at Buka Buka turn-off. [ ] A bus arrived in a cloud of dust.

Maximise your results in NAPLAN Online

STEP 1: USE THIS BOOK

How *Excel* has updated this book to help you revise

Tailored test design

- We can't replicate the digital experience in book form and offer you tailored tests, but with this series we do provide Intermediate and Advanced NAPLAN Online–style Literacy and Numeracy tests

- This means that a student using these tests will be able to prepare with confidence for tests at different ability levels.

- This makes it excellent preparation for the tailored NAPLAN Online Literacy and Numeracy tests.

Remember the advantages of revising in book form

There are many benefits to a child revising using books for the online test:

- One of the most important benefits is that writing on paper will help your child retain information. It can be a very effective way to memorise. High-quality educational research shows that using a keyboard is not as good as note-taking for learning.

- Students will be able to prepare thoroughly for topic revision using books and then practise computer skills easily. They will only succeed with sound knowledge of topics; this requires study and focus. Students will not succeed in tests simply because they know how to answer questions digitally.

- Also, some students find it easier to concentrate when reading a page in a book than when reading on a screen.

- Furthermore it can be more convenient to use a book, especially when a child doesn't have ready access to a digital device.

- You can be confident that *Excel* books will help students acquire the topic knowledge they need, as we have over 30 years experience in helping students prepare for tests. All our writers are experienced educators.

STEP 2: PRACTISE ON *Excel Test Zone*

How *Excel Test Zone* can help you practise online

We recommend you go to www.exceltestzone.com.au and register for practice in NAPLAN Online–style tests once you have completed this book. The reasons include:

- for optimal performance in the NAPLAN Online tests we recommend students gain practice at completing online tests as well as completing revision in book form

- students should practise answering questions on a digital device to become confident with this process

- students will be able to practise tailored tests like those in NAPLAN Online, as well as other types of tests

- students will also be able to gain valuable practice in onscreen skills such as dragging and dropping answers, using an online ruler to measure figures and using an online protractor to measure angles.

Remember that *Excel Test Zone* has been helping students prepare for NAPLAN since 2009; in fact we had NAPLAN online questions even before NAPLAN tests went online!

We also have updated our website along with our book range to ensure your preparation for NAPLAN Online is 100% up to date.

About the NAPLAN tests and this book

ABOUT THE TESTS

Test results

- The test results are used by teachers as a diagnostic tool. The results provide students, parents and teachers with information that can be used to improve student learning.

- The student report provides information about what students know and can do in the areas of Reading, Writing, Conventions of Language (spelling, grammar and punctuation) and the various strands of Numeracy. It also provides information on how each student has performed in relation to other students in their year group and against the national average and the national minimum standard.

- NAPLAN tests are not aptitude or intelligence tests. They focus on what has been achieved, especially on the knowledge and skills taught in the syllabus. These are often called KLAs (key learning areas).

- Official tests are trialled on selected groups to test the reliability of the questions. The questions in this book are representative of questions that you can expect to find in an official test. They have been prepared by professionals who have an understanding of teaching and of testing procedures.

- The NAPLAN results present an objective view of student performance and form the basis from which schools can make informed educational decisions about further school learning programs.

- Because NAPLAN tests are national tests they provide authorities with sufficient information to track student educational development from primary to high school, or when transferring from one Australian school to another.

TYPES OF TESTS

- There are four different types of tests in Year 5 NAPLAN Online.
  1. The Numeracy test (50 minutes)
  2. The Conventions of Language test (45 minutes)
  3. The Reading test (50 minutes)
  4. The Writing test (42 minutes)
  Tests 2–4 form the Literacy component of the test.

- The Writing test is held first, followed by the Reading test, the Conventions of Language test and finally the Numeracy test.

USING THIS BOOK

- This book is designed to be used over four weeks, with weekly exercises in various aspects of literacy and numeracy.

- Each session gives students an opportunity to Test their Skills, revise Key Points and practise a Real Test on a specific aspect of the curriculum.

- In a month the student will have covered much of the material that could be included in a NAPLAN Online test.

- Finally there are two Sample Test Papers based on the content used in past Year 5 NAPLAN test papers.

- Because NAPLAN tests are timed tests, times have been suggested for completing the various units in this book.

Let's start to revise!

Week

1

This is what we cover this week:

Day 1 **Number and Algebra:** ◎ Whole numbers

◎ Addition and subtraction

◎ Multiplication and division

Day 2 **Spelling:** ◎ Making plurals from nouns

◎ Common misspellings

Grammar and punctuation: ◎ Types of sentences and articles

Day 3 **Reading:** ◎ Understanding narratives

◎ Understanding explanations

Day 4 **Writing:** ◎ Persuasive texts

◎ Narrative texts

Test Your Skills

NUMBER AND ALGEBRA
Whole numbers

Circle the correct answer.

TEST 1

1 What is the place value of 5 in 15 389?
A units (ones)   B tens
C hundreds   D thousands

2 Which number is 100 greater than 2034?
A 2035   B 2044
C 2134   D 3034

3 What counting number comes just before 2020?
A 1020   B 2009
C 2010   D 2019

4 What number is midway between 54 and 76?
A 64   B 65
C 66   D 67

5 Which of these numbers is an odd number?
A 1335   B 2050
C 5792   D 5100

6 What is 102 507 in words?
A one million, two thousand and seven
B one hundred and two thousand, five hundred and seven
C one hundred and two thousand and fifty seven
D one million, two thousand, five hundred and seven

7 Which statement is correct?
A 64 > 45   B 94 < 19
C 26 = 62   D 75 < 75

8 Round 1526 to the nearest thousand.
A 1   B 2
C 1000   D 2000

9 What is the fifth number after 2178?
A 9   B 2173
C 2183   D 2228

TEST 2

1 What is the value 5000 + 600 + 7?
A 5067   B 5607
C 50 607   D 50 006 007

2 How many factors has 12?
A 6   B 5
C 4   D 3

3 What year will it be in 20 years from 2006?
A 2020   B 2026
C 2226   D 2260

4 Which of the following numbers is closest to 60?
A 64   B 53
C 61   D 69

5 Round 1364 to the nearest hundred.
A 1360   B 1370
C 1300   D 1400

6 What is the difference between the **place value** and the **face value** of 5 in 3508?
A 0   B 45
C 495   D 2008

7 Which of these is larger than five hundred but less than three thousand?
A 390   B 480
C 1200   D 3001

8 When an odd and even number are added the answer will be
A odd.   B even.
C mostly even.   D unable to tell.

9 Which of the following is true?
A 3 > 7   B 270 < 208
C 84 > 92   D 102 < 110

☞ **Explanations on page 146**

Answers: 1D 2C 3D 4B 5A 6B 7A 8D 9C

Answers: 1B 2A 3B 4C 5D 6C 7C 8A 9D

Key Points

NUMBER AND ALGEBRA
Whole numbers

① Counting numbers are either **odd** or **even**. Even numbers end with 2, 4, 6, 8 or 0. Odd numbers end with 1, 3, 5, 7 or 9. All even numbers can be divided exactly by 2. **Digits** are the symbols (0 to 9) we use to write numerals. The numeral 23 508 is made up of five digits.

② Numbers can also be **prime** or **composite**. Prime numbers are those without factors except 1 and the number itself (e.g. $5 = 5 \times 1$). Composite numbers have more than two **factors** (e.g. $6 = 6 \times 1$ and 2×3). Factors are numbers that go evenly into a given number. 1, 2, 3 and 6 are factors of 6. The first prime numbers are 2, 3, 5, 7, 11. The first composite numbers are 4, 6, 8, 9, 10. 1 is considered neither prime nor composite.

③ **Zero** has a special place in our system because it is a place holder. In the number 306 the zero is a place holder for the tens.

④ Our number system is a **base ten system**. It is built up on tens: units, tens (10), ten × ten (100), ten × ten × ten (1000) and so on. Learn to read and write (in numbers and words) numbers to ten million.

⑤ **Expanded notation** is the writing of numerals in an expanded form using the base ten system. It shows the place value of each digit.
Example: $2568 = 2000 + 500 + 60 + 8$ or $(2 \times 1000) + (5 \times 100) + (6 \times 10) + 8$

⑥ **Rounding off** allows us to estimate answers. For numbers 1 to 4 round to the lower number. For numbers 5 to 9 round to the higher number. Let us look at **23 837**.
Rounding to the nearest 10: The unit (7) is closer to the next ten (40), so round up to 40 (23 840).
Rounding to the nearest 100: The ten (3) is closer to the previous ten (30), so round down to 800 (23 800).
Rounding to the nearest 1000: The hundred (8) is closer to the next thousand, so round up (24 000).

⑦ Each digit has a **face value**: for example, 5 (five) represents five units. The value of a digit depends on its **place** in a numeral. In 3847 the 7 has a place value of 7 units, 4 has a value of 4 tens (40), 8 has a place value of 8 hundreds (800), 3 has a place value of 3000.

⑧ **Even numbers**, when added, subtracted or multiplied, always produce an answer that is even. Two odd numbers added or subtracted have an even answer but when multiplied the product is odd.

⑨ **Ordinal numbers** are used to order things from first to last (e.g. first, 1st; second, 2nd; third, 3rd). The ordinal number for 30 is 30th.

⑩ To find the number **midway** between two numbers, add the two numbers and then divide by 2.
The number midway between 16 and 22 is 19: $(16 + 22) \div 2 = 19$.

⑪ **Signs you should know include** (>) greater than; (<) less than; (=) equals.
Example: 56 > (is greater than) 54;
56 < (is less than) 57

Real Test

NUMBER AND ALGEBRA
Whole numbers

20 MIN

Circle the correct answer.

1 What number is eight thousand three hundred and nine?

A 8309 **B** 8390
C 80 309 **D** 80 003 009

2 Five numbers are written on cards:

| 706 | 1021 | 499 | 1100 | 998 |

Arrange the cards from smallest to largest.

smallest | | | | | | largest

3 What number does the arrow point to?

52   60

A 61 **B** 62 **C** 64 **D** 65

4 Which of these numbers is a factor of 18? Select **all** the possible answers.

| 2 | 3 | 6 | 8 | 18 |
| A | B | C | D | E |

5 Which number is equal to 4007?

A four thousand seven hundred
B four thousand and seventy
C four thousand and seven
D forty thousand and seven

6 Which of these shows numbers that are written from smallest to largest?

A 34 287 541 89
B 541 34 89 287
C 34 541 287 89
D 34 89 287 541

7 The number 32 400 is the same as

A 3 × 10 000 + 2 × 1000 + 4 × 100
B 3 × 1000 + 2 × 100 + 4 × 10
C 3 × 100 + 2 × 10 + 4 × 1
D 3 × 10 000 + 2 × 1000 + 4 × 1

8 Frances wrote the number 5430. She removed the zero at the end of the number. The new number is

A ten times smaller than 5430.
B ten times larger than 5430.
C one hundred times smaller than 5430.
D one hundred times larger than 5430.

9 Which number is closest to 70?

A 7 **B** 64 **C** 69 **D** 73

10 The grid shows the number 100. Which number is represented by the shaded squares?

A 24 **B** 33
C 34 **D** 36

11 What is the place value of the underlined number? 2<u>3</u> 547

A 3 ten thousands **B** 3 thousands
C 3 hundreds **D** 3 tens

12 How many dots are in the display?

A 38 **B** 39
C 49 **D** 51

13 What number is in the middle of 12 and 18?

A 6 **B** 14 **C** 15 **D** 16

14 The students from 5P are standing in a line waiting to catch a bus to the swimming pool. Samuel is third in line and Bronson is seventh in line.

B

How many students are standing between Samuel and Bronson?

15 Which of the number sentences are true? Select **all** the possible answers.

A 25 > 9 **B** 18 < 16
C 303 > 330 **D** 8 < 11

16 Sophie used these cards to make a three-digit number.

| 5 | 3 | 0 | 2 | 9 | 7 |

What is the largest three-digit number she can make from the cards?

Write your answer in the box.

☞ **Answers and explanations on pages 146–147**

NUMBER AND ALGEBRA
Addition and subtraction

20 MIN

Circle the correct answer.

ADDITION

1 7 + 8 + 5 + 6 = ?
  A 25   B 26   C 27   D 28

2 Add   312
            323
            ———
  A 623   B 625   C 635   D 645

3 Add   252
            438
            ———
  A 680   B 690   C 710   D 790

4 What is the missing number in this addition?

  149
  □5
  ———
  204

  A 4   B 5
  C 6   D 7

5 Add   8300
             82
            ———
  A 7262   B 8272
  C 8372   D 8382

6 Add $25.38
            $9.80
            $7.07
            ———
  A $31.15   B $31.25
  C $41.15   D $42.25

7 37 + □ = 73
  A 36   B 44
  C 46   D 110

SUBTRACTION

1 25 − 8 − 5 − 2 = ?
  A 9   B 10   C 11   D 24

2 Subtract   794
                − 602
                ———
  A 82   B 102   C 182   D 192

3 Subtract   539
                − 47
                ———
  A 492   B 493   C 512   D 592

4 What is the missing number in this subtraction?

  256
  − 8□
  ———
  167

  A 1   B 3   C 5   D 9

5   486
       − 68
        ———
  A 318   B 418
  C 421   D 422

6 $52.08
      − $39.67
        ———
  A $12.41   B $12.42
  C $13.00   D $13.41

7 81 − □ = 47
  A 34   B 40
  C 44   D 46

☞ **Explanations on page 147**

Key Points

NUMBER AND ALGEBRA
Addition and subtraction

ADDITION

1 **Addition** is the joining of two or more numbers together. The addition sign is + (plus).

2 When **two or more numbers are added**, we get a **total**: 23 + 35 = 58. The total of 23 and 35 is 58. Another term is **sum**. The sum of 23 and 35 is 58.

3 **Additions can be written horizontally** (23 + 40 + 7 = 70) or **vertically**:

This vertical addition has two columns: units (ones) and tens. Often the plus sign is left off vertical addition.

$$\begin{array}{r} 51 \\ + \ 44 \\ \hline \end{array}$$

4 When **working vertical additions with more than one column**, start with the right-hand column (units) and then work to the left (tens, hundreds and so on).

5 **Regrouping** or **carrying** is needed if the total of a column is more than 9. If the total of any column is from 10 to 19, the units are written in the answer section and the ten (1) is 'carried' to the next column to be included in that total (number of tens).

$$\begin{array}{r} 26 \\ + \ 36 \\ \hline 62 \end{array}$$
(6 + 6 = 12, write the 2 in the units column and the 1 is added in with the tens: 3 + 2 + 1 = 6).

$$\begin{array}{r} 26 \\ 38 \\ + \ 19 \\ \hline 83 \end{array}$$
If the total is from 20 to 29 then a 2 is carried to the next column. (6 + 8 + 9 = 23, write the 3 in the units column and the 2 is added in with the tens: 1 + 3 + 2 + 2 carried from the units = 8).

The same process applies to totals from 30 to 39 except that a 3 is carried.

6 Beware of **ragged ends**. Ragged ends describe operations where numbers are of different lengths in the columns. Don't stray out of the column when finding a total.

7 In finding the **number required to give a specific total**, the best method is to use subtraction.
Example: 3 + ? = 8. Solution: 8 – 3 = 5

SUBTRACTION

1 **Subtraction** is 'taking away', or finding what is left. The subtraction sign is – (minus).

2 When a **number is subtracted from another** number you get the difference. The difference between 7 and 15 is 8 (15 – 7 = 8).

3 **Subtractions** can be written horizontally (24 – 10 = 14) or vertically:

This subtraction has two columns: units (ones) and tens. The minus sign is never left off vertical subtraction.

$$\begin{array}{r} 51 \\ - \ 44 \\ \hline \end{array}$$

4 When **subtracting vertical subtractions** with more than one column, always start with the right-hand column (units) and then work to the left (tens, hundreds and so on).

5 **Regrouping** or **decomposing** is used in subtraction. Look at this subtraction:

In the units column the 7 'cannot' be subtracted from the 3. To work the solution, the numbers are regrouped. 53 becomes 40 + 13 (= 53), and the subtraction becomes:

$$\begin{array}{r} 53 \\ - \ 27 \\ \hline \end{array}$$

$$\begin{array}{rr} 4 \text{ (tens)} & 13 \\ - \ 2 \text{ (tens)} & 7 \\ \hline \text{Answer} = 26 & \end{array}$$
13 – 7 = 6 and 4 – 2 = 2

This process can be worked through any or all columns of a subtraction.

6 **Ragged ends** must be avoided. See Addition, point 6 (opposite).

7 In **finding the number required to give a specific difference** there are two methods you can use.

Example 1: 13 – ? = 8

Solution: 13 – 8 = 5

Example 2: ? – 12 = 10

Solution: 12 + 10 = 22

Real Test

NUMBER AND ALGEBRA
Addition and subtraction

Circle the correct answer.

1 Natasha added these numbers:
4 8 2 6 1
What was Natasha's total?
A 18   **B** 21   **C** 23   **D** 31

2 Rael added half of 24 to twice 13. What number did Rael get?
A 12   **B** 26   **C** 38   **D** 50

3 45 + ☐ = 67

What is the missing number?
A 20   **B** 18   **C** 22   **D** 28

4 Joel wrote down these numbers.
28   76   21   53   68
He added the smallest number to the largest number. What was Joel's answer?
A 21   **B** 76   **C** 96   **D** 97

5 Sarah's teacher wrote the following on her whiteboard:
326 add 7 add 23. The answer is 356.
Sarah then had to find the answer to this question:
826 add 7 add 23. The answer is ____
What is Sarah's answer?
A 30   **B** 830   **C** 850   **D** 856

6 Brodie is 11 years old. His grandmother is 59 years older than him. How old is Brodie's grandmother?
A 48   **B** 60   **C** 70   **D** 80

7 Which number sentences give a total between 25 and 35? Select **all** possible answers..
A 6 + 6 + 6 + 6 + 6   **B** 7 + 7 + 7 + 7
C 8 + 8 + 8   **D** 9 + 9 + 9

8 The following sum has missing numbers replaced with X and Y. Which of the following has the correct values of X and Y?

$$\begin{array}{r} 6\,8\,4 \\ +\ 2\,5\,3 \\ \hline X\,3\,Y \end{array}$$

A X = 8, Y = 1   **B** X = 8, Y = 7
C X = 9, Y = 1   **D** X = 9, Y = 7

9 What number is 6 less than 20?
A 4   **B** 14   **C** 16   **D** 26

10 A packet of lollypops contains 24 lollypops. On Monday, Mrs Harrison rewarded 4 students with a lollypop each. On Tuesday she rewarded another 6 students with a lollypop each. How many lollypops remain in the packet?
A 8   **B** 10   **C** 14   **D** 34

11 Joanne bought a pair of jeans which cost $65. She paid with a $100 note. How much change will she receive?

Write the answer in the box: $ ☐

12
$$\begin{array}{r} 9\,5 \\ -\ 4\,2 \\ \hline \boxed{}\,3 \end{array}$$

Write the missing number in the box: ☐

13 Sasha is counting backwards by 19.
161, 142, 123, 104 …
Which of these will be a number in Sasha's pattern? Select **all** the possible answers.
95   85   66   65   64
A   **B**   **C**   **D**   **E**

14 What number is 24 less than 42?
A 18   **B** 22
C 28   **D** 66

15 What is the difference between 4 × 18 and 5 × 18?
A 4   **B** 5
C 18   **D** 19

16 Jasmine organised the family's DVD collection into three piles according to the rating of the DVD. Sixteen of the DVDs were rated G, forty-three were rated PG and the remainder rated M. If she had a total of eighty DVDs, how many were rated M?   ☐

☞ **Answers and explanations on pages 147-148**

Test Your Skills

NUMBER AND ALGEBRA
Multiplication and division

20 MIN

Circle the correct answer.

MULTIPLICATION

1 13 + 13 + 13 + 13 = ?
   A 4 × 13   B 4 + 13
   C 13²   D 13 × 13 × 2

2 Multiply: 23
                 × 7

   A 40   B 151   C 161   D 1214

3   205
      × 40

   A 802   B 820   C 1200   D 8200

4 What is the missing number in this multiplication?
       35
     ×
     ───
     210

   A 2   B 4   C 6   D 8

5   51
      × 3

   A 84   B 153   C 181   D 183

6 $25.38
      ×   4
      ─────
      $

   A $91.32   B $100.22
   C $104.42   D $101.52

7 What number should replace the □?
   12 × □ = 108
   A 8   B 9   C 11   D 12

8 7² = ?
   A 9   B 14   C 28   D 49

DIVISION

1 96 ÷ 6 = ?
   A 8   B 12   C 14   D 16

2 $\frac{360}{10}$ = ?

   A 18   B 36   C 72   D 350

3 Excluding 24, what are the two highest factors of 24?
   A 6 and 8   B 6 and 12
   C 8 and 16   D 8 and 12

4 7)2135 = ?

   A 35   B 36
   C 305   D 350

5 What is 656 divided by 8?
   A 70 r 6   B 80 r 6
   C 82   D 83

6 What is the remainder when 110 is divided by 9?
   A 2   B 3
   C 9   D 11

7 What is the missing number in this division?
       117 r1
   7)82□

   A 0   B 1
   C 3   D 6

8 $29.16 ÷ 6 = ?
   A $4.01   B $4.86
   C $4.71   D $40.86

9 What is the average of 5, 9 and 4?
   A 3   B 6
   C 9   D 15

☞ **Explanations on pages 148-149**

8   *Excel* Revise in a Month Year 5 NAPLAN*-style Tests

NUMBER AND ALGEBRA
Multiplication and division

MULTIPLICATION

1 **Multiplication** is repeated addition of the same number. The multiplication sign is × (sometimes called 'times'). Another term is **lots of**. 5 lots of 8 equals 40.

2 **When two or more numbers are multiplied** we get a **product**. The product of 3 and 9 is 27.

3 **Multiplications can be written horizontally** (6 × 9 = 54) or vertically:

104

× 5   (This number is called the **multiplier**.)

This multiplication has three columns: units (ones), tens and hundreds.

4 Learn your **basic multiplication facts**. This table should help.

×	1	2	3	4	5	6	7	8	9	10
1	1	2	3	4	5	6	7	8	9	10
2	2	4	6	8	10	12	14	16	18	20
3	3	6	9	12	15	18	21	24	27	30
4	4	8	12	16	20	24	28	32	36	40
5	5	10	15	20	25	30	35	40	45	50
6	6	12	18	24	30	36	42	48	54	60
7	7	14	21	28	35	42	49	56	63	70
8	8	16	24	32	40	48	56	64	72	80
9	9	18	27	36	45	54	63	72	81	90
10	10	20	30	40	50	60	70	80	90	100

To use the table you read across and down. *Example:* 6 × 5 = 30 (follow the coloured boxes)

5 When working **vertical multiplications** with more than one column, start with the right-hand column (units) and then work to the left (tens, hundreds and so on).

6 The same rules for **carrying** apply to multiplication as for addition.

7 When **zero** is multiplied by any number the product is always **zero**: 23 × 0 = 0

DIVISION

1 **Division** is repeated subtraction of the same number. The division sign is ÷ . Another term is **share** (e.g. share $6 between 3 girls).

2 When one number is divided by another number we get a **quotient**.
The quotient when 8 is divided by 2 is 4.

3 **Division** can be written several ways: 36 ÷ 9 or $3\overline{)36}$ or $5\overline{)25}$ or $\dfrac{54}{9}$

4 Use the **multiplication table** to learn basic division facts.   7 × 8 = 56 → 56 ÷ 8 = 7 and 56 ÷ 7 = 8

5 **Factors** (See Whole Numbers Key Point 2 on page 3):
The factors of 12 are 1, 2, 3, 4, 6 and 12.

6 There are **several methods** of working a **division problem**.
  a Using repeated subtraction:
    37 ÷ 11 = (37 − 11 − 11 − 11 = 4)
        = 3 (11s) r 4
  b Using knowledge of basic multiplication facts, start with the left-hand column (thousands) and then work to the right (hundreds, tens and units):

$3\overline{)6903}$ = 2301

(3 into 6 = 2, 3 into 9 = 3,
3 into 0 = 0 and 3 into 3 = 1.)

7 **Trading (or carrying)** is used in division.

$5\overline{)75}$ = 15 (5 into 7 = 1 with remainder of two;
the 2 (tens) with the 5 (units) = 25;
5 into 25 = 5; Answer = 15)
Trading can continue across several number places (thousands, hundreds, tens, units).

8 When **dividing (sharing) money** don't be too concerned about the cent point. Divide the amount to be divided as if the decimal point has no value BUT place it in directly above the decimal point in the operation or two places to the left from the right-hand end.

9 Multiplying a whole number by 100 means that we write two zeros on the end of the number.

10 When **zero** is divided by any number the quotient is always **zero**: $14\overline{)0}^{\,0}$

11 **Averages** are found by adding all the 'amounts' in the set and dividing by the number of 'amounts'.
The average of $4, $4 and $1 is $3 ($9 ÷ 3).

Real Test

NUMBER AND ALGEBRA
Multiplication and division

20 MIN

Circle the correct answer.

1

Each plate has 3 biscuits. What is the total number of biscuits?

Write your answer in the box:

2 At the circus were 2 elephants and 3 monkeys. Melanie counted the total number of legs. What was Melanie's total?
A 5   B 11   C 12   D 14

3 Aziz is 8 years old and his uncle is 7 times his age. How old is his uncle?
A 15   B 56   C 60   D 87

4 A bag contains 6 oranges and is on sale for $2. What is the largest number of oranges Rachael can purchase for $10?
A 5   B 20
C 25   D 30

6 oranges for $2

5 Sharma multiplied 35 by 100. What is his answer?
A 65   B 135
C 350   D 3500

6 Dots are organised in an array. How many dots are in the array?
A 13   B 35
C 48   D 64

7 What is the missing digit?

$$\begin{array}{r} \boxed{8}\,\boxed{7} \times \\ \boxed{4} \\ \hline \boxed{3}\,\boxed{}\,\boxed{8} \end{array}$$

A 2   B 3   C 4   D 5

8 5515 ÷ 5 = _____
What answer is this?
A 13   B 111
C 113   D 1103

9 Sophie arranges cards in 4 rows of 6 cards each. She collects up the cards, and then lays all the cards down again using 3 rows. How many cards are in each row?
A 6   B 8   C 2   D 18

10 Gautam multiplied a whole number by 2. Which of these could be his answer? Select **all** the possible answers.
A 310   B 485   C 11 372   D 2041

11 Grace's family received 19 Christmas cards last year. If she arranged them into groups of 6, how many cards will she have left over?
A 1   B 2   C 3   D 5

12 A pizza shop offered a deal of '6 before 6'. This meant that pizzas cost $6 if ordered before 6 pm. What is the largest number of pizzas Courtney could order for $20?
A 3   B 4   C 5   D 6

PIZZA
6 before 6

13 Ramaranjan wrote a four-digit number.

3	6	8	?

When he divided the number by 4 there was no remainder. Which of these could be the missing digit? Select **all** the possible answers.

0	2	4	6	8
A	B	C	D	E

14 What is the average of 2, 6 and 7?

Write your answer in the box:

15
$$6\overline{)4\,2\,6}\quad 7\triangle$$

What number replaces the triangle?

16 Frida's mother orders a dozen cupcakes for $60 for a party. What is the price of each cupcake?
$

☞ **Answers and explanations on page 149**

SPELLING
Making plurals from nouns

 With most spelling rules there are exceptions. English words have many different origins (e.g. 'café' comes from French and 'kindergarten' comes from German).

Key Points

❶ With most words, to make a plural (more than one) you simply add an 's'.
Examples: dollars, displays, paintings, teachers, elephants, stages

❷ To make plurals with words that end with a consonant + 'y', change the 'y' to 'i' and add 'es'.
Examples: try → tries, jelly → jellies, berry → berries, canary → canaries, pony → ponies

❸ To make plurals of words that end with 's', 'ss', 'x', 'zz', 'ch' and 'sh', add 'es'.
Examples: gas → gases, glass → glasses, box → boxes, buzz → buzzes, church → churches, bush → bushes

❹ For quite a few words ending in 'f' or 'fe', change the 'f' to a 'v' and add 'es' or 's'.
Examples: life → lives, shelf → shelves, hoof → hooves

❺ For quite a few words that end with a single 'o', add 'es'.
Examples: potato → potatoes, tomato → tomatoes, volcano → volcanoes
Note, however, there are quite a few common exceptions to this rule: radios, solos, trios.

❻ A few words have unusual spellings. You will just have to know them.
Examples: child → children, foot → feet, man → men, goose → geese, mouse → mice

❼ A few words refer simply to the substance's mass. *Examples:* water, rice, flour

❽ A few common words don't change at all. *Examples:* deer, fish, sheep, tuna

Test Your Skills

Learn the words below. A common method of learning and self-testing is the **LOOK, SAY, COVER, WRITE, CHECK** method. If you make any mistakes, you should rewrite the word three times correctly, immediately. In this way you will become familiar with the correct spelling. If the word is particularly troublesome, rewrite it several more times or keep a list of words that you can check regularly.

This week's theme word: SCHOOL

library	_____	libraries	_____
brush	_____	vacation	_____
brushes	_____	vacations	_____
match	_____	domino	_____
matches	_____	dominoes	_____
survey	_____	address	_____
surveys	_____	addresses	_____

Write any troublesome word three times: _____ _____

_____ _____ _____

Real Test

SPELLING
Common misspellings

Please ask your parent or teacher to read to you the spelling words on page 201.
Write the correct spelling of each word in the box.

1 We wrote _____ next to all the names.

2 Your shirt is made from a soft _____.

3 My father _____ his shoes each morning.

4 After _____ from the pen the pig crossed the road.

5 The _____ is working in the kitchen.

6 David hurt his _____ when he was tackled.

Each line has one word that is incorrect. Write the correct spelling of the underlined word in the box.

7 Two new <u>deputys</u> were hired by the police force.

8 Did you have <u>rasberry</u> topping on the ice cream?

9 The <u>lighouse</u> was visible from the bow of the ship.

10 The cruise ship disappeared over the <u>horizen</u>.

11 A steep sand <u>june</u> rose up behind the beach.

12 Dad has a small <u>woodden</u> rowboat he uses for fishing.

Read the text *Broome*.
Each line has a word that is incorrect. Write the correct spelling of the word in the box.

Broome

13 Broome is a famous perling town on the north coast

14 of Western Australia. Many years ago divers speant

15 hours trudgeing the ocean floor in heavy gear to collect

16 shells. They were not beng collected because of

17 their precious contends. Shells were used to make

18 buttons. Broome depented on the buttons industry!

☞ **Answers on page 150**

GRAMMAR AND PUNCTUATION
Types of sentences and articles

15 min

Key Points

1 All sentences start with a capital letter. There are four main types of sentences.

  a **Statements** end with a full stop. A simple statement contains one verb and makes sense on its own. *Example:* The dog <u>ran</u> across the road.

  More complex sentences can contain two or more verbs and two or more ideas.
Example The dog <u>ran</u> across the road when it <u>saw</u> the dogcatcher arrive.

  b **Questions** end with a question mark. Questions usually need answers.
Example: Where <u>are</u> you going? (Answer: I am going home.)

  c **Exclamations** end with an exclamation mark. Exclamation sentences are often quite short.
Example: <u>Look</u> at the strange bird!

  d **Commands** end with a full stop (unless they are particularly sharp; then use an exclamation mark). *Example:* <u>Bring</u> your work over here.

2 The small words 'a', 'an' and 'the' are called articles.

  a We use the word '**the**' before specific objects or people. It is called a **definite article** because it refers to a definite object or person.
Examples: Dad put his coat on <u>the sofa</u> in the study. (By this we mean that Dad put his coat on one special sofa, not any old sofa.)
<u>The 8:30 bus</u> is always on time. (In this sentence the writer is referring to one special bus at one special time, not just any bus.)

  b The word '**a**' is an **indefinite article**. It is used when you are referring **not** to a particular object or person, but to things in general.
Examples: Dad put his coat on <u>a chair</u> in the kitchen. (We are not told if it was a particular chair.)
<u>A bus</u> should come along soon. (In this sentence the writer is not referring to any particular bus—he doesn't know which one will come.)

  c The word '**an**' is also an **indefinite article**. It is used before words that start with vowels: <u>an umbrella</u>, <u>an ice-cream</u>, <u>an old</u> lady. It is also used with silent 'h': <u>an hour</u>
Example: Dianne took an apple from the bowl. (The writer means that Dianne took no particular apple from the bowl, she just took any apple in general.)

Test Your Skills

1 Put the correct stop in the brackets at the end of these sentences.

  a I've told you not to do that ( ) Don't you listen to what you have been told ( )
  b Jack isn't coming, is he ( )
  c Dad asked if I was going to see the match ( ) I told him I wasn't ( )
  d Watch it ( ) I don't need milk all over the new carpet ( )
  e Take your clothes to the laundry ( ) We have visitors within the hour ( )

2 Write 'a', 'an' or 'the' in the spaces.

Greg has _____ orange sports car with _____ black hood. His wife drives _____ old Toyota. Greg also has _____ Holden. It is one of _____ early models. He has _____ new Honda on order. _____ salesman said there was _____ month's wait. _____ Holden is old but it will still be his favourite.

Real Test

GRAMMAR AND PUNCTUATION
Types of sentences and articles

1 Which of the following correctly completes this sentence?

I have a pet dog and cat. Last night [_____] dog made a hole under the fence!

an	a	one	the	his
A	**B**	**C**	**D**	**E**

2 Which of the following correctly completes this sentence?

Gina felt [_____] today than she did yesterday.

gooder	best	better	more better
A	**B**	**C**	**D**

3 Which of the following correctly completes this sentence?

The baby [_____] all the time we were at the show!

wept	weeped	weep	weept
A	**B**	**C**	**D**

4 Which of the following correctly completes this sentence?

[_____] you listened to the instructions, you didn't make a mistake!

Yet	Because	However	Although
A	**B**	**C**	**D**

5 Which of the following correctly completes this sentence?

Harry and Charlie [_____] school before I arrived.

have left	had leaved	leave	had left
A	**B**	**C**	**D**

6 Which of the following correctly completes this sentence?

Your dog chased our cat across the garden and [_____] the busy street!

in	onto	through	inside
A	**B**	**C**	**D**

Read the text *Death Cap*. The text has some gaps. Choose the correct word to fill each gap.

Death Cap

A Death Cap is not for putting on your head.
It is a [_____] poisonous ground fungi

7

greatly	mostly	very	awfully
A	**B**	**C**	**D**

[_____] grows in shady woodlands. The

8

which	who	what	how
A	**B**	**C**	**D**

Death Cap [_____] a yellow cap

9

have	has	had	how
A	**B**	**C**	**D**

☞ **Answers and explanations on pages 150-151**

a white stem with a frilly, droopy

ring. ▨▨▨▨ eaten, the poison causes

great pain, even death. There is no ▨▨▨▨

10 and	or	but	nor
A	B	C	D
11 if	however	If	However
A	B	C	D
12 cure?	Cure.	cure	cure.
A	B	C	D

13 Read this sentence.

A group of tourists made their way towards Bondi to see the famous beach.

Write any nouns from the sentences in the boxes. Use as many boxes as you need.

14 Which sentence has the correct punctuation?
A Most days this week there were no westerly winds but monday was different.
B Most days this week there were no Westerly winds but Monday was different.
C Most Days this Week there were no westerly winds but Monday was different.
D Most days this week there were no westerly winds but Monday was different.

15 Which word or words are unnecessary in this sentence?

Heavy rain came at a time when the creek was a series of waterholes.

Heavy	at a time	the	series of
A	B	C	D

16 Which word correctly completes the sentence? Write your answer in the box.

Last night frogs were croaking and the dog [   ] barking.

17 Which sentence is correct?
A They selled their old car to pays for the new TV screen.
B They sold their old car to paid for the new TV screen.
C They selled their old car to pay for the new TV screen.
D They sold their old car to pay for the new TV screen.

18 Shade a bubble to show where the missing comma (,) should go.

Jessie had to buy new ⬆ shoes ⬆ bag ⬆ and books ⬆ after the sudden storm.
　　　　　　　　　　　　Ⓐ　　Ⓑ　Ⓒ　　　　Ⓓ

☞ **Answers and explanations on pages 150-151**

A narrative is a form of prose writing that tells a story. Its main purpose is to entertain.

Writers of narratives create experiences that are shared with the reader. To do this the writer uses literary techniques such as figurative language (similes and metaphors), variety in sentence length and type, variety in paragraph length and direct speech.

In many narratives, the **author** is the person who wrote the story. The **narrator** is the person (I) *in* the story who tells the story.

Read this extract from *The Rats of Wolfe Island* by Alan Horsfield and answer the questions. Circle the correct answer.

Cautiously I made my way across the open space to the cabin.

'Kingy! Kingy!' I called tentatively. 'Anyone home?' I wasn't feeling very original.

No reply.

It was a bad sign. Kingy rarely went too far from his lab and his all-consuming work.

I reached the back door. It was <u>ajar</u>. I listened for a moment, then called with more <u>gusto</u> than I felt, 'Hey Kingy, it's me. You can come out now. I'll come in and get you!'

No reply.

I pushed the door open. The place smelt musty and dirty.

When I stepped into the cabin it was obvious that Kingy hadn't been there for a while. There were dirty teacups on the sink. Papers had blown from the table and spread across the floor. There were rat droppings everywhere.

Suddenly I was worried that Kingy had got sick or had had an accident and left the island. This was immediately followed by a horrible, sinking feeling that maybe his body was lying in a decomposing heap nearby. I had a mad urge to get out of the place as soon as possible.

I realised there were no rat noises coming from the lab. The ache in my stomach got worse.

---

❶ This extract is most likely from
   A a historical novel.   B a mystery novel.   C a scientific report.   D a legend.

❷ What is meant when a door is described as being ajar?
   A It is locked.   B It is wide open.   C It is coming off its hinges.   D It is slightly open.

❸ Which **two** terms best describe the narrator's behaviour?
uneasy	annoyed	confident	daring	cautious
A	B	C	D	E

❹ What discovery upset the narrator most?
   A rat droppings on the floor   B the ache in his stomach
   C the absence of Kingy   D the smell inside the cabin

❺ It is most likely Kingy was on the island because he was working as a
   A sailor.   B scientist.   C writer.   D doctor.

❻ Which word could best replace the word 'gusto'?
   A anger   B pleasure   C frustration   D enthusiasm

☞ **Answers and explanations on page 151**

Real Test

Read this extract from *Spooked* by Eric Broome and answer the questions. Circle the correct answer.

'What's the time?' Gerry asked.

'It's 1:28 a.m,' said Henk.

'Gee! Don't you feel tired?'

'Not really,' said Henk casually. 'I've never slept in the same room as a spook before.'

Henk would not admit that he was too scared to close his eyes. If he kept talking, he might be able to stay awake until the sun came up.

The door rattled again. <u>The boys' scalps prickled.</u> Surely, something moved inside the wardrobe? The boys held their breath. Nothing happened.

A faint sigh <u>rustled</u> through the wardrobe doors. Henk's eyes were as big as ping-pong balls. He clapped his hands over his mouth. The doors rattled again.

The shape inside moved—the boys were sure it moved!

Henk jumped out of bed and grabbed his clothes from the floor. 'I'm not staying here,' he said. 'I believe you—it is a spook! I'm going!'

'Where?'

'Home.'

1 Where did the incident in the extract occur? Write your answer on the line.

_____

2 Henk's eyes are described as being as big as ping-pong balls to show that he was

    A excited.   **B** surprised .   **C** terrified.   **D** thrilled

3 Which word best describes why Henk rushed from the room?

    A fear   **B** annoyance   **C** impatience   **D** disappointment

4 What made the boys' scalps prickle?

    A movement in the wardrobe   **B** a faint sigh

    C the sun coming up   **D** the rattling of doors

5 Henk kept talking because he was

    A feeling excited.   **B** trying to keep Gerry awake.

    C finishing a ghost story.   **D** trying to stay awake.

6 Which word is closest in meaning to the word 'rustled'?

    A rattled   **B** crackled   **C** whispered   **D** crunched

7 Which statement is correct?

    A The boys were trying to go to sleep.

    B Gerry was woken up by a noise in the wardrobe.

    C The boys knew there might be a spook in the wardrobe.

    D The incident in the passage took place as the sun came up.

☞ **Answers and explanations on page 152**

Real Test

READING
Understanding narratives

10 MIN

Read this extract from *Cadaver Dog* by Alan Horsfield and answer the questions. Circle the correct answer.

A wave of loneliness swept over Shane as soon as his father drove off. He knew no one at Ironbark Ridge. The bush looked uninviting. His father had taken the mobile phone to work and he had no contact with the real world.

The radio in the caravan was on batteries until his father returned home to hook the car's power up to the van. Batteries didn't last forever.

The last shop he had seen was kilometres away. It was no more than a bush garage and a grocery store sitting at one of the small crossroads they had passed on their way to the new farm. He couldn't remember the last person he had seen about his age, until he remembered the girl with the pram.

No one to talk to. Well, there was the girl with the pram, he thought with a <u>wry</u> smile.

And he wasn't the type to sit down and read all day. He wasn't sure how long his few Christmas present books might have to last. He was not really in a reading mood.

He wandered around the van hoping he might be distracted by some exciting discovery.

No such luck, but then he remembered the overgrown track that disappeared into the bush behind the van.

Picking up a stick, he made an instant decision to follow the track and do some bush exploring.

1 Why did Shane wander around the caravan?
   A He was bored.
   B He was looking for a stick.
   C He was expecting his father.
   D He was about to start reading.

2 Which term best describes Ironbark Ridge, the setting for the extract?
   A sheltered   **B** isolated   **C** barren   **D** exciting

3 Which word could best replace the word 'wry'?
   A crooked   **B** scornful   **C** delightful   **D** cheeky

4 Which word from the text indicates that the track near the caravan was rarely used?

   Write your answer in the box.

5 What was Shane missing most of all?
   A books to read   **B** a place to explore   **C** the mobile phone   **D** someone his own age

6 What is the importance of the grocery store for Shane?
   A The girl with the pram lived there.
   B It was a place for contact with other people.
   C Batteries for the radio could be purchased there.
   D It was where his father worked during the day.

7 What did Shane's father expect to do at Ironbark Ridge?
   A set up a shop   **B** explore   **C** farm   **D** build a garage

☞ **Answers and explanations on page 152**

Real Test

Read this extract from *The Incredible Experience of Megan Kingsley* by Pamela O'Connor and answer the questions. Circle the correct answer.

The small launch <u>bobbed</u> widely in the choppy water, like a toy duck in a baby's bath, as the captain steered skilfully towards the rocky forbidding cove of Stellar Island.

To the two small figures sitting in the bow, the cove appeared to have been carved out of two sheer black cliff faces that rose straight up from the sea. The children laughed suddenly as the cold spray splashed over them.

'Patrick and Annabel!' their mother called. 'Come back here!'

The pair reluctantly left the front of the boat and clambered down the small hatch to the cabin below, where their older sister sat quietly on a bench, staring stonily at the lapping water against the porthole.

'What's the matter with Megan?' asked Annabel.

'Nothing,' replied her mother. 'Just leave her alone.'

'I'm hungry,' announced Patrick. 'Can we have something to eat?'

'We'll be landing in a few minutes. We will have lunch when we get to the house.' Mrs Kingsley frowned as she looked at her elder daughter, wondering how much longer Megan could keep up this <u>stony silence</u>.

1 According to the information available, how many people were on the launch? Write a number in the box.

2 Why were the passengers on the launch heading for the cove?
   A to escape a storm
   C to have a picnic lunch
   B to commence a trip to a house
   D to get medical care for Megan

3 The best word to describe how Mrs Kingsley feels at the end of the passage is
   A hungry.　　　　B concerned.　　　　C frightened.　　　　D reluctant.

4 What could Patrick and Annabel see as they sat in the bow of the launch?
   A a baby's bath
   C a cove surrounded by a cliff
   B a house
   D the whole of Stellar Island

5 The term 'stony silence' implies that Megan was feeling
   A hostile.　　　　B stubborn.　　　　C lonely.　　　　D snobbish.

6 Which word from the passage means an entry hole in the deck of a boat?
   A porthole　　　　B cabin　　　　C hatch　　　　D bow

7 The word 'bobbed' could be best replaced with
   A bubbled.　　　　B bounced.　　　　C floated.　　　　D rocked.

8 The passage describes water as 'lapping against the porthole'. This means
   A the cabin was below water level.
   B the launch was in danger of sinking.
   C the seas were getting dangerously choppy.
   D water was splashing over the bow and onto the portholes.

☞ **Answers and explanations on page 152**

Real Test

READING
Understanding explanations

Read the passage from *Kites* by David Bowden and Jenny Dibley and answer the questions.

Kites come in many shapes and sizes. They can be constructed from a large variety of materials from the simplest, such as paper or cloth, to the most advanced, such as carbon fibre and tear-proof sailsheet.

Kites can be quite easy to make. As with most things it is best to <u>master</u> the simplest kites first before you advance to state-of-the-art kite building.

To build your kite you will need a few supplies. For the frame you will need timber. Hobby shops and timber yards are the best source of light timbers such as bamboo, pine and <u>Australian mountain ash</u>. The timber should be round; ask for dowel, they'll know what you'll need. Garden shops are a good source of bamboo.

For the covering skin you can use paper, plastic or cloth. Some of these materials will tear in strong winds, so you will need some reinforcing tape. The beauty of these materials is that they can be easily decorated with paint, drawings and pictures.

To fly a kite you will also need a good length of string. Most of the materials needed can be found in household recycle bins or scrap bins in the shed.

1 This information would most likely be found in a
  A novel.   B craft book.   C manual.   D newspaper.

2 What is the meaning of 'master' in this text?
  A an old teacher   B to rule or control
  C to be skilled in an activity   D an experienced tradesperson

3 According to the text the three most important requirements when making a kite are wood, skin covering and
  A string.   B paint.   C sailsheet.   D reinforcing tape.

4 Dowel can be obtained from
  A a decorator.   B an art store.   C a timber yard.   D a garden shop.

5 You are going to compare the texts *The Incredible Experience of Megan Kingsley* (page 20) and *Kites* (page 21). For what purposes were these texts written? Tick **two** options for each text.

	Incredible Experience	Kites
to recount	A ☐	A ☐
to explain	B ☐	B ☐
to persuade	C ☐	C ☐
to entertain	D ☐	D ☐

6 According to the text, what damage can strong winds do to a kite? Write your answer on the line.

_____

7 Which statement is true?
  A Kite flying is dangerous.   B New materials are best for kites.
  C Kites can be made from scraps   D It is costly to get started with kites.

☞ **Answers and explanations on pages 152–153**

GENERAL WRITING TIPS

> Each weekly writing plan provides four exercises. It is strongly suggested that you **attempt only three of the four exercises** in each practice period. This allows for three 42-minute writing sessions. The exercise not attempted in each unit can be used as additional practice at another time.

Writing Tests are designed to test your ability to express ideas, feelings and points of view. You will be assessed on:

- the thought and content of your writing
- the structure and organisation of your ideas
- the expression, style and appropriate use of language of your writing
- the amount you write in the given time.

To get the best results, follow these steps.

Step 1 – Before you start writing

- **Read the question.** Be sure you understand the type of writing requested by the assessors. If you are expected to write an explanation, there is little point in writing a story. Read the instructions carefully. Ask yourself if you should be describing, explaining, entertaining, telling a story, expressing a point of view, expressing an emotion or persuading the reader.
- **Check the stimulus material carefully.** Make sure the stimulus material forms the basis of your writing. You will likely be given a topic, picture, words/phrases, short poem or prose extract as stimulus material.
- **What writing style?** If you are given a choice of writing styles (text types), pick the style you are most comfortable with.
- **Warning:** Don't try to make a pre-planned response fit the stimulus material given.

Step 2 – Jot down points

Give yourself a few minutes before you start to get your thoughts in order and jot down points. You won't have time to write a draft. Depending on the style required, jot down points on:

- who (characters), why (reasons for action), where (setting), when (time)
- sequences of events/arguments/points
- any good ideas you suddenly have
- how to include the senses and your feelings.

Remember: You can discard ideas that don't fit into your final approach.

Step 3 – Make a brief outline

List the points or events in order. This will become your framework. It can be modified as you write.

GENERAL WRITING TIPS

Step 4 – Start writing

- Make your **paragraphing** work for you. New paragraphs are usually needed for
  - new incidents in stories
  - changes in time or place
  - descriptions that move from one sense to another (e.g. from sight to sound)
  - a change in the character using direct speech.

- The quality and extent of your **vocabulary** is being tested. Don't use unusual words or big words just to impress the assessor. A mistake here will expose your ignorance.

- It is important that you **complete your piece of writing**. Unfinished work will lose you marks, as will extremely short responses.

- Get as much of the **punctuation, spelling and grammar** right as you can, but allow yourself a couple of minutes after you finish to proofread your work. You won't have time for detailed editing.

- If you are writing a story, know the **ending** before you start. Your ending should not be trite or clichéd (e.g. *I woke up and found it was just a dream*).

- If you are asked to give a **point of view**, think through the evidence you can use to support your 'argument' so that you can build to a strong conclusion.

- If you are including **descriptions** in your writing, think about the importance and relevance of all the senses—sights, smells, tastes, sounds and physical feelings. You may also include an **emotional response**.

- Have a **concluding sentence** that 'rounds off' your work.

- Keep your **handwriting** reasonably neat (i.e. readable).

Step 5 – When you finish

When you finish, **re-read** your work and do a quick check for spelling, punctuation, capital letters and grammar.

Check the Writing section (www.nap.edu.au/naplan/writing) **of the official NAPLAN website for up-to-date and important information on the Writing Test**. Sample Writing Tests and marking guidelines that outline the criteria markers use when assessing your writing are also provided. Please note that, to date in NAPLAN, the types of texts that students have been tested on have been narrative and persuasive writing.

The Australian Curriculum for English requires students to be taught three main types of texts:

- imaginative writing (including narratives and descriptions)
- informative writing (including procedures and reports)
- persuasive writing (expositions).

Informative writing has not yet been tested by NAPLAN. The best preparation for writing is for students to read a range of texts and to get lots of practice in writing different types of texts. We have included information on all types of texts in this book.

TIPS FOR WRITING PERSUASIVE TEXTS

Persuasive texts (expositions or opinions) are used to 'argue' the case for or against a particular action, plan or point of view—to *persuade* others to see it your way. Persuasive texts need to be well organised and clear so that readers will understand and be convinced of your arguments.

When writing persuasive texts it is best to keep the following points in mind. They will help you get the best possible mark.

Before you start writing

- Read the question carefully. You will probably be asked to write your reaction to a particular question or statement, such as *Dogs should be kept out of parks*. Most of the topics that you will be asked to comment on are very general. This means you will probably be writing about something you know and can draw upon your experience. When writing your personal opinion you may include such phrases as *I think, I believe* and *It is important*. Remember to sound confident. Some common ways for the question to be worded are: *Give your opinion on …; Do you agree or disagree?; What do you think is/are … ?; What changes would you like to see … ?; Is … a good idea or a bad idea?*
- You will be expected to give your reasons. Sometimes the question may actually state *Give your reasons*. Remember: the stance taken in a persuasive text is not wrong, as long as the writer has evidence to support his or her opinion. How the opinion is supported is as important as the opinion itself.
- Give yourself a few minutes before you start writing to get your thoughts in order and jot down points.

The introduction

- Right from the beginning it is important to let the reader know what position you have taken or what you believe. You can do this via the title or in the first line or paragraph, which may include a brief preview of the main arguments and some background information.

The body

- **Follow the structure of persuasive texts.** As persuasive texts aim to convince readers, your reasons must be logical and easily understood. You must provide both arguments (points) and evidence to support the arguments.
- **Correctly paragraph your writing.** Use paragraphs with topic sentences to organise your information. Without paragraphs your arguments become confused and difficult to follow. Use one paragraph for each idea or argument. Arguments can be ordered according to your choice. They can be 'numbered', e.g. *firstly, secondly, finally*.
- **Make sure your arguments (or points) are relevant.** They must add to your case. 'Waffle' and unnecessary detail don't improve a persuasive text. It is better to stick to the facts without getting sidetracked. Once you have made a point there is no need to repeat it.
- **Use interesting, precise words.** Include strong persuasive words such as *must, believe, important* or *certainly*. Avoid common words that carry little or no meaning, such as *good*. You can state your arguments using sentences beginning with words such as *firstly, furthermore* or *finally*.
- **Vary the types and lengths of sentences and the words that begin each sentence.** If your writing includes a personal opinion, try to avoid too many sentences starting with *I*.
- **Use impersonal writing**, although personal opinions can be part of the text.

The conclusion

- The final paragraph must restate your position more forcefully and wrap up your case. It can include a recommendation.

When you have finished writing give yourself a few moments to read through your persuasive text. Quickly check spelling and punctuation and insert any words that have been accidentally left out. Direct speech is not a feature of persuasive texts. Indirect speech (reported speech) does not have speech marks (" ").

You will find a sample annotated persuasive text on the following page. The question is from Sample Test 1 on page 110. Read the persuasive text and the notes before you begin your first Writing Test. This piece of writing has been analysed based on the marking criteria used by markers to assess the NAPLAN Writing Test.

Remember: This sample was not written under exam conditions.

Vocabulary
- A good variety of precise verb types are used to establish strong, informed arguments.
- Nouns are used to make generalised statements.
- Adverbs and adjectives are well selected to qualify statements.
- The pronoun *I* is used sparingly.

Sentence structure
- A good variety of sentence beginnings (e.g. *Firstly, As*) are used.
- A variety of sentence types and lengths are used.
- Topic sentences are used to introduce each paragraph's main idea.
- Exclamations and questions are used to good effect.

Ideas
- Ideas are well balanced to create a sense of rational, logical argument.
- A rhetorical question is used to emphasise a point.
- A strong viewpoint is expressed with careful choice of words.
- Ideas are presented positively.

Punctuation
- Punctuation, including apostrophes and full stops, is correctly applied.

Spelling
- There are no spelling mistakes of common or unusual words.

Year 5 Sample Persuasive Writing
(a sample answer to the question on page 110)

Students should have fruit lunches rather than those based on bread products.

For me there is no real debate. Sandwiches and suitably filled rolls are much better for school lunches than fruit. There are just so many problems with a fruit-only lunch.

Firstly fruit is more difficult to carry to school than sandwiches. Apricots and peaches are so easily squashed unless treated with care. The juice from squashed fruit can ruin items kept in school bags. The juice attracts the ants!

Fruit is not a satisfactory source of food. Bananas are easily bruised and who likes eating brown, bruised bananas? Often other fruit has little 'real' taste. Oranges are often bitter and can be a bit dry. Peaches have furry skin. They have to be peeled. Who has a chance to peel peaches at school?

Then there are the skins of bananas and oranges to get rid of. Lunch wrappers can be quickly put into pockets but who would want a pocket full of orange or mandarin peels—or peach seeds?

The cost of fruit is unpredictable. Sandwiches usually are much the same price. They are simpler to budget for. Out-of-season fruit can be a great expense for families on low incomes.

As far as taste goes, fruit is fairly predicable. Sandwiches can be made interesting with little effort. A salad sandwich has as much goodness as a couple of pieces of fruit. Sandwiches with other fillings can provide a greater variety of necessary vitamins and minerals. End-of-season fruit or cold-store fruit can be quite unappetising.

I cannot find any important reason to insist that students have a fruit-only school lunch. Fruit is not very practical, it can be expensive and tasteless, and doesn't have the food value of a well-prepared and interesting sandwich. Fruit is best enjoyed at home.

This text is beyond what would be expected of a typical Year 5 student. It is provided here as a model. The assessment comments are based on the marking criteria used to assess the NAPLAN Writing Test.

Audience
- The audience is readily identified (students).
- Readers are quickly engaged in an issue relevant to primary school students.
- A brief statement is made outlining the issue to be discussed.
- Background information is provided to give context to the points raised.

Persuasive techniques
- Arguments for the writer's reaction are organised into separate paragraphs.
- Points raised are obviously important to the writer in a personal way.
- Evidence and examples are used to support the argument.
- Objectivity is maintained throughout the writing.

Text structure
- The text contains a well-organised introduction, body and conclusion.
- The writer refers regularly to words used in the topic and opening paragraph.

Paragraphing
- New paragraphs are used for new arguments and the summary.

Cohesion
- The final paragraph establishes where the writer stands on the issue.
- The concluding sentence is forceful and personal.

Before you start, read the General writing tips on pages 22–23 and the Tips for writing persuasive texts on page 24.

Today you are going to write a persuasive text, often called an exposition. The purpose of writing a persuasive text is to influence or change a reader's thoughts or opinions on a particular topic or subject. Your aim is to convince a reader that your opinion is sensible and logical. Successful persuasive writing is always well planned. Persuasive texts may include advertisements, letters to newspapers, speeches and newspaper editorials, as well as arguments in debates.

Skateboarding and rollerblading should be optional school sports.

What do you think about this idea? Do you support or reject this proposal?
Write to convince a reader of your opinions.

Before you start writing, give some thought to:
- whether you strongly agree or strongly disagree with this opinion
- reasons or evidence for your arguments
- a brief but definite conclusion—list some of your main points and add a personal opinion
- the structure of a persuasive text, which begins with a well-organised introduction, followed by a body of arguments or points, and finally a conclusion that restates the writer's position.

Don't forget to:
- plan your writing before you start—make a list of important points you wish to make
- write in correctly formed sentences and take care with paragraphing
- choose your words carefully, and pay attention to your spelling and punctuation
- write neatly but don't waste time
- quickly check your persuasive text once you have finished—your position must be clear to the reader.

Remember: The stance taken in a persuasive text is not wrong, as long as the writer has evidence to support his or her opinion. How the opinion is supported is as important as the opinion itself.

Start writing here or type your answer on a tablet or computer.

_____

_____

_____

_____

_____

_____

_____

_____

☞ **Marking guide on page 153**

Real Test and Tips

Before you start, read the General writing tips on pages 22–23 and the Tips for writing persuasive texts on page 24.

Today you are going to write a persuasive text, often called an exposition. The purpose of writing a persuasive text is to influence or change a reader's thoughts or opinions on a particular topic or subject. Your aim is to convince a reader that your opinion is sensible and logical. Successful persuasive writing is always well planned. Persuasive texts may include advertisements, letters to newspapers, speeches and newspaper editorials, as well as arguments in debates.

Walking to school is better than being driven.

What do you think of this idea? Which is the better way for most students?

Write to convince a reader of your opinions.

Before you start writing, give some thought to:
- whether you strongly agree or strongly disagree with this opinion
- reasons or evidence for your arguments
- a brief but definite conclusion—list some of your main points and add a personal opinion
- the structure of a persuasive text, which begins with a well-organised introduction, followed by a body of arguments or points, and finally a conclusion that restates the writer's position.

Don't forget to:
- plan your writing before you start—make a list of important points you wish to make
- write in correctly formed sentences and take care with paragraphing
- choose your words carefully, and pay attention to your spelling and punctuation
- write neatly but don't waste time
- quickly check your persuasive text once you have finished—your position must be clear to the reader.

Remember: The stance taken in a persuasive text is not wrong, as long as the writer has evidence to support his or her opinion. How the opinion is supported is as important as the opinion itself.

Start writing here or type your answer on a tablet or computer.

_____

_____

_____

_____

_____

_____

_____

_____

☞ **Marking guide on page 154**

TIPS FOR WRITING NARRATIVE TEXTS

A **narrative** is a form of prose writing that tells a story. Its main purpose is to entertain. Writers of narratives create experiences that are shared with the reader. To do this the writer uses literary techniques. Such techniques include figurative language (similes, metaphors, alliteration, onomatopoeia, rhetorical questions and repetition), variety in sentence length and type, variety in paragraph length, and direct speech.

In any narratives, the author is the person who wrote the story. The narrator is the person (*I*) who is both in the story and who tells the story.

When writing narratives it is best to keep the following points in mind. They will help you get the best possible mark.

Before you start writing

- Read the question and check the stimulus material carefully. *Stimulus material* means the topic, title, picture, words, phrases or extract of writing you are given to base your writing on.
- Write about something you know. Don't try to write about something way outside your experience.
- Decide if you are going to be writing in the first person (you become a character in your story) or in the third person (about other characters). When writing in the first person be careful not to overuse the pronoun *I* (e.g. *I did this, I did that*).
- Take a few moments to jot your ideas down on a piece of paper. Write down the order in which things happen. These could be the points in your story where you start new paragraphs.
- Remember: stories have a beginning, middle and end. It sounds simple but many stories fail because one of these three parts is not well written.

The introduction

- Don't start with *Once upon a time*—this is too clichéd and predictable.
- Don't tell the reader too much in the beginning. Make the reader want to read on to find out more. The beginning should **introduce a problem to be solved**.

The body

- **In the middle of your story include events that make solving the problem more difficult or doubtful.** This makes the story interesting.
- **Use a setting that you are familiar with**, e.g. home, school, sport, holiday place or shopping centre. You will then be able to describe the setting realistically.
- **Choose characters that are like people you know** because they are easier to imagine. You don't have to use their real names—it's probably best not to!
- **Use your imagination to make the story more interesting**, but don't try to fill it with weird or disgusting events.
- **Enhance your story with the use of literary techniques**, e.g. similes, metaphors, onomatopoeia and alliteration.
- **Make your paragraphing work for you**. New paragraphs are usually needed for new incidents in your story, changes in time or place, descriptions that move from one sense to another, or changes in the character who is speaking.

The conclusion

- The ending is the hardest part to write because it has to have something to do with the beginning.
- Have some idea of how your story will end before you start writing.
- Never end your stories with: *and it was just a dream; I was saved by a superhero (or by magic); I was dead; and they lived happily ever after!* Endings like these just tell the marker that you don't have a creative way to end your story.

When you have finished writing give yourself a few minutes to read through your story. Now is the time to check spelling and punctuation, and to insert words that have been accidentally left out.

WRITING
Narrative text 1

Before you start, read the General writing tips on pages 22–23 and the Tips for writing narrative texts on page 28.

Today you are going to write a narrative or story.

Look at the picture on the right.

The idea for your story is the discovery of something unusual. It could be a note hidden in a container, a wallet or small purse, a map, keys with a tag, a strange electronic device or some strange information.

Think about where your story takes place. It could on a beach, by a lake or river. It could be in a park or camping grounds.

Think about when your story takes place—daytime or dusk, summer or winter, holidays or school days.

Your story might be amusing or it might be serious. Think about how the people in your story react.

Before you start writing, give some thought to:
- where your story takes place
- the characters and what they do in your story
- the events that take place in your story and the problems that have to be resolved
- how your story begins, what happens in your story, and how your story ends.

Don't forget to:
- plan your story before you start writing
- write in correctly formed sentences and take care with paragraphing
- choose your words carefully and pay attention to your spelling and punctuation
- write neatly but don't waste time
- quickly check your story once you have finished.

Start writing here or type your answer on a tablet or computer.

_____

_____

_____

_____

_____

_____

_____

_____

_____

_____

_____

☞ **Marking guide on pages 154-155**

Before you start, read the General writing tips on pages 22–23 and the Tips for writing narrative texts on page 28.

Today you are going to write a narrative or story.
Choose one of the following phrases and use it as a basis for a story.
- A surprise parcel or message
- A surprise discovery
- A surprise party
- A surprise sighting

Think about all of the places where the surprise might unexpectedly turn up. It could be at home but it could be at school, at an event, while exploring or on holidays.
Your story could be about your experiences or different people in situations where they are faced with the surprise. Think about the way people react in your story.
Think about when your story takes place—daytime or night time, weekends or weekdays or while helping someone. Your story might be amusing or it might be serious.

Before you start writing, give some thought to:
- where your story takes place
- the characters and what they do in your story
- the events that take place in your story and the problems that have to be resolved
- how your story begins, what happens in your story, and how your story ends.

Don't forget to:
- plan your story before you start writing
- write in correctly formed sentences and take care with paragraphing
- choose your words carefully and pay attention to your spelling and punctuation
- write neatly but don't waste time
- quickly check your story once you have finished.

Start writing here or type your answer on a tablet or computer.

_____

_____

_____

_____

_____

_____

_____

_____

_____

_____

_____

☞ **Marking guide on page 155**

What's next?

Week 2

This is what we cover this week:

Day 1 **Number and Algebra:** ◎ Fractions, decimals and percentages

Measurement and Geometry: ◎ 2D shapes and position

◎ 3D shapes

Day 2 **Spelling:** ◎ Adding 'ing' or 'ed' to verbs

◎ Common misspellings

Grammar and punctuation: ◎ Types of nouns and adjectives

◎ Tenses, contractions and punctuation

Day 3 **Reading:** ◎ Understanding poetry

◎ Interpreting notices

◎ Following a procedure

Day 4 **Writing:** ◎ Recounts

Test Your Skills

NUMBER AND ALGEBRA
Fractions, decimals and percentages

20 MIN

Circle the correct answer.

1 What is the place value of 5 in 12.359?
A units (ones)   B tenths
C hundredths   D thousandths

2 Which of the following is not the same as $\frac{1}{2}$?
A $\frac{2}{3}$ B $\frac{2}{4}$ C $\frac{4}{8}$ D $\frac{3}{6}$

3 $\frac{1}{3} + \frac{1}{3} = ?$
A $\frac{1}{4}$ B $\frac{2}{5}$ C $\frac{2}{6}$ D $\frac{2}{3}$

4 $\frac{8}{12} = ?$
A $\frac{3}{4}$ B $\frac{1}{4}$ C $\frac{2}{3}$ D $\frac{5}{10}$

5 $1\frac{1}{2} + 1\frac{1}{2} = ?$
A 2   B 3   C $2\frac{1}{2}$ D $\frac{5}{4}$

6 How many quarters in 2 wholes?
A 4   B 5   C 6   D 8

7 $6 \times 0.3 = ?$
A 0.9   B 1.8   C 0.18   D 18

8 What part of this shape is shaded?
A 0.4   B 0.10
C 2.5   D 10.0

9 $0.5 + 1.2 + 0.3 + 1.1 = ?$
A 1.3   B 2.1   C 2.11   D 3.1

10 Which is the smallest decimal?
A 0.09   B 0.7   C 0.62   D 1.088

11 $\frac{1}{4} = ?$
A 0.04   B 0.25   C 0.4   D 1.4

12 Mary got 65% in a Maths test. How much more did she need to receive full marks?
A 5%   B 25%   C 35%   D 100%

13 $1.6 + 0.23 = ?$
A 1.83   B 0.39   C 3.9   D 1.623

14 Round 3.25 to the nearest whole number.
A 3   B 3.24   C 3.26   D 4

15
$$\begin{array}{r} 12.7 \\ -\ \ 3.9 \\ \hline \end{array}$$
A 7.8   B 8.2   C 8.8   D 9.2

16
$$\begin{array}{r} 8.6 \\ \times\ \ 9 \\ \hline \end{array}$$
A 73.4   B 76.4   C 77.4   D 72.54

17 What number is the arrow pointing at?

A 3.3   B 3.6   C 3.2   D 0.6

18 How many tenths in 2 wholes?
A 5   B 10   C 12   D 20

19 Which statement is correct?
A 0.5 < 0.06   B $\frac{1}{2} > \frac{1}{4}$

C 12.4 < 1.25   D $\frac{1}{4} > \frac{1}{3}$

☞ **Explanations on page 156**

Key Points

NUMBER AND ALGEBRA
Fractions, decimals and percentages

❶ A **fraction** is any part of a whole. A common fraction is written with a numerator over a denominator:

$$\frac{2}{5} \quad \frac{\text{numerator}}{\text{denominator}}$$

This fraction means 2 parts out of 5 equal parts.

Example: What fraction of the squares are shaded?

5 out of 12 squares are shaded. This means $\frac{5}{12}$ shaded.

❷ **Decimal fractions** are fractions that use a decimal point. Decimal fractions show the number of parts out of 10, 100, 1000 and so on (e.g. 7 equal parts out of 10 or $\frac{7}{10}$ or 0.7).

The correct way to say 3.56 is 'three point five six'.

Zeros at the extreme right of a decimal do not change the value of the decimal:
1.600 = 1.60 = 1.6

Here is the place value in decimals:
… hundreds tens units decimal point tenths hundredths thousandths …

Example: What is the value of 5 in 34.052? The value of the 5 is 5 hundredths.

❸ A **percentage** is a special fraction that is always out of 100 (e.g. $\frac{35}{100}$ = 0.35 = 35%).

❹ This table shows the relationships between some **common fractions**: halves, quarters, eighths, fifths and tenths.

One whole									
$\frac{1}{2}$					$\frac{1}{2}$				
$\frac{1}{4}$		$\frac{1}{4}$		$\frac{1}{4}$		$\frac{1}{4}$			
$\frac{1}{8}$	$\frac{1}{8}$	$\frac{1}{8}$	$\frac{1}{8}$	$\frac{1}{8}$	$\frac{1}{8}$	$\frac{1}{8}$	$\frac{1}{8}$		
$\frac{1}{5}$		$\frac{1}{5}$		$\frac{1}{5}$		$\frac{1}{5}$		$\frac{1}{5}$	
$\frac{1}{10}$	$\frac{1}{10}$	$\frac{1}{10}$	$\frac{1}{10}$	$\frac{1}{10}$	$\frac{1}{10}$	$\frac{1}{10}$	$\frac{1}{10}$	$\frac{1}{10}$	$\frac{1}{10}$

❺ Often fractions that look 'difficult' can be **simplified by cancelling**. This is done by dividing both the numerator and denominator by the **same number**.
Examples:

$\frac{15}{25}$ is simplified to $\frac{3}{5}$ when both numbers are divided by 5.

$\frac{2}{4}$ becomes $\frac{1}{2}$ when both numbers are divided by 2.

❻ Fractions and decimals can be placed on **number lines**:

Example: Locate $1\frac{3}{4}$ on the number line.

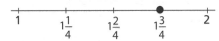

We can mark the section of the number line in quarters instead of halves:

Example: Locate 3.4 on the number line.

We can mark the section of the number line:

Real Test

NUMBER AND ALGEBRA
Fractions, decimals and percentages

20 min

Circle the correct answer.

1 What fraction of the diagram is not shaded?

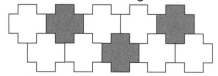

A $\frac{1}{10}$ B $\frac{3}{10}$ C $\frac{7}{10}$ D $\frac{9}{10}$

2 Fatima drew a number line.

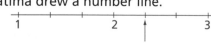

What number is the arrow pointing to?

A $\frac{1}{3}$ B $\frac{1}{2}$ C $2\frac{1}{3}$ D $3\frac{1}{2}$

3 Mila shades part of a rectangle. About what fraction is not shaded?

A quarter   B third
C half   D three quarters

4 A birthday cake is cut into eight equal pieces. If 2 pieces remain, what fraction of the cake has been removed?

A $\frac{1}{6}$ B $\frac{1}{4}$ C $\frac{1}{2}$ D $\frac{3}{4}$

5 Laura is paid an allowance of $10. If she spends half of her allowance on a magazine, how much did it cost?
A $2   B $4   C $5   D $8

6 Fractions are written on cards:

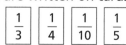

Rearrange these cards from smallest to largest.

smallest ☐ ☐ ☐ ☐ largest

7 What is the value of the 5 in 23.051?
A 5 hundredths   B 5 tenths
C 5 tens   D 5 hundreds

8 Here is a number line.

What number is the arrow pointing to?
A 0.3   B 0.4   C 0.5   D 0.6

9 Which card has the largest decimal?

A 0.27   B 0.7   C 0.63   D 0.08

10 1.68, 1.74, ____, 1.86, 1.92
What is the missing decimal?
A 1.8   B 1.08   C 1.78   D 1.82

11 The number 107.03 is the same as
A 1 hundred + 7 units + 3 hundredths.
B 1 ten + 7 units + 3 hundredths.
C 1 hundred + 7 units + 3 tenths.
D 1 hundred + 7 hundreds + 3 tenths.

12 Sarah buys a writing pad costing $3.25. What is the change from $5.00?
A $1.25 B $1.75   C $2.25   D $2.75

13 A carton of soft drink costs $6.50.

 $6.50

What is the cost of each can?
A $0.06 B $0.07   C $0.65   D $0.75

14 Which of these groups of decimals add to 1? Select **all** the possible answers.
A 0.4, 0.04, 0.002   B 0.3, 0.5, 0.2
C 0.06, 0.03, 0.01   D 0.7, 0.2, 0.1

15 Riann has $7.25 and wants to buy a bracelet which costs $10. $ ☐
How much more money does she need?

16 What percentage of the grid is shaded?

☐ %

☞ **Answers and explanations on pages 156-157**

MEASUREMENT AND GEOMETRY
2D shapes and position

Circle the correct answer.

1 Which shape is a pentagon?

A ◯   B ⬠

C ⬡   D ▢

2 Which shape contains parallel lines?

A △   B ▱

C ⬠   D ⏢

3 Here are four angles. Which angle is the obtuse angle?

4 How many degrees in a right angle?

A 45°   B 50°

C 90°   D 100°

5 Which line is perpendicular to the red line?

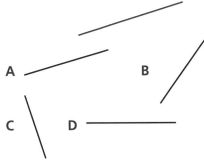

6 Which triangle has two equal angles and two equal sides?

A isosceles   B right angle

C scalene   D equilateral

7 How many diagonals can be drawn in this shape?

A 2   B 3

C 5   D 10

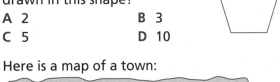

8 Here is a map of a town:

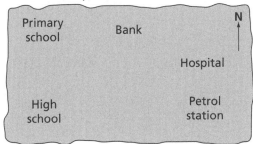

What direction is the Bank from the Petrol Station?

A south-east   B south

C north-west   D north-east

9 How many lines of symmetry can be drawn in this hexagon?

A 1   B 3

C 6   D 12

10 Which one of these shapes can make an all-over pattern without overlapping or gaps?

A ◯   B △

C ▱   D ⬠

11 How many triangles of any size are in this shape?

A 5   B 7

C 8   D 9

☞ **Explanations on page 157**

MEASUREMENT AND GEOMETRY
2D shapes and position

1 Basic **quadrilateral shapes** (4-sided)

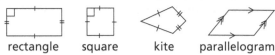

rectangle   square   kite   parallelogram

2 Types of **lines**

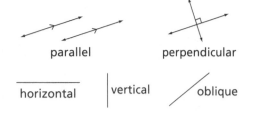

parallel   perpendicular

horizontal   vertical   oblique

3 In a **triangle**, the angles have a total of 180°. In a **quadrilateral**, the angles have a total of 360°.

4 **Diagonals** are lines that join the corners of 2D shapes. A square has two diagonals. A pentagon has five diagonals.

5 **Other shapes**

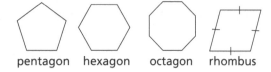

pentagon   hexagon   octagon   rhombus

6 Shapes that fit together without overlapping or gaps are said to **tessellate**. Squares tessellate but circles do not. This is a tessellating shape:

7 A shape has **symmetry** (is symmetrical) when one half of the shape fits exactly over the other half. This is a line of symmetry.

8 In making patterns with 2D shapes, the shapes can **flip**, **slide** or **turn** to new positions. A knowledge of right and left is important.

Example:

If the shape is to be turned, or rotated, a quarter of a turn in a clockwise direction, draw the new image?

9 A **mirror image** is the form a shape becomes when seen in a mirror. The letter H looks the same but the letter E is 'flipped' when viewed in a vertically placed mirror.

10 A **compass rose** is used for directions:

MEASUREMENT AND GEOMETRY
2D shapes and position

Circle the correct answer.

1 Aimee drew this shape. What is the name of the shape?
A triangle   **B** hexagon
C pentagon   **D** rhombus

2 The picture shows a flag. How many axes of symmetry has the flag?
A 0   **B** 1   **C** 2   **D** 3

3 Rhiannon drew 2 shapes and counted 12 sides in total. If one of the shapes was a square, what was the other shape?
A triangle   **B** pentagon
C hexagon   **D** octagon

4 Which of the following letters has a pair of parallel lines? Select **all** the possible answers.
V   T   H   K   M
A   **B**   **C**   **D**   **E**

5 Jake folds a piece of paper in half and cuts out a quarter of a circle. What does the paper look like when Jake unfolds it?
A   **B**
C   **D**

6 Which is the smallest angle?
A   **B**
C   **D**

7 How many rectangles are there in this shape?
A 3   **B** 4
C 5   **D** 6

8 The letter **F** is turned a quarter of a circle. What does the image looks like?
A   **B**   **C**   **D**

9 How many sides has a hexagon?
A 3   **B** 5   **C** 6   **D** 8

10 The letter **K** is painted on a sheet of paper. While the paint is still wet, the paper is folded to make an image. What does the paper look like?
A   **B**   **C**   **D**

The map shows the location of the homes of four friends.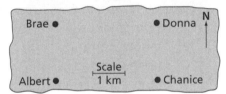

11 Which of the following is correct?
A Brae lives east of Albert
B Chanice lives south of Donna
C Donna lives west of Albert
D Donna lives north of Brae

12 The distance from Brae to Donna is closest to
A 3 cm.   **B** 3 m.   **C** 30 m.   **D** 3 km.

13 Ryan is north-east of a park. From Ryan, the park is
A south-east.   **B** south-west.
C north-east.   **D** north-west.

Aaron placed a coin on the grid.

14 What is the location of the coin?

15 Aaron then moved the coin down 2 squares and to the right 1 square. What is the new location of the coin?

16 What direction is the arrow pointing to?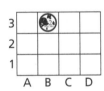
A north-east   **B** south-east
C north-west   **D** south-west

☞ **Answers and explanations on pages 157-158**

MEASUREMENT AND GEOMETRY
3D shapes

Circle the correct answer.

1 Which shape is a rectangular prism?

2 I am thinking of a shape.
It has 5 faces and 6 vertices. What is it?
A rectangular prism
B triangular prism
C square pyramid
D triangular pyramid

3 How many cubes are there in this stack?
There are no hidden gaps.

A 8   B 9
C 11   D 12

4 What shape can be made from this net?

A a rectangular prism
B a triangular prism
C a square pyramid
D a triangular pyramid

5 What would this block look like from above?

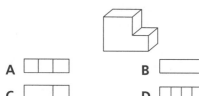

6 This shape is cut at an angle as shown by the dotted line. What shape will the cut faces be?

A   B

C   D

7 How many edges does a hexagonal prism have?
A 12
B 16
C 18
D 24

8 A tin of soup is most like a
A cylinder.
B sphere.
C cone.
D pyramid.

9 How many cubes would I need to build a stack that was 3 cubes long, 2 cubes high and 4 cubes deep?
A 9
B 10
C 14
D 24

10 One edge has been cut off this cube. How many faces does the shape have?
A 5
B 6
C 7
D 8

☞ **Explanations on page 158**

MEASUREMENT AND GEOMETRY
3D shapes

❶ **3D shapes** include:

cube

rectangular prism

triangular prism

octagonal prism

hexagonal pyramid

square pyramid

Pyramids are described by their base. The base is not necessarily the 'bottom' of the shape. A pyramid can have a variety of bases, e.g. a hexagonal pyramid.

Prisms are described by their base, e.g. an octagonal prism.

❷ The features of 3D shapes are **faces**, **edges** and **vertices** (corners). A cube has six faces, twelve edges and eight vertices. Faces must be flat. Surfaces can be curved or flat.

This rectangular prism has:

12 edges (4 at the top, 4 at the base and 4 up the sides)

6 faces (flat surfaces: top, base and 4 sides)

8 vertices (corners: 4 at the top, 4 at the base)

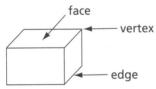
face

vertex

edge

❸ A **net** is a flat pattern that can be cut and folded to make a 3D shape.
This is a net for a cube.

❹ Some questions may ask the student to visualise (imagine) 3D shapes from other positions.

A **square pyramid** as viewed from above would look like this.

❺ You may also be asked to **count all the blocks in a stack** when all blocks are not visible.
There are nine blocks in this stack.

❻ A **cross-section** is the face that is made when a solid shape is cut straight through. When a cone is cut at an angle the shape of the face will look like this:

❼ This table gives a quick reference for the features of many **flat-faced 3D shapes**.

Shape	Faces	Edges	Vertices
Triangular pyramid	4	6	4
Square pyramid	5	8	5
Cube	6	12	8
Rectangular prism	6	12	8
Triangular prism	5	9	6
Hexagonal prism	8	18	12

❽ It is important to **recognise 3D shapes** in the environment. A soccer ball is much like a sphere.

Real Test

MEASUREMENT AND GEOMETRY
3D shapes

Circle the correct answer.

1 How many faces are on this solid?

A 4   **B** 5
C 6   **D** 8

The diagram shows a net of a cube. The cube is now made up.

2 What letter is on the opposite face to E?
A A   **B** B   **C** C   **D** D

3 What letter is on the opposite face to F?
A A   **B** B   **C** C   **D** D

4 Which of the following shapes is not a prism?

A **B** **C** **D**

5 Which shape is a cylinder?

A **B** **C** **D**

6 Which of these shows the net of a cylinder?

A **B** **C** **D**

7 Which of these nets would not make a cube?

A **B** **C** **D**

8 Bruce sketched the net of a triangular prism using triangles and some rectangles. How many rectangles did he use?
A 3   **B** 4   **C** 5   **D** 6

9 This is a sketch of a rectangular pyramid. What is the top view of the solid?

A **B** **C** **D**

10 A cylinder is cut in half as shown by the dotted line. What shape will the cut faces be most like?

A △   **B** ▭   **C** ◯   **D** ◯

11 Joanne has a tin of tomatoes in her pantry. What shape is the tin?
A sphere   **B** cylinder
C triangular prism   **D** cube

Hanif built this solid from small cubes.

12 Which is the top view?

A   **B**

C   **D**

13 What is the view from the left?

A   **B**

C   **D**

Blanco uses glue to join the bases of 2 square pyramids together.

14 How many faces does the new solid have?

15 How many edges does the new solid have?

16 Dhama made these solids.

Which solid was not made?
A cone   **B** cylinder
C sphere   **D** cube

☞ **Answers and explanations on pages 158-159**

 With most spelling rules there are exceptions. English words have many different origins (e.g. 'bunyip' comes from Aboriginal Australian and 'sarong' comes from Malaysia).

Key Points

1 With most words you simply add 'ing' or 'ed'.
Examples: camp → camping, camped; paint → painting, painted; peep → peeping, peeped

2 **a** For words that end with a consonant + 'y', simply add 'ing'.
Examples: try → trying, bury → burying, carry → carrying

   b When adding 'ed' to words that end in a consonant + 'y', change the 'y' to 'i' before adding 'ed'.
   Examples: tally → tallied, cry → cried, hurry → hurried

3 For words ending with a consonant + 'e', drop the 'e' and then add 'ing' or 'ed'.
Examples: hope → hoping, hoped; wave → waving, waved

4 For words ending in a single vowel + a consonant, simply double the last letter before adding 'ing' or 'ed'. *Examples:* hop → hopping, hopped; stab → stabbing, stabbed; beg → begging, begged

Main exceptions are words ending in 'w', 'x' and 'y':
Examples: show → showing, showed; box → boxing, boxed; play → playing, played

Test Your Skills

Learn the words below. A common method of learning and self-testing is the **LOOK, SAY, COVER, WRITE, CHECK** method. If you make any mistakes, you should rewrite the word three times correctly, immediately. In this way you will become familiar with the correct spelling. If the word is particularly troublesome, rewrite it several more times or keep a list of words that you can check regularly.

This week's theme word: GARDEN

bury	_____	burying	_____
buried	_____	plant	_____
planting	_____	planted	_____
crop	_____	cropping	_____
cropped	_____	fence	_____
fencing	_____	fenced	_____
water	_____	watering	_____
watered	_____	prune	_____
pruning	_____	pruned	_____
spray	_____	spraying	_____
sprayed	_____	prepare	_____
preparing	_____	prepared	_____

Write any troublesome word three times: _____ _____

_____ _____ _____ _____

Real Test

Please ask your parent or teacher to read to you the spelling words on page 201.
Write the correct spelling of each word in the box.

1 What did you _____ in your bag?

2 You are not _____ to walk on the grass!

3 I sometimes _____ why I go to training.

4 Year 3 students were playing with _____ bands.

5 The school _____ was shorter today.

6 Dad parked his car in the neighbour's _____.

Each line has one word that is incorrect.
Write the correct spelling of the underlined word in the box.

7 We were <u>worryed</u> for your safety.

8 Did you watch the <u>herdles</u> in the Olympic Games?

9 We were <u>hikeing</u> when we saw a scrub wallaby.

10 Jo twisted her <u>ankel</u> when she jumped from the step.

11 The <u>soul</u> of my left shoe has come unstuck.

12 Builders have to wear <u>steal</u>-capped boots.

Read the text *Iguana*.
Each line has a word that is incorrect. Write the correct spelling of the word in the box.

Iguana

13 The iguana is green in color and is a strong

14 swimmer. It is ussually found near streams and

15 rivers. As it is a cold blodded reptile it spends

16 much of its time in the forrest canopy, on branches and

17 basking in the sun. It has pointy spynes along its

18 back which give some pretection against predators.

☞ **Answers on page 159**

Key Points.

❶ There are four types of nouns.

a **Common nouns** are the names of everyday things around us.
Examples: coat, rat, clouds, toe, elephant, desert

b **Proper nouns** begin with a capital letter and are the names of particular persons, places or things. *Examples:* Napoleon, Melbourne, Ford, Opera House, Christmas Day, Russians

c **Abstract nouns** are things that can be recognised by the five senses.
Examples: beauty, hate, amazement, sadness, peace, exhaustion, health

d **Collective nouns** are used to name groups of individuals, places or things.
Examples: crowd, batch, bunch, herd, flock, kit

❷ a **Adjectives** are words that tell us more about nouns or describe them.
Examples: <u>weak</u> cordial, <u>ugly</u> boxer, <u>ten</u> houses, <u>brown</u> paint, the sky is <u>blue</u>

b **Proper adjectives** are formed from proper nouns.
Examples: Italy → Italian, France → French

c Adjectives have **three degrees of comparison**.
Example: Joan is tall. (One person is tall.)
Bill is taller than Joan. (Two people are compared.)
Helen is the tallest person in our class. (Three or more people are compared.)

❸ **Commas** are used in series or to indicate a pause. There is no comma between the last two items of a series that are separated by 'and'.
Examples: Commas in series: I bought eggs, meat, butter, milk and bread at the store.
Commas for pauses: My best friend, Jules Warner, is not at school today.

Test Your Skills

❶ Name the types of nouns.
wind _____, Tasmania _____, swarm _____, truth _____

❷ Draw a line through the adjectives in this sentence.
Jack was in severe pain after the hard match played on the dry, dusty oval.

❸ Write the correct word in the space.
a The _____ sea explorer was Captain Cook. (great, greater, greatest)
b John is a _____ worker. (fast, faster, fastest)

❹ Add commas to these sentences. Write the number you used in the box.

a Mr Jones my science teacher lets us do experiments. ☐

b Tony Trevor Mandy and Leo are waiting by the car ☐

Real Test

GRAMMAR AND PUNCTUATION
Tenses, contractions and punctuation

1 Which of the following correctly completes this sentence?

By lunch time Jackie and Joyce ▭ most of the mowing.

did	have done	does	had done	had of done
A	**B**	**C**	**D**	**E**

2 Which of the following correctly completes this sentence?

Yesterday I ▭ cleaned my room.

should of	should've	should off	should'er
A	**B**	**C**	**D**

3 Choose the pair of words that correctly complete this sentence.

The cleaner stated, " ▭ are bins in every room but the new boys have left ▭ wrappers on the floor!"

Their there	They're there	There their	They're their
A	**B**	**C**	**D**

4 Which of the following correctly completes this sentence?

The ▭ of the old man was understandable.

anger	angry	angrily	angered
A	**B**	**C**	**D**

5 Choose the word that is not required in this sentence.

Dad completed a survey and was given a free gift for his effort.

completed	given	free	gift
A	**B**	**C**	**D**

6 Which of the following correctly completes this sentence?

'How ▭ money to replace the motor?' asked Dad.

much	many	more	mutch
A	**B**	**C**	**D**

Read the text *Peta Hana, cartoonist*. The text has some gaps.
Choose the best option to fill each gap. Circle a letter to show your answer.

Peta Hana, cartoonist
Peta Hana is a cartoonist for the Daily News.

Peta has ▭ many famous

people for newspapers. She ▭

fun of ▭ cricket captain when

7
draw	drew	drawn	drawed
A	**B**	**C**	**D**

8
mades	makes	made	make
A	**B**	**C**	**D**

9
her	an	are	the
A	**B**	**C**	**D**

☞ **Answers and explanations on pages 159-160**

GRAMMAR AND PUNCTUATION
Tenses, contractions and punctuation

he was ░░░░░ using his mobile

phone ░░░░░ the cricket field.

He won't do that ░░░░░

10

seed	seen	saw	sawn
A	B	C	D

11

on	in	for	by
A	B	C	D

12

again?	Again	Again!	again!
A	B	C	D

13 Which sentence has the correct punctuation?
 A 'Take your time?' Dad warned.
 B 'Take your time,' Dad warned.
 C 'Take your time, Dad warned.'
 D Take your time, 'Dad warned.'

14 Which sentence has the correct punctuation?
 A Horses, cows, and sheep need more care than cats, and dogs.
 B Horses cows and sheep need more care than cats and dogs.
 C Horses, cows and sheep need more care than cats and dogs.
 D Horses, cows and sheep need more care than cats, and dogs.

15 Which of the following correctly completes the sentence?

 The weather turned cold and Marie began to ░░░░░ .

shatter	shiver	shudder	shutter
A	B	C	D

16 Which sentence is correct?
 A May I and james give out the pencils?
 B May James and me give out the pencils?
 C May me and James give out the pencils?
 D May James and I give out the pencils?

17 Shade a bubble to show where the missing exclamation mark (!) should go.

 'That's mine▲ ' ▲exclaimed▲ Reg as he dashed across the room▲
 　　　　　　　(A)(B)　　　(C)　　　　　　　　　　　　　　(D)

18 Which two words should start with a capital letter? Write your answers in the boxes.

 of all people, there is no star as famous as the top french soccer player.

 ┌─────────────┐　┌─────────────┐
 │   │　│   │
 └─────────────┘　└─────────────┘

☞ **Answers and explanations on pages 159-160**

Test Your Skills

READING
Understanding poetry

Poetry can take many forms. It can tell a story (narrative verse), paint a word picture, or be the format for a play.

Poets create experiences that are shared with the reader. To do this the poet uses literary techniques such as figurative language (similes and metaphors), rhyme and rhythm. Poetry does not have to rhyme.

Poetry is often described as the most personal form of expression. Poets choose their words carefully and economically. They create images and feelings with words.

Read the poem *Stray Dog* by Elaine Horsfield and answer the questions. Circle the correct answer.

> **Stray Dog**
> A <u>tentative bark</u>—
> And then she sniffed the stranger,
> Circling <u>warily</u>,
> Unsure,
> Afraid to venture close
> For fear of harm.
>
> He bent down,
> Calling softly.
> Yet still she held back,
> Not confident enough
> To risk a touch.
> She'd been hurt before.

❶ This poem
   A tells a story.   **B** portrays an incident.   **C** describes a landscape.
   D explains a situation.   **E** warns the reader.   **F** explains dog care.

❷ Which **two** words have a similar meaning to 'warily'?
     warmly   angrily   violently   suspiciously   distrustfully
      A   **B**   **C**   **D**   **E**

❸ What was the response of the stranger to the dog?
   A He was hostile towards it.   **B** He was trying to win its trust.
   C He was afraid of it.   **D** He was trying to avoid it.

❹ A 'tentative bark' is
   A a loud bark.   **B** an excited bark.   **C** a threatening bark.   **D** a cautious bark.

❺ Why was the stray dog afraid to let the stranger touch her?
   A The man had hurt her before.   **B** Strangers had been cruel to her.
   C The dog didn't know the man.   **D** The dog was injured.

❻ Speaking softly to the dog was meant to
   A put the dog at ease.   **B** trick the dog.
   C gain control over the dog.   **D** taunt the dog into acting savagely.

☞ **Answers and explanations on page 161**

Real Test

READING
Understanding poetry

11 min

Read the poem *Rain* by Elaine Horsfield and answer the questions. Circle the correct answer.

Rain
Today it rained—again.
Big fat drops of rain
That fell from a <u>leaden sky</u>,
Disturbing the dirty pools of water,
And splashing mud on the <u>drooping</u> plants.

I watched the drops
<u>Trickle</u> down the windowpane,
Stopping and starting like cars on the road.
I looked at the grey sky
And thought how well it matched my mood.
Today it rained—again.

---

1 This poem
   A tells a story. B paints a word picture. C describes a landscape.
   D explains an incident. E warns the reader F explains features of rain.

2 Which word has a similar meaning to 'drooping'?
   A dropping B flowering C sagging D bending

3 How did the poet feel about the weather? She was feeling
   A dejected. B stressed. C thrilled. D thoughtful.

4 A 'leaden sky' is one that
   A is dark with heavy cloud. B causes traffic problems.
   C is full of thunder and lightning. D makes the windowpanes foggy.

5 The last line suggests that the
   A rain was very welcome. B poet's mood will continue.
   C windows will be well washed. D poet cannot go driving.

6 Which word has a similar meaning to 'trickle'?
   A gush B tickle C dribble D gurgle

7 The raindrops on the windowpane are like the traffic because they
   A are big and fat. B splash through mud puddles.
   C make the puddles dirty. D often start and stop.

8 The poet was watching the raindrops on the windowpane. She most likely did this because
   A it helped pass the time. B she found it exciting.
   C she was waiting for a car. D it was dark in the house.

☞ **Answers and explanations on page 161**

Many organisations hand out notices to advertise coming events. Notices, as well as fliers and posters, try to capture the reader's attention and provide information with a minimum of reading.

Study this Cockatoo School Fete notice and answer the questions. Circle the correct answer.

Plenty of parking at the **2020**   **FREE ENTRY**

COCKATOO SCHOOL FETE

Lucky Dip for pre-school children
Mystery visit by children's book author in the library

Jumping castle
Laughing clowns

Where: Cockatoo School Oval
When: Saturday 20 June
at 1 pm

Year 5 ART SHOW

1:00 Gates open for our Annual Fete
2:30 Official opening by Lord Mayor
3:00 Tug-of-war competition (adults' and children's teams)
3:30 Scottish Dancing Year 4 in the school gym
3:45 Pet Parade with Miss Kitty
3:45 Monster Hamper Draw (tickets: see Bob Blue)
3:50 Students v Parents Soccer

• Fabulous Food Stalls
• Mothers' Club BBQ
• Dad's Hot Dogs
• Year 6 Cold Drinks
• Fairy Floss

---

1 An annual event is one that is held
  A often.   **B** weekly.   **C** yearly.   **D** rarely.

2 In which location are most Cockatoo School fete activities held?
  A car park   **B** school oval   **C** school gym   **D** school library

3 The most likely reason for the stars on the notice is to show that
  A the fete is at night.   **B** the mystery author is a star.
  C the fete will be a fun event.   **D** some activities are dangerous.

4 A hamper is
  A an animal.   **B** pig meat.   **C** a raffle.   **D** a food basket.

5 What is Year 6 organising at the fete? Write your answer on the line.

6 Which activity is especially for pre-school children?
  A lucky dip   **B** Scottish dancing   **C** tug-of-war   **D** jumping castle

☞ **Answers and explanations on page 161**

Real Test

10 MIN

Many small businesses distribute information about their services or products through 'mail drops'. These are usually half-page fliers, often referred to as junk mail.

Study this flier from Betty's Big Spaghetti and answer the questions. Circle the correct answer.

Open every day 10 am

Betty's Big Spaghetti
176 Beach Road Camdenville
Eat-in, take-away or delivered
Phone: 11 11 2323 00

Last deliveries 10:30 pm

PASTA DISHES $14
Bolognese: tomato, beef, herbs
Puttanesca: tomato, olives, anchovies, capers
Marinara: tuna, clams, mussels, prawns, white wine sauce
Carbonara: bacon, cream, eggs, Parmesan cheese sauce

PIZZA $15 (large) $12 (small)
Napoli: spicy, cheesy and extra garlic!
Vegetarian: juicy, fresh vegetables only
Spinacci: spinach-flavoured topping
Funghi: mushrooms, oysters amd more!
Calzoni: rich with Italian sausage
Americano: a favourite in the USA

BREADS
Olive bread $6
Garlic bread $6
Tomato paste bread $7

SALADS
Italian $7
Greek $8
Green $5

SOUP of the day $4

Local area delivery fee:
$2.00 per delivery (orders less than $20)
Orders over $20 FREE

---

1 The word 'rich', as used in the flier, means
   A wealthy.   **B** spicy.   **C** thick.   **D** full flavoured.

2 What is the cheapest item on the menu? Write your answer on the line.

_____

3 The most likely reason for the arrows on the flier is to
   A draw attention to the name.   **B** show that service is quick.
   C suggest that the place is busy.   **D** give directions to Camdenville.

4 Which pasta dish is a seafood dish?
   A Bolognese   **B** Puttanesca   **C** Marinara   **D** Carbonara

5 The flier for Betty's Big Spaghetti, LEAST creates the impression of
   A home cooking.   **B** friendly service.
   C expensive dining.   **D** lengthy waits for service.

6 Which dish has an **extra** serve of garlic?
   A garlic bread   **B** Napoli pizza   **C** Puttanesca pasta   **D** Italian salad

7 How much would a Greek salad cost if delivered?

   Write your answer in the box.

☞ **Answers and explanations on page 161**

Real Test

Read the recipe for making Crunchy Apple Balls and answer the questions.

Crunchy Apple Balls (makes 16 balls)
You will need:
3/4 cup of crushed plain biscuit crumbs
1 cup of Corn Flakes
1/2 cup of dried coconut
250 g of finely chopped white chocolate
1 tablespoon of cooking oil
3 tablespoons of apple jam
3/4 cup of hundreds and thousands
Tip: Coconut or crushed nuts may be used instead of hundreds and thousands.

Method:
1. Put biscuit crumbs, Corn Flakes and coconut in a bowl and mix gently.
2. Melt chocolate in a bowl over hot water. (Do not melt with hot plate.)
3. Remove melted chocolate from heat and add oil. Stir until smooth.
4. Warm jam in a pot.
5. Make a hole about as round as a small glass in the dry mixture.
6. Pour jam and melted chocolate into hole and mix in gently.
7. Make balls by rolling a large spoonful of mixture.
8. Roll balls in hundreds and thousands and allow to <u>set</u> at room temperature.

1 What word could be used to replace the heading 'Method'?

   A Steps   **B** Style   **C** Plan   **D** Process

2 Write the numbers 1, 2, 3 and 4 in the boxes to show the order in which things should be done.

   ☐ Melt white chocolate.

   ☐ Mix chocolate and warm jam.

   ☐ Mix dry ingredients.

   ☐ Add hundreds and thousands to balls.

3 Which word would best describe the taste of Crunchy Apple Balls?

   A bland   **B** bitter   **C** plain   **D** sweet

4 What is meant by letting the Crunchy Apple Balls 'set'?

   A melt   **B** finish   **C** settle   **D** harden

5 What is the pot needed for?

   A to warm the jam   **B** to melt the chocolate
   C to store the hundreds and thousands   **D** to mix the biscuit, Corn Flakes and coconut

6 Which ingredient is required in the smallest quantity?

   A biscuit   **B** cooking oil   **C** coconut   **D** apple jam

7 What is the purpose of the hole in the dry mixture? Write your answer on the lines.

_____

_____

☞ **Answers and explanations on page 162**

TIPS FOR WRITING RECOUNTS

A **recount** tells about events that have happened to you or other people. The purpose of a factual recount is to record a series of events in the order they happened and evaluate their importance in some way. A recount can also be fictitious. Whether the recount is factual or fictitious remember to tell who, what, when, where and why. There are many types of recount—diaries, newspaper reports, letters and biographies. Recounts can be the easiest texts to write if you are given the choice. They don't need much planning or organisation as they are a straightforward record of events.

When writing recounts it is best to keep these points in mind. They will help you get the best possible mark.

Before you start writing

- Read the question and check the stimulus material carefully. *Stimulus material* means the topic, title, picture, words, phrases or extract of writing you are given to base your writing on.
- Remember that a recount is usually told in the past tense because the events described have already happened.
- Write about something you know. Don't try to write about something way outside your experience.
- Use a setting you are familiar with, e.g. home, school, sport, holiday place or shopping centre.
- When you have chosen your topic it might be helpful to jot down a few ideas quickly on paper so you don't forget them. Make up your mind quickly if you are writing a first-person recount (using *I* as the main character) or a third-person recount. If it is a personal recount, try to avoid too many sentences beginning with *I*.

The introduction

- A striking title gives impact to a recount. Newspaper reports do this well.

The body

- **Use conjunctions and connectives**, e.g. *when, then, first* or *next*. Because recounts can record either events that happen over a short period or events that happen over a lifetime, you need conjunctions and connectives to link and order the events.
- **Correctly paragraph your writing.** You need a new paragraph when there is a change in time or place, or a new idea. You may want to comment on the events as you write about them.
- **Include personal comments**, e.g. about your feelings, your opinions and your reactions, but only include comments that add to your recount. 'Waffle' and unnecessary detail don't improve a recount. It is better to stick to the facts without getting sidetracked.
- **Use language imaginatively** so that the recount is interesting, but don't try to fill it with weird or disgusting events.

The conclusion

- **Include a conclusion**. This tells how the experience ended. You may give your opinion about what happened and some thoughts you may have had about it. This final comment on the events or experiences is a way to wrap up your recount.

When you have finished writing give yourself a few moments to read through your recount. Quickly check spelling and punctuation, and insert words that have been accidentally left out.

WRITING
Recount 1

There is no way of knowing for certain what type of writing will be included in the NAPLAN Tests in years to come. This is an opportunity for you to practise different types of writing.

Before you start, read the General writing tips on pages 22–23 and the Tips for writing recounts on page 51.

A recount tells about events that have happened to you or other people. It is usually a record of events as they have happened. Events are told in order. A recount can conclude with a personal opinion of the event. Write your recount as a report; that is, tell what happened but don't write it in the first person (using personal pronouns such as *I* or *we*).

Today you are going to write a recount of a CLUB (or FAMILY) ACTIVITY. It could be a trip to a special place, a visit to a theme park, a picnic, a sporting event or a concert. Think about where you went for the activity and how you got there. Was it by bus or by train? Did you go in a private car or were you able to walk? It might be an activity for a few friends or a whole crowd. It can be just a few hours long or it could be an all-day event. Did anything unusual happen on the way? How did people react? How did you feel about the event? In what way was it a success or fun? Did anything happen to make the excursion less pleasant?

Before you start writing, give some thought to:
- where your recount takes place
- the characters and what they do in your recount
- the events that take place in your recount and the problems that have to be resolved
- how you, and others, felt about the activity—you may comment on events as you write about them.

Don't forget to:
- plan your recount before you start writing
- write in correctly formed sentences and take care with paragraphing
- choose your words carefully and pay attention to your spelling and punctuation
- write neatly but don't waste time
- quickly check your recount once you have finished.

Start writing here or type your answer on a tablet or computer.

Title: _____

_____

_____

_____

_____

_____

_____

_____

_____

☞ **Marking guide on page 162**

Real Test and Tips

There is no way of knowing for certain what type of writing will be included in the NAPLAN Tests in years to come. This is an opportunity for you to practise different types of writing.

Before you start, read the General writing tips on pages 22–23 and the Tips for writing recounts on page 51.

A recount tells about events that have happened to you or other people. It is usually a record of events as they have happened. Events are told in order. A recount can conclude with a personal opinion of the event.

Today you are going to write a personal recount about AN UNUSUAL DAY. Focus on the weather on that day. What was so extreme about the weather? Was it hotter or colder than usual? Were there extreme winds or rain? Did it snow or hail? Was it an unusual storm? An electrical storm? A fire storm? How did you react?

How did things change during the day? Did you go to the beach or build a snowman? How did the weather make you feel? Think about what you had to wear, and how you protected yourself against the sun, the wind or the cold. How did other people react? Was there a sudden and unexpected change in the weather?

Before you start writing, give some thought to:
- where your recount takes place
- the characters and what they do in your recount
- the events that take place in your recount and the problems that have to be resolved
- how you, and others, reacted to the extreme weather—you may comment on events as you write about them.

Don't forget to:
- plan your recount before you start writing
- write in correctly formed sentences and take care with paragraphing
- choose your words carefully and pay attention to your spelling and punctuation
- write neatly but don't waste time
- quickly check your recount once you have finished.

Start writing here or type your answer on a tablet or computer.

Title: _____

_____

_____

_____

_____

_____

_____

_____

☞ **Marking guide on page 163**

There is no way of knowing for certain what type of writing will be included in the NAPLAN Tests in years to come. This is an opportunity for you to practise different types of writing.

Before you start, read the General writing tips on pages 22–23 and the Tips for writing recounts on page 51.

A recount is a retelling of an event. It usually retells an event in the order the incidents happened. Choose one of the following events and write several paragraphs, with a conclusion based on your opinion of the event.

- My first time fishing
- My first day in a new class
- My best (or worst) day out

Before you start writing, give some thought to:
- where your recount takes place
- the characters and what they do in your recount
- the events that take place in your personal recount and the problems that have to be resolved
- how you, and others, felt about the event—you may comment on events as you write about them.

Don't forget to:
- plan your recount before you start writing
- write in correctly formed sentences and take care with paragraphing
- choose your words carefully and pay attention to your spelling and punctuation
- write neatly but don't waste time
- quickly check your recount once you have finished.

Start writing here or type your answer on a tablet or computer.

Title: _____

_____

_____

_____

_____

_____

_____

_____

_____

_____

_____

_____

_____

☞ **Marking guide on pages 163-164**

There is no way of knowing for certain what type of writing will be included in the NAPLAN Tests in years to come. This is an opportunity for you to practise different types of writing.

Before you start, read the General writing tips on pages 22–23 and the Tips for writing recounts on page 51.

Recounts can also recall historical (real) events, the lives of interesting people and other events the writer may not be directly involved in. Such recounts are written from an impersonal point of view.

Choose one of the following events and write several paragraphs, with a conclusion based on an opinion of or comment on the event.
- A school swimming carnival
- An inter-school (or inter-class) sports match
- An event you found particularly interesting or amusing

 Before you start writing, give some thought to:
- where your recount takes place
- the characters and what they do in your recount
- the events that take place in your recount and the problems that have to be resolved
- how you, and others, felt about the activity—you may comment on events as you write about them.

Don't forget to:
- plan your recount before you start writing
- write in correctly formed sentences and take care with paragraphing
- choose your words carefully and pay attention to your spelling and punctuation
- write neatly but don't waste time
- quickly check your recount once you have finished.

Start writing here or type your answer on a tablet or computer.

Title: _____

_____

_____

_____

_____

_____

_____

_____

_____

_____

_____

☞ **Marking guide on page 164**

We're halfway there!

Week 3

This is what we cover this week:

Day 1   **Measurement and Geometry:** ◎ Length and mass
◎ Area, volume and capacity
◎ Time

Day 2   **Spelling:** ◎ 'ie' and 'ei' words and the suffix 'ful'
◎ Common misspellings

Grammar and punctuation: ◎ Verbs and using 'of', 'have' and 'off'

Day 3   **Reading:** ◎ Understanding recounts
◎ Understanding explanations
◎ Understanding narratives

Day 4   **Writing:** ◎ Description of a scene
◎ Description of a person
◎ Book review
◎ Review of a production

MEASUREMENT AND GEOMETRY
Length and mass

Circle the correct answer.

1 What is the best measure for a hen's egg?
- **A** 60 g
- **B** 6 kg
- **C** 6 mg
- **D** 60 mg

2 The height of a household door is about
- **A** 1 m.
- **B** 1.5 m.
- **C** 2 m.
- **D** 2.5 m.

3 How many centimetres are there in 3.5 m?
- **A** 35
- **B** 305
- **C** 350
- **D** 3500

4 What is the perimeter of an 8 cm square?
- **A** 2 cm
- **B** 16 cm
- **C** 32 cm
- **D** 64 cm

5 What is the perimeter of this rectangle?
- **A** 18 cm
- **B** 31 cm
- **C** 36 cm
- **D** 65 cm

13 cm
5 cm

6 What is the perimeter of the shape?

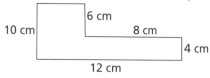

6 cm
10 cm
8 cm
4 cm
12 cm

- **A** 44 cm
- **B** 40 cm
- **C** 36 cm
- **D** 48 cm

7 The perimeter of a rectangular lawn is 36 m. One side is 6 m. What is the length of the other side?
- **A** 12 m
- **B** 15 m
- **C** 16 m
- **D** 30 m

8 All sides of a triangle have the same length. If the perimeter of the triangle is 36 cm, how long is each side?
- **A** 9 cm
- **B** 12 cm
- **C** 18 cm
- **D** 24 cm

9 Malcolm has three spheres and four cubes on a balance beam, as shown. All the spheres have the same mass and all the cubes have the same mass. If each sphere has a mass of 8 kg, what is the mass of each cube?

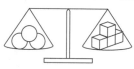

- **A** 3 kg
- **B** 4 kg
- **C** 6 kg
- **D** 8 kg

10 What would be the best way to measure the length of a winding garden path?
- **A** trundle wheel
- **B** tape measure
- **C** paces
- **D** school ruler

11 This is a small part of a road map.

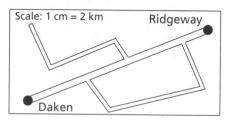

Scale: 1 cm = 2 km
Ridgeway
Daken

The real distance between Daken and Ridgeway is about
- **A** 4 km.
- **B** 5 km.
- **C** 8 km.
- **D** 10 km.

12 Estimate the length of this path.

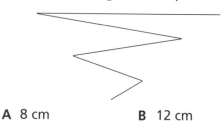

- **A** 8 cm
- **B** 12 cm
- **C** 10 cm
- **D** 15 cm

☞ **Explanations on page 165**

Key Points

MEASUREMENT AND GEOMETRY
Length and mass

❶ In **metric units** the prefix tells you the size.

Prefix	Symbol	Value	Example
milli	m	$\frac{1}{1000}$	milligram (mg)
centi	c	$\frac{1}{100}$	centimetre (cm)
Basic unit (1)			
kilo	k	$1000\times$	kilogram (kg)

❷ **Common measurements:**

$$10 \text{ mm} = 1 \text{ cm}$$
$$100 \text{ cm} = 1 \text{ m}$$
$$1000 \text{ mm} = 1 \text{ m}$$
$$1000 \text{ m} = 1 \text{ km}$$

$$1000 \text{ mg} = 1 \text{ g}$$
$$1000 \text{ g} = 1 \text{ kg}$$
$$1000 \text{ kg} = 1 \text{ t}$$

❸ **Perimeter** is the distance around a 2D shape. The perimeter of a 6 cm square is 24 cm. There are four sides each 6 cm long:
4×6 cm = 24 cm or
6 cm + 6 cm + 6 cm + 6 cm = 24 cm

6 cm

6 cm

The perimeter of a 4 cm × 7 cm rectangle is 22 cm: $(2 \times 4 \text{ cm}) + (2 \times 7 \text{ cm})$.

❹ Different devices are used to measure length and mass.

Length: rules, tapes, trundle wheels

Mass: balance beams, scales

❺ **Measurements** can be **converted** (changed) from one form to another.
To convert kilometres to metres or kilograms to grams, multiply by 1000:

13 km = 13 000 m
3 kg = 3000 g

❻ To **convert** metres to kilometres or grams to kilograms, divide by 1000:

13 000 m = 13 km
1458 m = 1.458 km
5000 g = 5 kg
5207 g = 5.207 kg

❼ **Estimating** is an important measurement skill. To make good comparisons it is useful to know the terms used and the sizes of some common objects (e.g. a kilogram of butter, a long step (about 1 m), the mass of a mobile phone).

❽ The **scale** on a map or diagram shows the amount of reduction or enlargement. A map may have this scale: 1 cm = 1 km. This means every centimetre of the map is the same as 1 km on land. If a map has the scale 1 cm = 2 km, then 3 cm on the map would be 6 km on land.

MEASUREMENT AND GEOMETRY
Length and mass

Circle the correct answer.

Parvati lays her pencil and her eraser along her ruler.

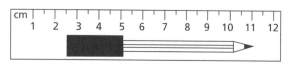

1 What is the length of the pencil? ⬚ cm

2 Estimate the length of the eraser?
A 25 mm **B** 50 mm **C** 75 mm **D** 100 mm

3 Year 5 students used a ruler to measure their handspans. Which of these is the best estimate for the length of one of their handspans?
A 1 mm **B** 1 cm **C** 10 cm **D** 100 cm

4 Sebastian is trying to lose weight and he wore a pedometer to count his number of steps. In one day it counted 7000 steps. Which of these would be the best estimate of the distance he walked?
A 600 m **B** 6 km **C** 60 km **D** 600 km

A grid is drawn from small squares. On the grid is a rectangle and triangle.

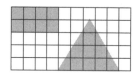

5 What is the perimeter of the rectangle? ⬚ units

6 If the sides of the triangle are equal, what is the perimeter of the triangle?
A 5 units **B** 6 units
C 10 units **D** 15 units

7 While training for a fun run, Ivan ran 5 times around a 600 metre running circuit. What was the total distance Ivan ran?
A 1 km **B** 1.1 km **C** 3 km **D** 6 km

8 The length of this book would be closest to
A 50 mm. **B** 30 cm. **C** 70 cm. **D** 250 cm.

9 How many centimetres in 50 metres?
A 0.5 **B** 5 **C** 500 **D** 5000

10 What is the perimeter of this shape?
A 50 cm
B 57 cm
C 66 cm
D 70 cm

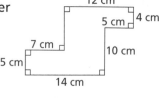

The grid shows the location of 3 towns. The distance from Elderslie to Stanhope is 12 km.

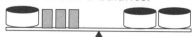

11 What is the distance from Elderslie to Glendon?
A 4 km **B** 6 km **C** 12 km **D** 24 km

12 What is the best estimate for the distance from Stanhope to Glendon?
A 5 km **B** 10 km **C** 18 km **D** 27 km

13 The sketch shows a balance.

This means that 1 cylinder is the same mass as
A ▮ **B** ▮▮
C ▮▮▮ **D** ▮▮▮▮

14 The masses of four objects are written on cards:

| 0.5 tonne | 600 grams | 1.7 kilograms | 90 grams |

Rearrange these masses from lightest to heaviest.

| | | | |

lightest   **heaviest**

15 From a 1 kg bag of rice, Jerome pours out 350 grams. What is the mass of rice remaining in the bag? ⬚ grams

16 The total mass of a 715 g book, a 280 g calculator and a 985 g lunchbox is closest to
A 1 kg. **B** 1.5 kg. **C** 2 kg. **D** 3 kg.

☞ **Answers and explanations on pages 165-166**

MEASUREMENT AND GEOMETRY
Area, volume and capacity

20 MIN

Circle the correct answer.

1 What is the area of this rectangle?

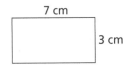

7 cm

3 cm

A 10 cm²   B 20 cm²
C 21 cm²   D 42 cm²

2 This shape is made up of 1 cm squares. What is its area?

A 6 cm²   B 7 cm²
C 8 cm²   D 16 cm²

3 What is the area of the shaded object?

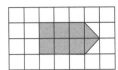

A 6 square units   B 7 square units
C 8 square units   D 10 square units

4 A jug contains a litre of water. If 350 mL is poured out, how much remains?
A 65 mL   B 75 mL
C 650 mL   D 750 mL

5 What is the volume of this 3 cm cube?

3 cm

A 3 cm³   B 6 cm³
C 9 cm³   D 27 cm³

6 The capacity of a bucket is about:
A 100 mL   B 10 L
C 60 L   D 200 L

7 Which shape has an area of 6 square units?

A   B

C   D

8 Find the area of the square with side 4 cm.

4 cm

4 cm

A 8 square centimetres
B 16 square centimetres
C 12 square centimetres
D 24 square centimetres

9 What is the volume of this solid?

A 9 cubic units
B 10 cubic units
C 12 cubic units
D 13 cubic units

10 What is the best unit of measurement for the amount of water in a cup?
A kilolitres
B millilitres
C centimetres
D grams

☞ **Explanations on page 166**

Key Points

MEASUREMENT AND GEOMETRY
Area, volume and capacity

1 **Revise your metric facts** (see Length and mass Key Point 1 on page 59).

2 **Common measurement relationships:**

$$1000 \text{ mL} = 1 \text{ L}$$
$$1000 \text{ L} = 1 \text{ kL}$$

3 **Area** is the amount of surface of a face or 2D shape.
Area is then recorded as cm^2 or m^2.
The area of this 6 cm square is thirty-six (36) 1 cm squares,
or 36 cm^2 (6 cm × 6 cm = 36 cm^2).

6 cm

The area of a 4 cm × 7 cm rectangle is 28 cm^2 (7 cm × 4 cm).

4 **Volume** is the space inside a container or the amount of space an object takes up.
The volume of this container is found by multiplying length × width × height (2 cm × 2 cm × 2 cm = 8 cm^3)

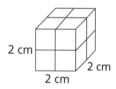

2 cm
2 cm
2 cm

5 Volume for **liquids** (**fluids**) is measured in mL, L and kL (capital L is used for litres so that the small l is not confused with numeral 1). Volume for **solids** is measured in cm^3 (cubic centimetres) or m^3 (cubic metres).

6 **Estimating** is an important measurement skill. You should know the measurement of some common objects (e.g. a litre of milk has a mass of about 1 kg or a volume of 1000 cm^3, a soccer ground has an area of about 1 ha).
A centicube has the volume of 1 cm^3.

7 All 2D shapes, including the faces of 3D shapes, have area. Curved surfaces also have area. All 3D shapes have volume, including 3D shapes with curved surfaces.

8 Students should be able to **convert** (change) between the various forms of measurement.
Example: To convert kilolitres to litres, multiply by 1000: 3 kL = 3000 L

Real Test

MEASUREMENT AND GEOMETRY
Area, volume and capacity

20 MIN

Circle the correct answer.

1 The diagram shows a grid containing a shaded shape. What is the area of the shape?

A 6 square units   **B** 8 square units
C 10 square units   **D** 12 square units

2 A square has an area of 20 square metres. How many squares are needed to cover an area of 260 square metres?

A 12   **B** 13   **C** 20   **D** 24

3 Belinda is covering a rectangle with small squares. How many more squares will she need to cover the entire rectangle?

A 2   **B** 4   **C** 9   **D** 18

The grid contains three shaded shapes.

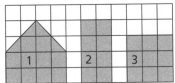

4 The shaded area of shape 1

A 10 square units.   **B** 12 square units.
C 14 square units.   **D** 16 square units.

5 What is the difference, in square units, in the areas of shapes 2 and 3?

A 1   **B** 2   **C** 8   **D** 9

6 The grid is to be completely covered with stickers. How many more stickers are needed?

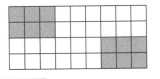

[ ] stickers

7 Which shape has the smallest area?

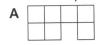 **A**

 **B**

 C

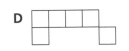 **D**

8 Giovanni shades a rectangle on the grid. If each side of the rectangle is doubled, what will happen to the area?

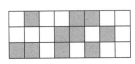

A The area will remain the same.
B The area will be multiplied by 2.
C The area will be multiplied by 3.
D The area will be multiplied by 4.

9 Tiffany wants half the squares shaded. How many more squares need to be shaded?

A 2   **B** 3   **C** 4   **D** 12

10 What is the volume of this solid?

A 6 cubic units   **B** 7 cubic units
C 8 cubic units   **D** 9 cubic units

11 What is the volume of this solid?
A 10 cubic units
B 20 cubic units
C 25 cubic units
D 30 cubic units

12 How many millilitres in half a litre?
A 5   **B** 50   **C** 200   **D** 500

13 The capacity of a teaspoon is closest to
A 5 millilitres.   **B** 100 millilitres.
C 500 millilitres.   **D** 5000 millilitres.

14 Andrew's petrol gauge is showing $\frac{1}{2}$ full. To fill the petrol tank, he pumps 30 litres into the tank. How much petrol is in the tank when it is full?

[ ] L

15 A cup contains exactly 250 millilitres. How many cups are needed to hold 2 litres?

[ ]

16 Mary opens a 1-litre carton of custard and pours 650 mL into a jug. How much custard remains in the carton?

[ ] mL

☞ **Answers and explanations on pages 166-167**

Test Your Skills

MEASUREMENT AND GEOMETRY
Time

Circle the correct answer.

1 James started his homework at 4:05 and finished 65 minutes later. At what time did he finish?

A 4:10 B 4:70
C 5 o'clock D 5:10

2 What is this time on a digital clock?

A 10:08 B 11:20
C 10:40 D 20:11

3 What is the time at a quarter to six?

A 5:15 B 5:25
C 5:45 D 6:15

4 What is the date 3 weeks after 10 November?

A 30 November B 31 November
C 1 December D 2 December

5 Mr Ryan was born in 1857. He died 78 years later. In what year did he die?

A 1945 B 1935
C 1925 D 1835

6 How many seconds are there in 2.5 minutes?

A 90 B 125
C 150 D 250

7 Mrs Brogan lived 13 years less than one century. How long did she live?

A 77 years B 83 years
C 87 years D 93 years

8 Marcia ran a long distance fun run in 256 minutes. How long is this in hours and minutes?

A 2 hrs 56 mins
B 4 hrs 16 mins
C 4 hrs 56 mins
D 5 hrs 6 mins

9

		JULY				
S	M	T	W	T	F	S
	1	2	3	4	5	6
7	8	9	10	11	12	13
14	15	16	17	18	19	20
21	22	23	24	25	26	27
28	29	30	31			

On 25th July, Jerome's teacher gave the class a project that was due four weeks later. What date was the project due?

A 14th August
B 15th August
C 21st August
D 22nd August

10 How many days in February in 2026?

A 28 B 29
C 30 D 31

11 A clock is showing the time as quarter past six. We know that it is 10 minutes slow. What is the correct time?

A 6:05 B 6:25
C 6:30 D 6:55

12 Bobbie was born in 1998. In what year will he celebrate his 50th birthday?

A 2040 B 2048
C 2049 D 2050

☞ **Explanations on page 167**

Key Points

MEASUREMENT AND GEOMETRY
Time

1 **Time** facts include:

60 seconds	=	1 minute
60 minutes	=	1 hour
24 hours	=	1 day
7 days	=	1 week
12 months	=	1 year
52 weeks	=	1 year
365 days	=	1 year
366 days	=	1 leap year
1 century	=	100 years

2 Know the **days of the week** (Monday, Tuesday, Wednesday, Thursday, Friday, Saturday, Sunday) and the months of the year (January, February, March, April, May, June, July, August, September, October, November, December). Know how many days in each month.

Months with 30 days: April, June, September, November

Months with 31 days: January, March, May, July, August, October, December

Months with 28 days: February (except for leap years when it has 29 days)

To work out what the date will be one week after 28 November: 2 days (November has 30 days) + 5 days = 5 December.

3 **Leap years** are every four years. To determine if a year is a leap year, the year must be evenly divisible by 4. 2016 was a leap year: 2016 ÷ 4 = 504.

4 **The day** is divided into **am** and **pm**: am refers to that part of a day between midnight and noon, and pm is the time between noon and midnight:

half past 6 in the morning = 6:30 am.

These labels are only used with 12-hour time.

5 **Years** are conventionally numbered from the birth of Christ (year 1). The year 2005 is 2005 years since the birth of Christ. This can be written as 2005 AD if there is a chance it will be confused with time before the birth of Christ. Years before the birth of Christ are referred to as BC (before Christ). The ancient Greeks, for example, lived in the BC period. The BC is also referred to as BCE (Before Common Era) and the AD period is also referred to as CE (Common Era).

6 Conversions between **analog and digital time** should be known as well as an understanding of the phrases 'quarter to the hour' and 'quarter past the hour'.

Example: Express the time 'A quarter to 8' in analog and digital time.

7 In Australia, the months are divided into **four seasons**.

Summer	Autumn
December	March
January	April
February	May
Winter	Spring
June	September
July	October
August	November

8 At the commencement of **daylight saving**, clocks are put forward one hour and at the end of daylight saving they are put back one hour.

Real Test

MEASUREMENT AND GEOMETRY
Time

20 MIN

Circle the correct answer.

1 How many minutes are there in 2 hours?
A 6   B 12   C 60   D 120

2 This is the time on the clock in Cedric's kitchen. What time is showing on the clock?

A 5 to 8   B 8 to 5
C 11 to 8   D 11 to 9

3 The time on Cedric's bedroom clock is 10 minutes ahead of the kitchen clock. What time is showing on his bedroom clock?
A 7:45   B 7:55   C 8:05   D 8:55

4 When Mike looks at his watch, the big hand is pointing to the 4. After 20 minutes, what number is the big hand pointing to?
A 5   B 6   C 7   D 8

5 The time is 4:30 and the library closes in two hours. Which clock shows the closing time?

A   B

C    D

6 Which of these is not true?
A There are 7 days in 1 week.
B There are 24 hours in 1 day.
C There are 60 seconds in 1 hour.
D There are 31 days in March.

7 Eliza's netball practice starts at 4:15 and lasts for one and a half hours. What time does training finish?
A 4:30   B 4:45   C 5:30   D 5:45

8 The night before daylight saving starts, Erica changes the clock on her kitchen clock. The time on her clock is 8:28 pm and she adds one hour to the time on her clock. What will be the new time?
A 8:29 pm   B 9:00 pm
C 9:28 pm   D 8:28 am

9 A movie runs for 2 hours 20 minutes. It commences at 5:35. What time will it finish?
A 5:55   B 5:57   C 7:35   D 7:55

10 Bree's mobile phone company charges her at the rate of 25 cents for every 30 seconds. How much will it cost Bree for a phone call that lasts for 2 minutes?
A 55 cents   B 75 cents
C 80 cents   D $1.00

11 Today is Manu's 11th birthday and his sister is 18. How old was his sister when Manu was born?

The month of July is shown.

JULY						
S	M	T	W	T	F	S
	1	2	3	4	5	6
7	8	9	10	11	12	13
14	15	16	17	18	19	20
21	22	23	24	25	26	27
28	29	30	31			

12 Lucas's birthday is on 17th July. If today is 3rd July, how many days until his birthday?

13 Use the calendar above to find what day of the week is 4th August.
A Thursday   B Saturday
C Sunday   D Tuesday

14 Pablo's family go on a ski holiday on the third Sunday in July. What is the date the holiday starts?
A 14th July   B 20th July
C 21st July   D 28th July

15 Today is 5th July. What day of the week is the day after tomorrow?
A Sunday   B Wednesday
C Saturday   D Monday

☞ **Answers and explanations on pages 167-168**

Key Points and Test Your Skills

SPELLING
'ie' and 'ei' words and the suffix 'ful'

15 min

 With most spelling rules there are exceptions. English words have many different origins (e.g. 'balaclava' comes from Central Europe and 'spaghetti' comes from Italy).

Key Points

❶ a In '**ie**' and '**ei**' words, the 'i' usually comes before 'e' when the sound is 'ee'.
Examples: piece, niece, field, diesel *but* ceiling is an exception

b In words where the sound is not 'ee', the 'e' comes before 'i'.
Example: height

c In words where the sound is 'ay', the spelling is usually 'ei'.
Examples: neighbour, eight, eighty, feint

❷ a The suffix '**ful**' means 'full' but is spelt with only one 'l'.
Examples: full of care → careful, full of use → useful, full of hate → hateful

b If the word ends with a consonant + 'y', then the 'y' is changed to 'i' before adding 'ful'.
Examples: beauty → beautiful, plenty → plentiful

Test Your Skills

Learn the words below. A common method of learning and self-testing is the **LOOK, SAY, COVER, WRITE, CHECK** method. If you make any mistakes, you should rewrite the word three times correctly, immediately. In this way you will become familiar with the correct spelling. If the word is particularly troublesome, rewrite it several more times or keep a list of words that you can check regularly.

This week's theme words: 'ie'/'ei' and 'ful' words

diet	_____	receipt	_____
heir	_____	hopeful	_____
dreadful	_____	lied	_____
mindful	_____	grief	_____
relief	_____	wonderful	_____
pliers	_____	tried	_____
receive	_____	neighbourly	_____
pitiful	_____	client	_____
friend	_____	spiteful	_____
review	_____	soldier	_____
plentiful	_____	brief	_____
pier	_____	meaningful	_____

Write any troublesome word three times: _____ _____ _____

_____ _____ _____

Real Test

Please ask your parent or teacher to read to you the spelling words on page 201.
Write the correct spelling of each word in the box.

1 Can you _____ that new tag to your bag?

2 There was some sort of _____ on the sports oval.

3 Andy spent a week in _____ after the accident.

4 There were _____ reasons for staying at home.

5 Mary felt _____ after the long hike.

6 The first letter of the alphabet is a _____.

Each line has one word that is incorrect.
Write the correct spelling of the underlined word in the box.

7 Scientists checked the <u>quallity</u> of the water.

8 Will the <u>govenor</u> arrive with the mayor?

9 The <u>berbar</u> was too busy to cut my hair today

10 I should <u>cumbe</u> my hair before going to school!

11 Always use the sharp <u>sisscors</u> to cut paper.

12 Dad has a rocking <u>chiare</u> on the back verandah.

Read the text *River Voyage*.
Each line has a word that is incorrect. Write the correct spelling of the word in the box.

River Voyage

13 Latter that afternoon Rod was out on the river in

14 a large boat with a powerfull outboard motor. A

15 smaller boat he towd behind. He was a long way

16 from the noises of town it felled very peaceful.

17 He bated a couple of hooks to catch some fish, then

18 lay back as the boat drifted gently down stream.

☞ **Answers on page 168**

Key Points and Test Your Skills

GRAMMAR AND PUNCTUATION
Verbs and using 'of', 'have' and 'off'

Key Points.

❶ **a** **Verbs** are often called **doing** words or **action** words. Doing verbs include verbs for thinking and speaking.
Examples: called, swam, collect, study, think, prepare, digest, compete

b There is a small group of verbs that are not doing or action verbs. These are often called **having** or **being** verbs. They do not involve actions or behaviour.
Examples: is, are, am, was, were
Sometimes these verbs combine with other verbs to make two-word verbs.
Examples: was running, is eating

❷ **a** Verbs can tell us when an action is, was or will be. This is called **tense**. Tense can be **past**, **present** or **future**. When an action happens can change the form of the verb.
Examples: Yesterday I <u>kicked</u> the ball. I <u>am kicking</u> the ball now. I <u>will kick</u> the ball soon.

b Some verbs change when the tense changes.
Example: dig, dug, will dig

❸ Troublesome words: People are often confused about when to use '**of**', '**have**' and '**off**'.
a When speaking, contractions such as 'could've', 'should've' and 'would've' can sound as if they end with 'of' (e.g. could of). This is never right. They should be 'could have' 'should have' and 'would have'.

b At times '**of**' is confused with '**off**', often in writing.
Example: 'The glass fell <u>off</u> the table.' (correct)   'The glass fell <u>of</u> the table.' (incorrect)

Test Your Skills

❶ Write the correct word (of, off, have) in the spaces.
a The boys could _____ finished on time if they had hurried.
b I took a book _____ the library shelf.
c Jenny is part _____ the school relay team.
d I would _____ used a spoon but I could not find one.

❷ Underline the five verbs in this passage.
Monday was hot and windy. Dad looked at the horizon and then at the dry paddock. He was hoping for rain. A flock of sheep grazed near a windmill. There was little grass covering the red soil.

❸ Write the tense (past, present or future) for each of these sentences.
a Jamie found his ball behind the carport. _____
b Julian will fly to New Zealand tomorrow. _____
c I am watching my favourite television show. _____

❹ Choose **see**, **sees**, **seen**, **seeing** or **saw** to fill the space.
All the students _____ the play.

❺ Choose the best 've type contraction for the space.
Jan _____ have been at school when the bell rang. She was late.

Real Test

GRAMMAR AND PUNCTUATION
Verbs and using 'of', 'have' and 'off'

❶ Which of the following correctly completes this sentence?

The Wong family now ▢▢▢▢ at the new supermarket.

shops	shop	shopped	shopping
A	**B**	**C**	**D**

❷ Choose the word that is not required in this sentence.

The State Emergency Service gave advance warning of the king tides.

Emergency	advance	warning	king
A	**B**	**C**	**D**

❸ Shade a bubble to show where the missing commas (,) should go.

I went to see ▲ Batman 4 ▲ the new movie ▲ at the Star ▲ Cinema.

Ⓐ   Ⓑ   Ⓒ   Ⓓ

❹ Which of the following correctly completes this sentence?

Kevin's interests are ▢▢▢▢ collecting model cars and racing posters.

on	for	with	in
A	**B**	**C**	**D**

❺ Which of the following correctly completes this sentence?

Has Sandra ▢▢▢▢ any of the cleaning?

did	done	does	do
A	**B**	**C**	**D**

❻ Which of the following correctly completes this sentence?

Who is the ▢▢▢▢ of the two witches?

ulgier	ulgiest	more ulgy	most uglier	more ugliest
A	**B**	**C**	**D**	**E**

Read the text *Table Hockey*. The text has some gaps.
Choose the best option to fill each gap.

Table Hockey

Table hockey is an indoor game.

It is a fast and rowdy game ▢▢▢▢ as

❼
and	but	yet	while
A	**B**	**C**	**D**

exciting as the outdoor ▢▢▢▢ but

❽
game.	game,	game!	Game
A	**B**	**C**	**D**

▢▢▢▢ much safer. To start, a referee

❾
as	also	it	so
A	**B**	**C**	**D**

☞ **Answers and explanations on pages 168-170**

Real Test

GRAMMAR AND PUNCTUATION
Verbs and using 'of', 'have' and 'off'

places the ball ▨▨▨ two players

⑩   in   among   at   between
      A   B   C   D

in ▨▨▨ centre of the board then

⑪   a   an   the   right
      A   B   C   D

▨▨▨ a signal for the game to start.

⑫   gives   gave   given   giving
      A   B   C   D

⑬ Which sentence has the correct punctuation?
   A Ask Casey for a hand? She's not doing anything.
   B Ask Casey for a hand. She's not doing anything.
   C Ask Casey for a hand. She's not doing anything?
   D Ask Casey 'for a hand?' She's not doing anything.

⑭ Which words should start with a capital letter? Use as many boxes as you need.

when we reached mt victoria the team could see lithgow in the distance.

⑮ Choose the word that best completes this sentence.

   The sun was ▨▨▨ brightly off the still water.
     flickering   sparkling   shining   glowing
       A   B   C   D

⑯ Which of the following correctly completes this sentence?

The school team walked ▨▨▨ from the field.
     slowly   slower   slow   slowing
      A   B   C   D

⑰ Draw a line to show which option correctly begins this sentence.
   A My brother and me are
   B My brother and I are | in the school choir. |
   C Me brother and I are
   D Me and my brother are

⑱ Brackets ( ) are required in this sentence. Which part of the sentence needs brackets?

On his second voyage of discovery 1772–1775 Captain Cook crossed the Antarctic Circle and almost reached the mainland of Antarctica.
     second   Captain   1772–1775   crossed the Antarctic Circle
       A   B   C   D

☞ **Answers and explanations on pages 168-170**

Test Your Skills

READING
Understanding recounts

A recount is a record of events that happened in sequence. A recount has several forms. It can be personal or historical. It may also contain opinions or personal comments on the events. Many newspaper articles are recounts.

Read this extract from *The Face on Mars* by Rachael Collinson and answer the questions. Circle the correct answer.

A photograph of the surface on Mars, taken in 1976 by the Viking spacecraft, clearly shows a face 2 km long. It could have been carved out of a Martian mountain 500 000 years ago.

Richard Hoagland, founder of an organization of scientists called The Mars Project, said that members of the National Aeronautics and Space Administration (NASA) had found the stone formation in the Viking photographs.

They did not take the face seriously at first. Dr Hoagland did. After studying the photographs for years, Dr Hoagland made other exciting discoveries. As well as the face there was 'a complex of unusual objects' that he believes could have been built by 'intelligent design'. The complex, which he called a 'city', included a five-sided mountain like a pyramid, and a grouping of rocks that could be a fortress.

Later, a computer enhancement of the Viking photographs showed that the face and other features could not just be 'a trick of light and shadow'.

Is it possible there had been a race of 'intelligent beings' on Mars?

The probe, Mars Observer, launched in 1993, carried a special camera that answered some of the questions about the face on Mars.

---

1 What is Dr Hoagland?
   A a scientist   **B** an astronaut   **C** a photographer   **D** a designer

2 What was one discovery Dr Hoagland made from the Mars photographs?
   A a spaceship   **B** a cliff   **C** a 'pyramid'   **D** a city

3 At the beginning of line 6 the word 'They' is underlined.
   Who does the word 'They' refer to? Write your answer on the line.

   _____

4 In the passage the word 'complex' refers to
   A buildings.   **B** difficulties.   **C** colours.   **D** hallways.

5 What is 'a trick of light and shadow'?
   A a fuzzy photograph   **B** a false impression
   C a wrong conclusion   **D** a light display

6 The article raises questions about
   A the quality of photographs.   **B** the importance of space research.
   C the work of Dr Hoagland.   **D** images transmitted from space probes.

7 The purpose of a space probe was to
   A take supplies to Mars.   **B** gather space information.
   C find aliens on Mars.   **D** return scientists to Earth.

☞ **Answers and explanations on page 170**

Real Test

READING
Understanding recounts

Read this passage from 'As The Wind Blows' by John Ruffles and answer the questions.
Circle the correct answer.

The successful Bondi Beach's Festival of the Winds has been running for more than 26 years. It is held every year in September. John Silk is the founder of The Festival of the Winds.

John was born in Nowra in 1949. He recalls his schoolteacher father trying to fly a homemade kite for him. It didn't get off the ground, and disappointed, John noted that, 'the wind was all wrong and my father did not have his heart in it anyway'.

After a course at Sydney University in 1971, John worked, making displays. One day, while in his bath, he was thinking of his father and *that* kite when he heard a voice tell him he should start a kite flying festival.

In early 1978, he told a journalist friend of his idea and word spread via the now <u>defunct</u> newspaper, 'Sydney Shout'. John met ceramic artist and kite sculpture maker Peter Travis, who he invited to be involved in his dream for a kite festival.

John put up $2,500 to fund his first festival and organised a display of Peter's kite sculptures. He made two dozen kites to ensure the festival would have kites to fly. He designed the festival to be a tribute to pioneer Australian box kite designer and aviator Lawrence Hargrave.

The first 'Festival of the Winds' was a huge success. The festival poster, dated September 1978, with an illustration of Hargrave and his box kites, has become a collector's item. The Sydney Kite Flyers Association has taken over the organization of the festival. In 2004, John Silk remains an interested and proud bystander.

1 The Festival of the Winds came about because
  A of a display of kites by Peter Travis.   **B** Lawrence Hargrave had built box kites.
  C Sydney University has kite making courses.
  D of the failure of a schoolteacher to get a kite to fly.

2 Who organised the latest kite festival at Bondi Beach?
  A Lawrence Hargrave   **B** Sydney Kite Flyers Association
  C Peter Travis   **D** John Silk

3 In which year was the first festival poster produced?
Write your answer in the box.

4 Where was the first Festival of the Winds held?
  A Nowra   **B** Bondi Beach   **C** a school   **D** Sydney University

5 Which term, with a similar meaning, could best replace 'defunct'?
  A broken   **B** not sold   **C** lost   **D** not produced

6 John Silk's attitude to Lawrence Hargrave could best be described as one of
  A respect.   **B** contempt.   **C** loyalty.   **D** wonder.

7 Draw lines to match each person with a fact.

| **1** Lawrence Hargrave | **2** John Silk | **3** Peter Travis |

| **A** creator of kite sculptures | **B** box kite designer | **C** founder of the kite festival |

☞ **Answers and explanations on page 170**

Test Your Skills

READING
Understanding explanations

The purpose of an explanation is to tell how or why something happens. Explanations can be about natural or scientific phenomena, how things work or events.

Read this passage on the Olympic Games and answer the questions. Circle the correct answer.

In 2004 the Olympic Games returned to Greece. The <u>previous</u> time the Games were held in Greece was over one hundred years earlier, in 1896. Those games were the start of the Modern Olympics.

In 776 BC the first Olympic Games were held at Olympia to honour the Greeks' most important god, Zeus. The ancient Greeks emphasised physical fitness and strength in their education of youth. Therefore, contests in running, jumping, boxing, discus and javelin throwing, and horse and chariot racing were held in cities of the Greek states and winners competed every four years at Olympia.

The winners were greatly honoured by having an olive <u>wreath</u> placed on their heads and having poems sung about their deeds. Gold, silver and bronze medals were not awarded.

Originally these were games of friendship and any wars in progress between any of the Greek states were halted to allow the games to take place.

The Greeks attached so much importance to these games that they calculated time in four-year cycles called 'Olympiads' starting with the 776 BC games.

---

1 The word 'previous', as used in this explanation, has a similar meaning to

later.	prior.	prevalent.	only.	foregoing.
A	**B**	**C**	**D**	**E**

2 Which of the following events was NOT held in the original games?

A swimming   **B** boxing   **C** horse racing   **D** discus throwing

3 Winners of events in the ancient games

A received gold medals.   **B** were congratulated by Zeus.
C became soldiers.   **D** had songs sung in their honour.

4 Which word, with a similar meaning, could best replace 'wreath'?

A garland   **B** headdress   **C** headband   **D** wrath

5 While the ancient Games were in progress

A schools had holidays.   **B** athletes climbed Mt Olympus.
C competitors formed friendships.   **D** wars between states halted.

6 A good title for the passage would be

A 'The 2004 Olympic Games'.   **B** 'In Memory of Zeus'.
C 'The First Olympic Medals'.   **D** 'Greece and the Olympics'.

7 Which statement is correct?

A Zeus was the founder of the first Olympic Games.
B The ancient Greeks valued physical fitness in education.
C The ancient games were held on Mount Olympus.
D There have only been three Olympic Games held in Greece.

☞ **Answers and explanations on pages 170-171**

Real Test

READING
Understanding explanations

Read this passage from *What a Waste!* by Stephen Jones and answer the questions. Circle the correct answer.

Hazardous wastes—solid and liquid wastes

It is well known that some wastes can be a danger to the health and lives of humans and all other living things. They can also damage the environment. These wastes may be poisonous, infectious (produce disease), flammable (burn readily) or explosive. Some may cause cancer and other forms of sickness.

Some of these wastes are produced by industries such as those making electronics, cloth and paper. Hospitals have materials that can spread disease if they are not disposed of carefully. These include bandages, syringes and materials infected by sick persons. Surprisingly, a lot of dangerous waste comes from our homes. Paints, cleaning fluids, drain cleaners, bleaches and insect sprays all contain dangerous chemicals. Batteries contain mercury and lead, which are dangerous to health.

The best way of dealing with dangerous waste is to produce less of it. If it is produced, it should be incinerated or put in a properly constructed tip. Liquids should be converted into solids before they are put into tips.

Gaseous waste

Most solid and liquid waste can be easily collected and disposed of and lots can be recycled. Gaseous waste, on the other hand, usually goes straight out into the air. Much of the gaseous waste is a product of industry. Gases are doing a great amount of damage to the environment all over the world. Important gaseous wastes are carbon dioxide, sulphur dioxide and fluorocarbons.

1 The purpose of the extract is to
A inform readers of the dangers of waste disposal.
B explain methods for recycling waste.
C show that gaseous wastes are the most dangerous waste.
D encourage homeowners to dispose of all waste products.

2 The most difficult waste products to manage are
A solids.   B syringes.   C gases.   D liquids.

3 Which products are NOT included in the list of dangerous waste?

Write your answer on the line. _____

4 According to the passage, where do most gaseous wastes come from?
A homes   B vehicles   C factories   D tips

5 Which word, with a similar meaning, could best replace 'incinerated'?
A buried   B dumped   C recycled   D burnt

6 Infectious wastes are most likely to be a product of
A hospitals.   B homes.   C tips.   D garages.

7 The information in the passage would most likely be found in
A a medical journal.
B an environmental booklet.
C a factory safety manual.
D a scientific magazine.

☞ **Answers and explanations on page 171**

Real Test

READING
Understanding narratives

Read the extract from *Show Off* by Hazel Edwards and answer the questions.

'Grade 5. Put your entries on the side table, please.' Mrs Black pointed to the long table, already <u>piled</u> with plates of cakes, monster masks and rainbow-coloured knitted squares. My lop-sided purple pottery mug was there too.

Mrs Black believed that all her children should enter something in the show.

'Make sure your name and the section you want to enter is on the entry form,' she said, fumbling for extra pens. Since losing her glasses on Monday, Mrs Black couldn't see too well. Students chatted excitedly as they filled in forms.

In last year's Grade 5, Amanda Brown won the prize for 'Most imaginative creature' in the Art and Craft section. Her entry was a pineapple stuck with toothpicks to look like an echidna.

Mrs Black kept mentioning that. 'Perhaps this year's Grade 5 will win something too'—she must have said it ten times a day in the week before the show. 'Especially since we have Amanda's cousin in the class this year.'

Matthew Brown just kept staring at the spider crawling on the windowsill.

Amanda was known for the things she did well. People always remembered Matthew for his mistakes.

1 Where are the events in the extract taking place?
- **A** in a classroom
- **B** in a cake shop
- **C** at Mrs Black's house
- **D** at an Art and Craft show

2 What did Amanda win a prize for? Write your answer on the line.

_____

3 Why did Mrs Black fumble for pens?
- **A** She was old and clumsy.
- **B** She had lost her glasses.
- **C** She was busy filling in a form.
- **D** She was excited about the show.

4 Which word could best replace 'piled'?
- **A** topped
- **B** covered
- **C** filled
- **D** heaped

5 What were the toothpicks used for?
- **A** to fill in entry forms
- **B** to make monster masks
- **C** to clean cake from teeth
- **D** as spikes for a model echidna

6 Why did Mrs Black think her class might do well in the show?
- **A** Her class always won a prize.
- **B** She had many entries on the table.
- **C** Amanda's cousin was in the class.
- **D** Students had filled in entry forms correctly.

7 This extract is most likely from a
- **A** humorous story.
- **B** myth or legend.
- **C** personal recount.
- **D** newspaper report.

☞ **Answers and explanations on page 171**

TIPS FOR WRITING DESCRIPTIONS

Descriptions function as pictures in words of people, places or things. In a description you aim to give the reader a clear and vivid picture of what you are describing. After reading your description the reader should be able to close his or her eyes and picture the subject.

Descriptions are seldom written to stand alone in the same way as, say, narratives or recounts. Descriptions are often part of another kind of writing; they help to make other text types interesting.

When writing descriptions, it is best to keep the following points in mind. They will help you get the best possible mark.

Before you start writing

- Read the question and check the stimulus material carefully. *Stimulus material* means the topic, title, picture, words, phrases or extract of writing you are given to base your writing on.
- Decide how you are going to present your description. It could be in the first person or third person. Take care when using the first person not to overuse the pronoun *I*.
- Decide on the tense you are going to use. Descriptions are usually written in the present tense but feel free to use past or future tenses if this suits your purpose.

The introduction

- Introduce the subject early in your writing. The title should put the subject in focus.

The body

- **Always include some facts**. Descriptions in an information report may consist entirely of facts.
- **Don't just focus on what can be seen**. Enhance your writing by adding 'imagined' sounds and smells—you can even describe how something feels.
- **Make full use of adjectives and adverbs**. Use a short series of adjectives to paint a vivid picture.
- **Use action verbs to describe behaviour**. This adds interest to your description.
- **Use figurative language such as similes and metaphors** to make your description clear and interesting. Avoid clichés.

The conclusion

- The final paragraph may include some brief personal opinions in your description—the best place for this is often in the form of a concluding comment.

When you have finished writing give yourself a few minutes to read through your description. Quickly check spelling and punctuation, and insert any words that have been accidentally left out.

WRITING
Description of a scene

42 MIN

There is no way of knowing for certain what type of writing will be included in the NAPLAN Tests in years to come. This is an opportunity for you to practise different types of writing.

Before you start, read the General writing tips on pages 22–23 and the Tips for writing descriptions on page 77.

The aim of a description is to give the reader a clear and vivid word picture of a person, thing, place or scene. Descriptions of scenes are often important in narratives. They can help create different moods and atmosphere.

Today you are going to write a description of a GARDEN. Think of a garden you know well. Is it a private garden or a public garden? Is it a big or little garden? Is it well maintained? Is it a flower garden, a vegetable garden or a native garden? Start your description with a sentence naming what you are about to describe. Then think about colours, sounds and smells. Think about how the garden is used and the effort required to care for it. What birds and other animals enjoy the garden? Is the weather important?

Before you start writing, give some thought to:
- the setting—what you are describing
- the special features of the garden
- what value the garden has to the owners and the community.

Don't forget to:
- plan your description before you start writing.
- write in correctly formed sentences and take care with paragraphing
- choose your words carefully and pay attention to your spelling and punctuation
- write neatly but don't waste time
- quickly check your description once you have finished.

Start writing here or type your answer on a tablet or computer.

_____

_____

_____

_____

_____

_____

_____

_____

_____

_____

_____

☞ **Marking guide on pages 171-172**

There is no way of knowing for certain what type of writing will be included in the NAPLAN Tests in years to come. This is an opportunity for you to practise different types of writing.

Before you start, read the General writing tips on pages 22–23 and the Tips for writing descriptions on page 77.

The aim of a description is to give the reader a clear and vivid word picture of a person, thing, place or scene. Descriptions of scenes are often important in narratives. They can help create different moods and atmosphere.

Today you are going to write a description of an AMATEUR SPORTSPERSON or a friend you play sport with. (An amateur is not a paid sportsperson.)

Think about what makes the person interesting or different. You can write about the person's appearance. Think about their hair, eyes, their stature (height and size) and anything you notice or remember about them. Then think about their mannerisms (the way they do things), habits and behaviour, especially on the field. Think about what they like doing and what seems to upset them. What do they do for relaxation? How do they speak? Are they noisy and outgoing, or quiet? Do they have other interests?

Before you start writing, give some thought to:
- where the person spends some or a lot of their time
- the character of the sportsperson—attitude towards other players, the opposition and team members
- how you or other sportspeople relate to the person.

Don't forget to:
- plan your description before you start writing.
- write in correctly formed sentences and take care with paragraphing
- choose your words carefully and pay attention to your spelling and punctuation
- write neatly but don't waste time
- quickly check your description once you have finished.

Start writing here or type your answer on a tablet or computer.

_____

_____

_____

_____

_____

_____

_____

_____

_____

_____

_____

☞ **Marking guide on page 172**

WRITING
Book review

The aim of a review is to give readers information about a book, play, film, electronic game or concert. Reviews are often found in newspapers.

> Write a review of a novel or children's story you have read recently. A book review should include: the book's title and author, a brief summary of the plot that doesn't give away too much, and the reviewer's personal opinion of the book with specific examples to support praise or criticism. You could mention the quality of any illustrations.

Before you start writing, give some thought to:
- the material you are reviewing: the strengths and weaknesses of the subject matter
- the style, setting, characters, illustrations and main events of the book
- a concluding personal judgment and recommendation.

Don't forget to:
- plan your book review before you start writing
- identify the book and author, and the type of book
- write in correctly formed sentences and take care with paragraphing
- choose your words carefully and pay attention to your spelling and punctuation
- write neatly but don't waste time
- quickly check your book review once you have finished.

Start writing here or type your answer on a tablet or computer.

Book/story: _____ Author: _____

_____

_____

_____

_____

_____

_____

_____

_____

_____

_____

_____

_____

_____

_____

_____

☞ **Marking guide on page 173**

Real Test and Tips

WRITING
Review of a production

42 MIN

Write a review of a television show, film or play you have seen recently.

Before you start writing, give some thought to:
- the name of the production, its location and who was in it
- your reaction to the staging, cost and enjoyment of the show, and the ability of the participants (actors).

Don't forget to:
- plan your review before you start writing
- write in correctly formed sentences and take care with paragraphing
- choose your words carefully and pay attention to your spelling and punctuation
- write neatly but don't waste time
- quickly check your review once you have finished.

Start writing here or type your answer on a tablet or computer.

Name of film/show: _____

_____

_____

_____

_____

_____

_____

_____

_____

_____

_____

_____

_____

_____

_____

_____

_____

_____

_____

_____

_____

☞ **Marking guide on pages 173-174**

Let's start to revise!

Week

4

This is what we cover this week:

Day 1 **Number and Algebra:** ◎ Patterns

Statistics and Probability: ◎ Graphs, tables and data

◎ Probability

Day 2 **Spelling:** ◎ Words ending in 'y', homophones and 'demon' words

◎ Common misspellings

Grammar and punctuation: ◎ Pronouns, prepositions, adverbs and apostrophes

◎ Pronouns, prepositions and punctuation

Day 3 **Reading:** ◎ Following procedures

◎ Understanding a book review, a table of contents and poetry

Day 4 **Writing:** ◎ Procedure

◎ Explanation

◎ Report from an outline

◎ Response to a picture

Test Your Skills

NUMBER AND ALGEBRA
Patterns

20 MIN

Circle the correct answer.

1 $5 \times 8 = 2 \times \square$
$\square = ?$

A 10   B 11
C 16   D 20

2 Which pattern is an example of doubling?
A 3, 6, 12, 24, 48
B 2, 4, 6, 8, 10, 12
C 1, 2, 3, 6, 10, 15
D 64, 32, 16, 8, 4, 2

3 If $72 \div 6 = 12$, then $6 \times \square = 72$
$\square = ?$

A 8   B 9
C 12   D 64

4 What is the next term in this sequence?
1.1, 1.9, 2.7, 3.5, 4.3, 5.1, ?
A 5.8   B 5.9
C 6.1   D 6.9

5 This is the start of a number pattern.
34, 41, 48, 55, ...
If the pattern is continued what will the tenth term be?
A 90   B 95
C 96   D 97

6 $16 + 25 - \square = 29$
$\square = ?$

A 2   B 11
C 12   D 31

7 $29 + 29 + 29 + 29 + 29 = \square \times 5$
$\square = ?$

A 15   B 19
C 29   D 58

8 $8 + 7 \times 9$ is the same as
A $8 \times 7 + 9$
B $9 \times 7 + 8$
C $9 + 8 \times 7$
D $8 \times 7 \times 9$

9 What is the first number in this sequence?
?, 89, 77, 65, 53, 41
A 90
B 99
C 100
D 101

10 Find $\square$ so that $13 + 9 = \square - 6$
A 16
B 22
C 28
D 32

11 What is the rule for this sequence?
3, 6, 12, 15, 30, 33, 66, 69
A Double each term.
B Add 3 then double, and so on.
C Multiply by 2 then by 3, and so on.
D Add 3 then 6 then 9, and so on.

12 Find the missing number in this number pattern.

5	6	8	10	13
12	14	18	22	?

A 23   B 24
C 26   D 28

13 Find the missing number in this number pattern.

27	21	18	12	?
9	7	6	4	1

A 0   B 2   C 3   D 4

☞ **Explanations on page 174**

Key Points

NUMBER AND ALGEBRA
Patterns

1 **Relating addition to subtraction:**
The total of two (or more) numbers produces a number of facts,
e.g. 6 + 7 = 13, 7 + 6 = 13, 13 − 6 = 7, 13 − 7 = 6

2 **Relating multiplication to division:**
The product of two (or more) numbers produces a number of facts,
e.g. 3 × 5 = 15, 5 × 3 = 15, 15 ÷ 3 = 5, 15 ÷ 5 = 3

3 **Multiplication** is repeated addition:
8 + 8 + 8 + 8 + 8 + 8 + 8 = 7 × 8 because there are seven lots of eight to be added.

4 **Number sequences** can be made up of increasing numbers (e.g. 2, 4, 6, 8, ...) or decreasing numbers (e.g. 21, 20, 19, 18, ...). Sequences can be devised on all four operations.

5 More **difficult sequences** may involve two or more steps. In the following sequence you first add 3 and then multiply by 2 (double).
5, 8, 16, 19, 38, 41, 82, ...

6 **Sequences may involve fractions** and decimals, e.g. $\frac{1}{2}, \frac{1}{4}, \frac{1}{8}, \frac{1}{16}, ...$

7 You should be able to find the **missing number in a number sentence**.
Examples: 6 + ? = 13
The missing number is 7.

2 × 8 = 3 + □
Then □ = 13 (2 × 8 = 16 and 3 + 13 = 16)

The missing number can be in any position.

Example:
□ ÷ 8 = 16 − 7.
Then □ = 72 (72 ÷ 8 = 9 and 16 − 7 = 9)

8 **Order of operations:**
When calculating the value of number sentences there is an order in which the various operations must be done. This order is to do **brackets** first, then **multiplying** (of) and **dividing**, finally **addition** and **subtraction**.

This means you should work out the terms in brackets first, then multiplication and division, addition and subtraction:
(6 − 2) × 8 + 5 = (4) × 8 + 5 = 32 + 5 = 37

9 The **signs + and −** are called **weak signs**. The **signs × and ÷** are called **strong signs**. In any calculation with mixed signs the strong signs are calculated first.
To calculate 6 + 9 × 2, first multiply 9 × 2 and then add 6 + 18.

10 In **number patterns** you are asked to find a number after you have been given a set of numbers.

1	6	8	11	13
2	7	9	12	?

In this pattern, the missing number is 14. The lower row is one greater than the top row.

11 **Number patterns** (as with sequences) can be based on any of the **four operations** or can involve two-step operations.

1	6	8	11	20
7	22	28	37	?

In this pattern the missing number is 64 (× 3, then + 4).

12 **Number patterns** can be created around **many shapes**.

1	2		4	5		7	8		10	11
2	4		8	7		14	10		?	13

The missing number is 20 (the operations are +1, +2 and doubling).

13 You may be asked to describe **single step** and **two-step sequences**. What is the rule for this sequence?
1, 9, 17, 25, 33, 41
It is a single step sequence. The numbers are increasing by 8.

Real Test

NUMBER AND ALGEBRA
Patterns

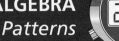

Circle the correct answer.

1 The pattern is made by adding 11 to each number:

17   28   39   □

What is the next number?

A 40   **B** 50   **C** 51   **D** 60

2 Complete the pattern:

85   76   67   58   □

A 9   **B** 11   **C** 49   **D** 47

3 The same number is written in each circle to make the number sentence correct.

◯ + ◯ + ◯ = 24

What number is placed in the circles?

A 8   **B** 12
C 14   **D** 72

4 Melanie coloured squares on this chart in an ascending order. What will be the seventh number shaded?

1	2	3	4	5
6	7	8	9	10
11	12	13	14	15
16	17	18	19	20
21	22	23	24	25

A 1   **B** 21   **C** 24   **D** 25

5 What is the missing number in the table?

1	2	3	4	5
6	12	18	?	30

A 20   **B** 24   **C** 25   **D** 26

6 Yolanda wrote this pattern of numbers

□, 32, 16, 8, 4, 2

What is the missing number?

Write the answer in the box.

7 Which pattern is counting forward by 11?

A 11, 21, 31, 41   **B** 6, 16, 116, 1116
C 20, 31, 43, 57   **D** 3, 14, 25, 36

8 12 × 3 = 4 × □

What number is written in the box to make the number sentence correct?

A 6   **B** 8   **C** 9   **D** 36

9 Complete this pattern:

30 – 12 = 18
40 – 12 = 28
50 – 12 = 38
80 – 12 = □

What number is written in the box?

A 8   **B** 48   **C** 58   **D** 68

10 How many squares are there in the next diagram?

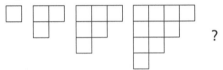

?

A 5   **B** 10   **C** 12   **D** 15

11 Geoff wrote this pattern of numbers.

90, 82, 74, 66, ? , 50, ?

Which two of these numbers will be in his pattern? Select **both** answers.

8   58   48   44   42
A   **B**   **C**   **D**   **E**

12 Look at these number sentences:

△ + △ = 12   △ – ◯ = 4

What is the value of the circle?

A 1   **B** 2   **C** 3   **D** 6

13 20 □ 5 = 4

What mathematical symbol must be written in the box to make the number sentence true?

A +   **B** –   **C** ×   **D** ÷

14 Here is Victor's number pattern:

3, 6, 9, 12, 15, …

What is the eighth number in Victor's pattern?

A 18   **B** 21   **C** 24   **D** 27

15 0.3, 0.5, 0.7, 0.9, □

What is the next number in the pattern?

Write your answer in the box.

16 Arpita called out this pattern. Starting at 100 and counting backwards by 5. What was the fourth number she called out?

☞ **Answers and explanations on pages 174-175**

STATISTICS AND PROBABILITY
Graphs, tables and data

20 MIN

Circle the correct answer.

① What does this tally represent? ⊪⊪ ⊪⊪ |||
   A 2.5   **B** 8
   C 11   **D** 13

② In a number of tests out of 10, Jake scored 6, 8, 9, 5 and 7. What was Jake's average score?
   A 5   **B** 7
   C 14   **D** 35

③ In a cricket competition Judy scored 12, 30, 2 and 0. What must she score in her next match to have an average of 12?
   A 11   **B** 12
   C 16   **D** 60

④ Jamie received a gift of $80. This graph shows how he spent his money. How much money did Jamie spend on fast food?

   A $10   **B** $20
   C $30   **D** $40

⑤ This pictograph shows the number of ski lifts in four alpine ski towns. What is the total number of ski lifts?

Skiville	❅❅❅❅❅
Hilltop	❅❅❅
Whitely	❅❅
Chalet	❅❅❅❅

❅ = 2 ski lifts

   A 28   **B** 26
   C 14   **D** 10

⑥ This graph shows the sales of family paintings by classes at a school fete. How many paintings did 4H sell?

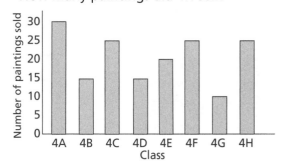

   A 25   **B** 20
   C 15   **D** 10

⑦ Members of the local sports club sold tickets in two raffles. This table shows the results. Who sold the most raffle tickets?

	Sue	Joe	Leo	Eve
Raffle 1	23	21	19	20
Raffle 2	18	14	26	15

   A Sue   **B** Joe
   C Leo   **D** Eve

⑧ Refer to the above table. How many tickets were sold in Raffle 2 by the members of the club?
   A 83   **B** 82
   C 74   **D** 73

⑨ This divided bar graph shows how Mr Brown spends his Sunday. About how much time does Mr Brown spend playing golf?

Time spent on Sunday

| TV | golf | garden-ing | meals | sleeping |

   A 1 hour   **B** 3 hours
   C 8 hours   **D** 12 hours

☞ **Explanations on page 175**

Answers: 1 D **2** B **3** C **4** B **5** A **6** A **7** C **8** D **9** B

STATISTICS AND PROBABILITY
Graphs, tables and data

1 Types of graphs:

a **Bar graphs** can be organised vertically or horizontally. Take care with the horizontal and vertical labels.

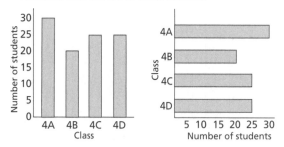

b **Pie graphs** (or circle graphs or sector graphs) show portions or sections of a whole. This graph shows how Les spent two hours doing homework. Les spent half his time doing Maths.

c **Line graphs** show data joined by segments of a line. This graph shows that the temperature at noon was about 23 °C.

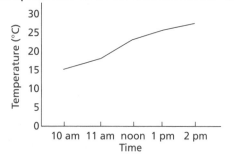

d **Divided bar graphs** are similar to pie graphs but show data in a bar form. this shows that Ms Lily has fewer orchids than violets.

Flowers in Ms Lily's garden

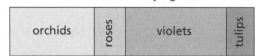

e **Pictographs** (or picture graphs) use pictures to display data. Halves are shown by half pictures.

NSW					
Qld					

 = 4 skiers

There were 22 skiers from Queensland $(5 \times 4 + \frac{1}{2} \times 4)$.

2 Types of tables:

a **One-way tables**. These show one line of data.

Betty	Tracey	Holly	Joyce	Dave
$12	$16	$21	$7	$32

Dave saved the most money.

b **Two-way tables**. These tables can be read down and across.

	Sue	Joe	Leo	Eve
Test 1	66%	51%	48%	76%
Test 2	68%	57%	58%	78%

Sue's total score was greater than Leo's total score.

3 A **tally** is a quick way to keep a record or a score and add up totals. Tallies are made with four vertical marks and one cross mark equalling five.
Examples: ||||| = 5; ||||| || = 7

4 An **average** is a score that represents the whole collection. It is found by adding all the individual scores and dividing the total by the number of scores.

The average of 2, 8 and 8 is 6
(2 + 8 + 8 = 18; 18 ÷ 3 = 6)

Another word for average is **mean**.

Real Test

STATISTICS AND PROBABILITY
Graphs, tables and data

20 MIN

Circle the correct answer.

The school held a pie drive. The sales were recorded in this pictograph.

Pie sales

Yr 3	Yr 4	Yr 5	Yr 6

🥧 = 10 pies

1 How many pies were sold by year 5?
A 10 **B** 40 **C** 45 **D** 55

2 How many year groups sold more than 45 pies?
A 1 **B** 2 **C** 3 **D** 4

3 How many more pies were sold by Year 5 than Year 4?
A 5 **B** 15 **C** 25 **D** 35

4 What was the total number of pies sold by the school students?
A 17 **B** 160 **C** 170 **D** 200

5 If the school made a $3 profit on each pie sold, which year group made $75 profit for the school?
A Yr 3 **B** Yr 4 **C** Yr 5 **D** Yr 6

120 students were surveyed. The graph represents their favourite sports.

6 What was the favourite sport?
A basketball
B soccer
C swimming
D netball

swimming · basketball · soccer · netball

7 Estimate the number that chose basketball
A 25 **B** 30 **C** 40 **D** 60

8 What is the best estimate for those who chose soccer?
A 20 **B** 50 **C** 60 **D** 80

Suzi recorded the ages of the children at the holiday camp in the table below.

Age	7	8	9	10	11	12
Children	5	8	11	14	10	2

9 How many 11-year-olds attended the camp?
A 9 **B** 10 **C** 12 **D** 16

10 How many children attended the camp?
A 14 **B** 40 **C** 50 **D** 140

11 How many children were aged more than 10 years old?
A 2 **B** 11 **C** 12 **D** 26

The table shows the number of sit-ups Shayne completed over 5 days.

Mon	Tue	Wed	Thu	Fri
10	8	?	12	10

Over the 5 days Shayne completed 50 sit-ups.

12 How many sit-ups did Shayne complete on Wednesday?

13 On the Saturday he completed twice as many sit-ups as he had completed on Tuesday. What was the total number of sit-ups completed by Shayne across the six days?

This table shows the amount of money that four students spent at the canteen.

Josie	Max	Angie	Jack
$3.30	$1.05	$2.90	$1.85

14 Who spent the largest amount of money?
A Josie **B** Max **C** Angie **D** Jack

15 How many students spent at least $2?

Write your answer in the box.

16 What was the total spent by Angie and Jack?
$

☞ **Answers and explanations on pages 175-176**

STATISTICS AND PROBABILITY
Probability

Circle the correct answer.

1 If a dice is tossed, what is the chance of throwing a five?
A 1 chance in 2 B 1 chance in 3
C 1 chance in 5 D 1 chance in 6

2 Which term best describes the possibility of warm days in spring?
A unlikely B most likely
C not likely D certain

3 A coin is tossed. What is the chance of getting a tail?
A 1 out of 2 B 1 out of 3
C 1 out of 5 D 1 out of 10

4 Tim has 4 red blocks, 5 green blocks and 3 black blocks in a bag. Without looking he takes one out. What are the chances it is a red block?
A 1 in 3 B 1 in 4
C 1 in 8 D 1 in 12

5 These cards are turned over and mixed around.

| 3 | 2 | 4 | 4 | 2 | 1 |

What is the chance of selecting a 3?
A 1 out of 2 B 1 out of 3
C 1 out of 6 D 3 out of 6

6 Peter made this spinner.

He painted it these colours. What colour is Peter most likely to get when he spins his spinner?
A red B black
C green D blue

7 A bag contains 6 balls. Two of the balls are black and the rest are white. If a ball is chosen at random, what is the chance that it is white?
A likely B unlikely
C impossible D certain

8 Which of these events has a fifty-fifty chance of happening?
A Someone will have a party today.
B The next baby born will be a girl.
C The news will not be on television.
D Aliens will land on Bondi Beach.

9 A raffle consists of 20 tickets. There is only one prize. How many tickets will Jo buy if the chance of her winning the prize is 'fifty-fifty'?
A 1 B 10
C 15 D 20

10 A dice is tossed. What is the chance of throwing a number less than 4?
A 1 in 6 B 1 in 3
C 1 in 2 D 3 in 5

11 5B conducted a survey of cars passing the school in one hour. These were their results.

Car	Number
Holden	3
Hyundai	12
Mazda	17
Toyota	8
Kia	1

The next car to go past will most likely be a
A Mazda. B Hyundai.
C Holden. D Kia.

☞ **Explanations on page 176**

Answers: 1D 2B 3A 4A 5C 6A 7A 8B 9B 10C 11A

Key Points

1 **Probability** refers to the chance of an event occurring. It is usually expressed as a fraction, decimal or percentage but can also be expressed in terms such as '1 chance in 3'.

2 The probability of an event occurring can be placed on a scale of 0 (zero) to 1 (one).

```
0                           1
impossible              certain
```

The probability of a female cat having at least 10 kittens would be closer to 0 than 1.

3 Some common objects used in **games of chance** are dice, coins, spinners and playing cards.

4 The chance of tossing a coin and getting a head is 1 chance in 2, or 50%.
The chance of getting a two with the roll of a dice is 1 chance in 6, or about 16%.
The chance of cutting a Queen of Hearts from a pack of cards is 1 chance in 52.

5 Often you will be asked to determine the **chance with a number of variables**.

Example:
In a bag Jack has 3 blue counters, 2 black counters and 5 white counters. If he takes a counter without looking, what are the chances it will be blue?
The answer is 3 chances out of 10 (counters). What are the chances of it being white?
1 chance in 2 because there were 5 white counters ($\frac{5}{10}$).

6 From data (information) gained, the likelihood of an event happening can be **predicted**. Weather records allow scientists to predict what the weather will be like at a particular time of the year.

7 **Surveys** are often used to collect data. A survey of what children eat after school may allow nutritionists to predict future health problems.

This was the result of a survey of pets that students in five classes have at home.

Class	Cats	Dogs
4A	8	2
4C	12	5
5A	9	8
5F	11	4
6T	10	6

If a student in 6T is chosen at random, it is more likely that the student has a cat than a dog at home.

8 **You should be familiar with these terms**: possible/impossible; certain/uncertain; likely/unlikely; probable; likelihood.

Real Test

STATISTICS AND PROBABILITY
Probability

20 MIN

Circle the correct answer.

1 What is the chance that the sun will rise tomorrow?
A impossible   **B** likely
C possible   **D** certain

2 Sam wears a blindfold and chooses a ball from a bag. It is likely but not certain that Sam will choose a white ball. Which is Sam's bag?

A **B** **C** **D**

3 A spinner is made and a section is shaded. What word describes the chance of landing on the shaded section?

A impossible   **B** unlikely
C likely   **D** certain

4 Six cards are placed in a bag. Three are yellow and three are green. Without looking, Marc chooses a card from the bag. What term describes the chance that it is yellow?
A impossible   **B** equal chance
C very likely   **D** certain

The picture shows a standard dice. Mary rolls the dice.

5 What is the chance she rolls a 4?
A 1 chance in 2   **B** 1 chance in 4
C 1 chance in 5   **D** 1 chance in 6

6 Suppose Mary rolls the dice again. What is the chance she rolls another 4?
A 1 chance in 2   **B** 1 chance in 4
C 1 chance in 5   **D** 1 chance in 6

7 Imran tosses 2 coins and writes down the results. Which of these is not possible?
A head then a tail   **B** 2 tails
C head, tail then a head   **D** 2 heads

8 A bag contains three times as many red balls as blue balls. What is the chance of selecting a red ball?
A 1 in 3   **B** 1 in 4   **C** 2 in 3   **D** 3 in 4

9 Hayden made this spinner and painted it these colours.

What colour is he most likely to get on his next spin?
A red   **B** blue   **C** yellow   **D** pink

A bag contains 20 jelly beans. In the bag there are 12 black jelly beans, 3 red jelly beans and the rest are green.

10 How many jelly beans are green?
Write your answer in the box. ☐

11 Without looking, Raj chooses a jelly bean from the bag. What is the chance that it is red?
A 3 in 12   **B** 3 in 15
C 3 in 20   **D** 1 in 3

These cards are the same size. Ricki-Lee turns them over and mixes them up. She selects one card at random.

2	1	5	2	3	4
1	0	2	4	4	3

12 What is the probability that the card is a 5?
A $\frac{1}{12}$ **B** $\frac{1}{5}$ **C** $\frac{5}{12}$ **D** $\frac{5}{10}$

13 What is the probability that the card is a 4?
A $\frac{1}{12}$ **B** $\frac{1}{6}$ **C** $\frac{1}{4}$ **D** $\frac{1}{3}$

14 What is the probability that the card is less than 3?
A $\frac{1}{2}$ **B** $\frac{1}{3}$ **C** $\frac{1}{4}$ **D** $\frac{1}{6}$

The picture shows 9 balls. Some of these balls are painted red and the rest are painted blue. All the balls are placed in a bucket and one is selected at random. The chance that the ball is red is 1 out of 3.

15 Write down the number of red balls in the bucket:
☐ red balls

16 What is the chance of selecting a blue ball?
A 2 out of 3   **B** 1 out of 2
C 1 out of 4   **D** 1 out of 6

☞ **Answers and explanations on pages 176-177**

**Key Points
and
Test Your
Skills**

SPELLING
*Words ending in 'y', homophones
and 'demon' words*

 With most spelling rules there are exceptions. English words have many different origins (e.g. 'siesta' comes from Spain and 'kayak' is an Inuit word from North America).

Key Points.

❶ To add a suffix to a word ending with a 'y', change the 'y' to an 'i' before adding the suffix. Some common suffixes are 'ly', 'less', 'ness', 'est', 'ful' (See page 67 for 'ful'.)
Examples: happiness, happily, tidily, penniless, dizziness, laziest, angrily
An exception to this rule is adding 'ing' (keep the 'y').

❷ Homophones are words that sound the same but have different spelling. You need to be able to use them correctly in context.
Examples: berry, bury; knew, new, gnu; scent, sent, cent; there, their

❸ 'Demon' words are words commonly misspelt. It is wise to know the spelling of these words.

umbrella	science	burglar	athletics	library
almost	Wednesday	February	woollen	wooden
film	separate	safety	misspelt	women
they're	ninth	guard	forty	won't
truly	legend	handkerchief	column	doubt

Test Your Skills

Learn the words below. A common method of learning and self-testing is the **LOOK, SAY, COVER, WRITE, CHECK** method. If you make any mistakes, you should rewrite the word three times correctly, immediately. In this way you will become familiar with the correct spelling. If the word is particularly troublesome, rewrite it several more times or keep a list of words that you can check regularly.

This week's theme word: CLOTHING

woollen	_____	nylon	_____
synthetic	_____	buckle	_____
jacket	_____	scarves	_____
blouse	_____	tuxedo	_____
casual	_____	formal	_____
attire	_____	uniform	_____
costume	_____	wardrobe	_____
menswear	_____	tunic	_____
matching	_____	bikini	_____
slacks	_____	helmet	_____
sleeveless	_____	cardigan	_____

Write any troublesome word three times: _____ _____ _____

_____ _____ _____

Real Test

15 MIN

Please ask your parent or teacher to read to you the spelling words on page 201.
Write the correct spelling of each word in the box.

1 Did you _____ the top score for Maths?

2 A solid _____ is essential for camping holidays.

3 Emma was huddled under a warm _____.

4 Not a _____ day passes without a complaint.

5 Did you see how Pat _____ after winning the prize!

6 The kayak was caught in a _____ near the rapids.

Each line has one word that is incorrect.
Write the correct spelling of the underlined word in the box.

7 The diver was just a <u>blurr</u> in my photograph.

8 Who will be the <u>foretyeth</u> leader of the nation?

9 The <u>bough</u> of a ship is at the front.

10 An <u>outbord</u> motor was attached to the rowing boat.

11 Some planes have just one <u>prepellor</u>!

12 There was a great gash in the <u>harl</u> of the yacht.

Read the text *The Search*.
Each line has a word that is incorrect. Write the correct spelling in the box.

The Search

13 Rod knew he was strainded. After a rest, he and

14 his dogs set off up the river to lokate fresh water.

15 It was dificcult and very tiring but finally they

16 managed to find freash water. When they had all

17 had a drink Rod looked for a campsight. A nearby

18 bank was levell and grassy, and back from the river.

☞ **Answers on page 177**

**Key Points
and
Test Your
Skills**

GRAMMAR AND PUNCTUATION
*Pronouns, prepositions, adverbs
and apostrophes*

15 MIN

Key Points.

1 **Pronouns** are words that take the place of nouns.
Example: John gave the ball to Jill. He gave it to her. ('He' and 'her' are pronouns.)
Here are some common pronouns: I, we, me, us, you, they, them, he, she, him, her, it.

2 **Prepositions** show the relationship between a noun or pronoun and another word. They show the position (preposition).
Examples: at, above, among, under, off, until, into, up, upon, beside, between

3 **Adverbs** help verbs. They add extra meaning to the verbs. They tell how, when or where something happened. *Examples:* quickly, lately, there, silently, patiently, roughly

4 **Apostrophes** have two uses.
a To show **ownership**: when something belongs to someone (or something), ownership is shown with 's. *Examples:* Bob's apple, dog's collar, Holden's tyre, doctor's fee, table's legs
b To indicate **contractions** (shortened words): when letters are left out of a word, an apostrophe is put in its place.
Examples: was not → wasn't, he will → he'll, they are → they're, I am → I'm,   it is → it's
Note: the word **it's** stands for 'it is'. (It's a fine day.) **Its**, without an apostrophe, is a pronoun like 'hers', 'his' and 'their'. (The cat licked its fur.)

Test Your Skills

1 Underline the **pronouns** in this passage.
Tony and Anna were lost. They could not see the house. It was hidden in the valley. Tony tried to climb a tree but he was too small. Anna sat on a log. She tried to remember which way they had come but her head ached.

2 Underline the **prepositions** in this passage.
Rover hid behind the kennel when he saw the family cat coming round the corner. The cat stopped by the door, looked at the kennel and then went into the house. Her tail was in the air.

3 Underline the **adverbs** in this passage.
Smiling widely, Kim waved enthusiastically to her team walking proudly onto the field. Shortly they would start the game. Both teams were known to fight bravely until the final whistle, but only one team would take the cup home.

4 Choose the correct **preposition** to fill the spaces.

a I picked the apple _____ the tree. (at, from, by)

b The kangaroo jumped _____ the fallen log. (over, below, in)

5 Write these words in shortened form.

We are _____ where is _____ I will _____ you have _____

she is _____ I am _____ we will _____ cannot _____

Answers: **1** They, It, She, they, her **2** behind, around, by, at, into, in **3** widely, enthusiastically, proudly, shortly, bravely **4a** from **b** over **5** we're, where's, I'll, you've, she's, I'm, we'll, can't

Real Test

GRAMMAR AND PUNCTUATION
Pronouns, prepositions and punctuation

15 MIN

1 Which of the following correctly completes this sentence?

The detective suspected [_____] the man behind the car was a thief.

but	that	who	what
A	**B**	**C**	**D**

2 Which of the following correctly completes this sentence?

Lara was ill [_____] I stayed in the spare room.

so	yet	in case	because
A	**B**	**C**	**D**

3 Which of the following correctly completes this sentence?

The sailor [_____] a watch from the market stall.

stealt	stold	stealed	stole
A	**B**	**C**	**D**

4 Which of the following correctly completes this sentence?

Bev's twenty-first birthday party is [_____] the weekend.

in	on	into	at
A	**B**	**C**	**D**

5 Choose the word that is a verb in this sentence.

After the sudden storm the raging creek carried off tons of good soil.

sudden	raging	carried	off
A	**B**	**C**	**D**

6 Which sentence has the correct punctuation?
A Mum, Pat and Kim crossed Lake Louise in a kayak.
B Mum, pat and kim crossed Lake Louise in a kayak.
C Mum, Pat and Kim crossed Lake Louise in a Kayak.
D Mum, pat and Kim crossed Lake Louise in a kayak.

Read the text *It is April Fools' Day*. The text has some gaps.

Choose the best option to fill each gap.

It is April Fools' Day

The first day of April is celebrated across the world.

April Fools' day is [_____] to have

7
say	sayed	says	said
A	**B**	**C**	**D**

[_____] in France, a long time ago.

8
begin	beginned	begun	begins
A	**B**	**C**	**D**

It [_____] when a French king decided

9
were	was	is	are
A	**B**	**C**	**D**

☞ **Answers and explanations on pages 178–179**

GRAMMAR AND PUNCTUATION

Pronouns, prepositions and punctuation

to change the calendar. ______ new

10 the (A) a (B) A (C) The (D)

calendar moved New Year ______ the

11 to (A) over (B) at (C) on (D)

the first day in January from ______

12 march (A) March (B) march (C) March. (D)

13 Some punctuation has been left out of the text below.

Shade one bubble to show the best place for the question mark (?).

I heard you knock (A) What (B) do you want (C) I am very busy right now (D)

14 Which sentence has the correct punctuation?

A How far are you going? asked Jason.
B "How far are you going?" asked Jason.
C "How far are you going," asked Jason?
D "how far are you going?" asked Jason.

15 Choose the pair of words that correctly complete this statement.

I had a choice. I could ______ pump up my bike tyre ______ walk to the beach.

either and	either or	neither but	neither and	either if
A	B	C	D	E

16 Which of the following correctly completes the sentence?

Martin had a ______ slice of toast under his egg.

long	thick	tall	narrow
A	B	C	D

17 Draw a line to show which option correctly begins this sentence.

A He's brother and he
B Him and his brother
C His brother and him
D He and his brother

work in Richmond.

18 Shade two bubbles to show where the missing commas (,) should go.

The new coach (A) for our team (B) from Newcastle (C) was late (D) for his first meeting.

☞ Answers and explanations on pages 178–179

A procedure is a set of instructions on how to do something. These are often called 'steps'. Procedures will often include the materials and tools needed and helpful hints. A recipe is a common form of procedure.

Read these instructions on how to make a pirate hook for Captain Hook and answer the questions. Circle the correct answer.

You will need
Scissors; 1.25-litre plastic soft drink bottle; plaster of Paris (Polyfilla); cup hook (from the local hardware store); quick-drying paints suitable for plastic; strip of material (10 × 2 cm) or plastic handle as on washing powder boxes

Instructions
1. Buy a cup hook from any hardware store. (They sometimes come in small packets.)
2. Using the scissors, cut the end with the cap off the bottle. Check that the bottle is wide enough to clench your fist in and that it will fit into a long-sleeved shirt.
3. Make a handle from the material, or remove the handle from a washing powder box.
4. Screw the cup hook into the outside centre of the base of the bottle.
5. Mix the plaster of Paris, following the given instructions, and pour it into the base of the bottle to a depth of 3 cm. <u>Embed the handle</u> in the wet plaster. Allow to set.
6. After the plaster hardens, paint the bottle base to look like a wooden stump. Wear your 'stump' coming out from the sleeve of a loose jacket or coat. Lock your fingers through the inside handle so that the hook hand cannot fall.

1 How many steps are needed to make the Captain Hook hand?
    A two   **B** five   **C** six   **D** eleven

2 What tool does the maker of the Captain Hook hand need?

Write your answer in the box.

3 The term 'embed the handle' means to
    A set it firmly in the plaster.   **B** leave it lying on the plaster.
    C lay the handle on material.   **D** pull the handle into position.

4 When you are wearing the hook hand the soft drink bottle should be hidden by
    A paint.   **B** a bandage.   **C** plastic.   **D** a sleeve.

5 What should be done once the handle is secured in the plaster of Paris?
    A Screw in the cup hook.   **B** Paint the end of the bottle.
    C Wait for the plaster to dry.   **D** Test the handle for strength.

6 A Captain Hook hand could best be worn
    A at a football match.   **B** to a fancy-dress party.
    C when rowing a boat.   **D** going to bed.

7 Which **two** items are NOT required to make the Captain Hook hand? Circle two answers.
      paint   wood   material   plaster of Paris   string
      A   **B**   **C**   **D**   **E**

☞ **Answers and explanations on page 179**

Real Test

READING
Following procedures

Read the instructions on making a worm farm from *Unusual Pets* by Chris Madsen and Julie Cooke and answer the questions. Circle the correct answer.

1. **Why bother having a worm farm?** Earthworms are the greatest gardeners on earth. They feed by swallowing soil and digesting the dead plant stuff in it. Although nobody knows why, it is an amazing fact that soil that has been through a worm's body is especially good for growing things. As well as being easy pets to keep, your worms will magically transform useless kitchen waste into better potting soil than money can buy.

2. **How to begin.** If you want to watch your worms working, the best place to keep them is in a terrarium. Put it in a shady, warm spot and half fill it with ordinary, moist garden soil. There are many different kinds of earthworms. The best ones for a worm farm are the short, soft, pale ones that live in compost or under dead leaves.

3. **Feeding.** You can begin by adding scraps of vegetable waste from the kitchen. Any old leaves and vegetable peelings will do, but it's best to chop them up quite small. Just drop the food on top of the soil and let the worms do the work. As time goes by, and your worms get into their stride, you can give them more and more to eat. Spray with a little water from time to time (don't drown them!), and just watch what they do.

4. **What next?** Eventually you will have a terrarium full of lovely, soft, dark coloured soil, heaving with worms, but there won't be room for any more food! What you do next is spread a large plastic sheet on the ground and simply tip out the whole lot, worms and all, onto the sheet. You can then pick out the worms and put them in a jar while you collect the compost to store in a plastic bag until it is needed. Put more soil into the terrarium and begin all over again.

1 Worms need soil, food scraps, water and

    A daily care.   **B** sunlight.   **C** shade.   **D** plastic sheets.

2 The word 'eventually' could best be replaced with

    A often.   **B** finally.   **C** repeatedly.   **D** occasionally.

3 What is meant by the term 'worms get into their stride'?

    A They start leaving the farm.   **B** They get used to their surroundings.

    C They get old and die.   **D** They learn to live together peacefully.

4 Which numbered point in the passage explains how to start a new worm farm? Write your answer in the box.

5 What is the plastic sheet used for?

    A to shade the worm farm   **B** to stop the worms from escaping

    C to keep the worm farm dry   **D** to sort the worms from the soil

5 What is a 'terrarium'?

    A a container like a fish-tank   **B** a large garden pot

    C a hole in the ground   **D** a compost bin

6 Which of the following items is least required when caring for a worm farm?

    A fertiliser   **B** plastic bag   **C** jar   **D** watering can

☞ **Answers and explanations on page 179**

READING
Understanding a book review

Book reviews appear in magazines and newspapers. An independent reader gives his or her opinion of the book. Book reviews can be positive (good) or negative (bad).

Read this review of *Disturbing Discoveries* and answer the questions. Circle the correct answer.

Disturbing Discoveries by Rowan Singh, B & T Books, 2004, $8.75

Great cover. Interesting title. The idea behind the book, young people making journeys of discovery, was intriguing. It sounded so promising but... The only disturbing discovery I made was of a group of fairly ordinary children trying to act (badly) like spoilt teenagers.

The book is a collection of short stories written by a little known writer. The book presents issues that concern many children—bullying, working parents, rejection, school results, conforming and so on. Although Singh has selected pertinent issues he offers rather corny solutions. In some stories I almost expected the ending 'and they lived happily ever after'.

Stories include children from inner suburbs, country towns and isolated rural properties. Some of the characters are little more than kids plonked down in strange environments and expected to cope with situations that are a little unreal. The best story, 'Annie Smith and the Dolphin', is set on Western Australia's north coast.

The stories do have one saving factor and that is the detailed descriptions of school grounds and council parks. It would be hard to convince the young reader to buy this book just to read a good description of their everyday environment.

M Gilroy

---

1 Who wrote the review of *Disturbing Discoveries*?
A Annie Smith   **B** R Singh   **C** B & T Books   **D** M Gilroy

2 The book review could best be described as
A positive.   **B** disturbing.   **C** negative.   **D** unexpected.

3 What does the reviewer suggest by the term 'It sounded so promising but ...'?
A She was disappointed.   **B** She was confused.
C She hasn't read the book.   **D** She is unsure of what to say.

4 What did the reviewer like most about the book?
title	cover	stories	setting	illustrations
A	B	C	D	E

5 What does the reviewer consider is the author's best writing feature?
A personal issues   **B** portraying the concerns of children
C unexpected story endings   **D** descriptions of local environment

6 How would the author, R Singh, most likely feel about the review?
A excited   **B** pleased   **C** unhappy   **D** uncaring

7 How did the reviewer rate the stories in the book?
A enjoyable   **B** exciting   **C** humorous   **D** disappointing

☞ **Answers and explanations on page 180**

Real Test

READING
Understanding a table of contents

Read this table of contents from *What a Waste!* by Stephen Jones and answer the questions. Circle the correct answer.

CONTENTS	page
Introduction	2
Recycling waste in nature	4
Waste through the ages	8
The throwaway society	15
What we throw away	18
How we dispose of solid and liquid waste	25
Difficult wastes	30
Gaseous waste	31
Beyond the throwaway society	37
Understanding packaging	40
Materials that can be recycled	42
Recycling – the benefits, the problems	50
Beyond recycling	52
Solving problems of the future	54
How much do we waste, how much do we recycle?	58
Glossary	60
Index	61
Pronunciation guide	62

1 On which page would I find information about liquid wastes? Write your answer in the box.

2 If I wanted to know the meaning of the word 'resource', I would look in the
   A Introduction.   **B** Glossary.   **C** Index.   **D** Pronunciation guide.

3 Which section is most likely to give information about the history of waste?
   A Waste through the ages   **B** Difficult wastes
   C The throwaway society   **D** Beyond recycling

4 If I wanted to know how to say the term 'polyvinyl chloride', I would look in the
   A Introduction.   **B** Glossary.   **C** Index.   **D** Pronunciation guide.

5 What is meant by a throwaway society? It is a society that
   A uses recycle bins.   **B** buys goods that are replaced, not repaired.
   C drops litter.   **D** has no respect for public places.

6 The *What a Waste!* book would be most useful for
   A scientists.   **B** artists.   **C** home owners.   **D** builders.

7 Which of the following sections is only one page long?
   A Beyond recycling   **B** What we throw away
   C Difficult wastes   **D** The throwaway society

☞ **Answers and explanations on page 180**

Real Test

READING
Understanding poetry

10 MIN

Read the poem 'Washing the Car' by Elaine Horsfield and answer the questions.

Washing the Car
Washing the car is lots of fun
Into my swimmers then into the sun.
Pick up the bucket and turn on the hose.
First make sure the windows are closed.
Suds in the bucket then <u>swish</u> it around
Try not to spill too much on the ground.
Dip in the chamois and splash on the car
A <u>bucket of suds doesn't go very far</u>.
When all of the dirt is washed away
It's back to the hose and give it a spray.
Look for the bits I might have missed
Then hose it all with a spray like mist.

Dad has a look to see if it's clean.
He likes to see the windows gleam.
Two dollars pay for a job well <u>done</u>
Washing the car is lots of fun.

1 Why do the car cleaners wear swimmers to wash the car?
  A The car is dirty.
  B The weather is hot.
  C Swimmers are easy to wash.
  D They know they will get wet washing the car.

2 Which word best describes the mood of the children cleaning the car?
  A eager
  B impatient
  C frenzied
  D careful

3 What does the word 'swish' mean, as used in the poem?
  A spill carelessly
  B stir around noisily
  C shake up and down
  D splash on the ground

4 What is the first thing the children should do when they have to wash the car?
  A Pick up a bucket.
  B Turn on the hose.
  C Clean the windows.
  D Close the car windows.

5 What part does Dad play in cleaning the car? Write your answer on the lines.

_____

_____

6 Which **two** words rhyme with 'done'?
  fun   gone   on   bone   won
   A   **B**   **C**   **D**   **E**

7 What is the most likely reason that a 'bucket of suds doesn't go very far'?
  A The bucket is small.
  B The car is big and dirty.
  C The car is not cleaned very often.
  D The children spill a lot while having fun.

☞ **Answers and explanations on page 180**

TIPS FOR WRITING PROCEDURES

Procedures tell us how to do something. This might include instructions on how to carry out a task or play a game. More complicated procedures involve several phases, directions for getting to a place or rules to be followed.

The purpose of a procedure is to provide instructions. Written procedures aim to tell the reader how to make or do something. Procedures usually have two main parts:

- the materials and tools needed (these are often called *requirements* or, in recipes, *ingredients*)
- the steps to be followed.

When writing procedures, it is best to keep the following points in mind. They will help you get the best possible mark.

Before you start writing

- Read the question and check the stimulus material carefully. *Stimulus material* means the topic, title, picture, words, phrases or extract of writing you are given to base your writing on.
- Write about something you know. Don't pick a complicated topic. Even the steps in a simple everyday procedure can be difficult to explain simply and precisely.

The introduction

- Start by stating what will happen in the end—the goal of the activity. This is often contained in the title.

The body

- **You may add personal opinions and comments** to brighten up the largely impersonal language used in procedures.
- **Follow the structure of procedures.** The materials and tools required are listed first, followed by short, concise sentences describing the steps in chronological order. The steps may be numbered.
- Correctly paragraph your writing. This is important: put each step in a separate paragraph.
- **Lay out your instructions clearly.** The reader must be able to follow the steps easily in order.
- **Add diagrams.** These can be very useful, as they can often clearly illustrate a step that would take many words to explain.
- **Include additional material** such as safety notes and explanations.
- **Use precise terms** such as *lukewarm, spread evenly, hold for two minutes* or *sharp turn right*.
- **Use command sentences.** These are sentences starting with infinitive verbs without *to*, such as *put, place* and *allow*. This is known as the imperative mood.
- **Use sequencing words**, such as *then, after* and *while*, that establish the sequence of steps clearly.
- **Include optional stages as necessary**, such as explaining reasons, providing alternative steps, giving warnings or mentioning possible consequences.

The conclusion

- The final paragraph may include a comment on what will have been achieved by following the steps.

When you have finished writing give yourself a few minutes to read through your procedure. Quickly check spelling and punctuation, and insert any words that have been accidentally left out.

WRITING
Procedure

There is no way of knowing for certain what type of writing will be included in the NAPLAN Tests in years to come. This is an opportunity for you to practise different types of writing.

Before you start, read the General writing tips on pages 22–23 and the Tips for writing procedures on page 103.

The aim of a procedure is to provide someone with instructions on how to make or do something. It might include instructions on how to carry out a task or play a game. More complicated procedures involve several phases, directions for getting to a place or rules to follow. Procedures usually have two main parts: the materials and tools needed and the steps to be followed.

Today you can choose one of the following topics.
- preparing a slice of toast spread with your favourite topping
- cleaning a pair of shoes or joggers
- starting a petrol-engine lawn mower
- writing and sending an email
- borrowing a book from a library

Imagine actually doing the task from your steps. Has anything been left out or is the wording unclear?

Before you start writing, give some thought to:
- every step involved in carrying out the task
- any safety hints or precautions you can offer
- what you achieved by following the instructions.

Don't forget to:
- plan your procedure before you start writing
- make a list of materials needed and command-type sentences in your instructions
- choose your words carefully and pay attention to your spelling and punctuation
- write neatly but don't waste time
- quickly check your procedure once you have finished.

Start writing here or type your answer on a tablet or computer.

_____

_____

_____

_____

_____

_____

_____

_____

_____

☞ **Marking guide on pages 180-181**

WRITING
Explanation

Before you start, read the General writing tips on pages 22–23.

An explanation tells **how** or **why** something happens or works.
Explanations are often about scientific, technical or natural phenomena.
The importance of the subject matter is stated.

Write an explanation of one of these topics.

■ Alarm clocks
■ Kitchen timers
■ Stop watches

Before you start writing, give some thought to:
● what you are describing
● the special features of the subject and how it operates
● the value or importance of the object.

Don't forget to:
● plan your explanation before you start writing
● write in correctly formed sentences and take care with paragraphing
● choose your words carefully and pay attention to your spelling and punctuation
● write neatly but don't waste time
● quickly check your explanation once you have finished.

Start writing here or type your answer on a tablet or computer.

_____

_____

_____

_____

_____

_____

_____

_____

_____

_____

_____

_____

_____

_____

_____

_____

_____

_____

☞ **Marking guide on pages 181-182**

Real Test and Tips

WRITING
Report from an outline

42 MIN

A report is an account based on research or investigation of a particular topic or incident. In some reports information is collected from a number of sources.

Before you start, read the General writing tips on pages 22–23.

Read the notes of the following incident and then write up a report of what happened.

> Date: Sunday 26 December
> Time: 11:45 am
> Location: South end Bondi Beach
> Persons involved: Jim Vale (British tourist), Nick Appinni (lifesaver)
> Incident: Mr Vale swam outside flagged area—got into difficulties when caught in a rip near rocks. Waved for assistance. Surf club rescue.
> Injuries: Mr Vale treated for cuts and exhaustion at clubhouse and then transported to nearby medical centre

Before you start writing, give some thought to:
- the details of the report: what, where, when, why, who
- which aspects of the scene are relevant to the incident (these are what you should write about).

Don't forget to:
- plan your report before you start writing
- use mostly short sentences that contain one fact each
- choose your words carefully and pay attention to your spelling and punctuation
- write neatly but don't waste time
- quickly check your report once you have finished.

Start writing here or type your answer on a tablet or computer.

Title: _____

_____

_____

_____

_____

_____

_____

_____

_____

_____

_____

☞ **Marking guide on page 182**

WRITING
Response to a picture

Before you start, read the General writing tips on pages 22–23.

You may be asked to write a response to a picture or some other stimulus, such as lines of poetry or the beginning of a story.

Look at this picture and then write your response to it.

Before you start writing, give some thought to:
- what you see in the picture and what you think about this
- what you feel about the picture: your impressions when you look at it
- what will happen next.

Don't forget to:
- plan your response before you start writing
- write in correctly formed sentences and take care with paragraphing
- choose your words carefully and pay attention to your spelling and punctuation
- write neatly but don't waste time
- quickly check your response once you have finished.

Start writing here or type your answer on a tablet or computer.

_____

_____

_____

_____

_____

_____

_____

_____

_____

_____

_____

_____

_____

_____

_____

_____

_____

_____

☞ **Marking guide on pages 182–183**

Sample NAPLAN Online-style tests

DIFFERENT TEST LEVELS

- There are eight tests for students to complete in this section. These sample tests have been classified as either Intermediate or Advanced according to the level of the majority of questions. This will broadly reflect the NAPLAN Online tailored testing experience where students are guided into answering questions that match their ability.
- The following tests are included in this section:
  - one Intermediate-level Test for each of Reading, Conventions of Language and Numeracy
  - one Advanced-level Test for each of Reading, Conventions of Language and Numeracy
  - two Writing Tests.

CHECKS

- The NAPLAN Online Reading, Conventions of Language and Numeracy tests will be divided into different sections.
- Students will have one last opportunity to check their answers in each section when they have reached the end of that section.
- Once they have moved onto a new section, they will not be able to go back and check their work again.
- We have included reminders for students to check their work at specific points in the Sample Tests so they become familiar with this process before they take the NAPLAN Online tests.

EXCEL TEST ZONE

- After students have consolidated their topic knowledge by completing this book, we recommend they practise NAPLAN Online–style questions on our website at www.exceltestzone.com.au.
- Students will be able to gain valuable practice in digital skills such as dragging text across a screen, using an onscreen ruler, protractor and calculator to answer questions, or listening to an audio recording of a spelling word which they then type into a box.
- Students will also become confident in using a computer or tablet to complete NAPLAN Online–style tests so they will be fully prepared for the actual NAPLAN Online tests.

Today you are going to write a persuasive text, often called an exposition. The purpose of writing a persuasive text is to influence or change a reader's thoughts or opinions on a particular topic or subject. Your aim is to convince a reader that your opinion is sensible and logical. Successful persuasive writing is always well planned. Persuasive texts may include advertisements, letters to newspapers, speeches and newspaper editorials, as well as arguments in debates.

Students should have fruit lunches rather than those based on bread products.
What do you think about this opinion? Do you support or reject this idea?
Write to convince a reader of your opinions.

Before you start writing, give some thought to:
- whether you strongly agree or strongly disagree with this opinion
- reasons or evidence for your arguments
- a brief but definite conclusion—list some of your main points and add a personal opinion
- the structure of a persuasive text, which begins with a well-organised introduction, followed by a body of arguments or points, and finally a conclusion that restates the writer's position.

Don't forget to:
- plan your writing before you start—make a list of important points you wish to make
- write in correctly formed sentences and take care with paragraphing
- choose your words carefully, and pay attention to your spelling and punctuation
- write neatly but don't waste time
- quickly check your persuasive text once you have finished—your position must be clear to the reader.

Remember: The stance taken in a persuasive text is not wrong, as long as the writer has evidence to support his or her opinion. How the opinion is supported is as important as the opinion itself.

Start writing here or type your answer on a tablet or computer.

_____
_____
_____
_____
_____
_____
_____
_____
_____
_____
_____
_____
_____
_____

☞ **Marking guide on pages 183–184 and sample response on page 25**

Read *Bush Stone-Curlew* and answer questions 1 to 6.

Bush Stone-Curlew

Status: NSW and Victoria: endangered

The Bush Stone-Curlew (*Burhinus grallarius*) is a large, ground-dwelling bird. It is endemic to Australia and nearby islands.

Although the Bush Stone-Curlew looks rather like a wading bird it is a dry-land predator, a winged terrestrial carnivore.

The Stone-Curlew is mainly nocturnal. It hunts small grassland animals: frogs, spiders, insects, molluscs, crustaceans, snakes, lizards and small mammals, mostly probed from soft soil or rotting wood. It will eat seeds or soft roots in drought years. Birds forage individually or in pairs over a large home territory, particularly on moonlit nights.

During the day, Bush Stone-Curlews tend to remain inactive, sheltering among tall grass or low shrubs and relying on their plumage to protect them from their only natural predators, raptors (eagles and hawks).

When disturbed, they freeze motionless, often in odd-looking postures. For visual predators like raptors this works well. It is useless with introduced feral animals that hunt by scent, notably foxes, their main predator. They are sure-footed, fast on the ground. They seldom fly during daylight hours. In the air, flight is swift and direct on long, broad wings.

(Information courtesy of Victorian Wildlife Service)

Distribution

1 Where are Bush Stone-Curlews found?
- **A** Australia wide
- **C** mostly in New South Wales and Victoria
- **B** only near gardens
- **D** all Australian states except Tasmania

2 The curlew's main method of survival is to
- **A** attack threats directly.
- **C** use camouflage tactics.
- **B** defend its chicks with sharp claws.
- **D** leave no scent.

3 According to the text which fact about curlews is correct? The curlew is
- **A** a wading bird.
- **C** a coastal sea bird.
- **B** a meat eater.
- **D** an insect-eating swamp bird.

4 Why are foxes a threat to curlews?
- **A** Foxes are an introduced animal to Australia.
- **C** Foxes are much larger than curlews.
- **B** Foxes hunt when it gets dark.
- **D** Foxes hunt by scent.

5 Complete this sentence. Curlews are
- **A** night hunters.
- **C** easily startled into fleeing.
- **B** garden scavengers.
- **D** awkward in flight.

6 The passage could best be described as
- **A** a narrative.
- **C** a historical record.
- **B** a description from a story.
- **D** an information report.

☞ **Answers and explanations on page 184**

Read *Growing tulips* and answer questions 7 to 12.

Growing tulips
Tulips are popular flowers. Look at the picture. These are tulips. Tulips come in many colours, including bi-colours. Avid tulip growers create works of art in planting their tulip beds. Some tulip beds are masterpieces in design.

The origin of tulips
In the sixteenth century, tulips were brought from Central Asia and Turkey to Holland. They quickly became so popular that 'Tulipmania' occurred in Holland in the seventeenth century. Trade in tulip bulbs became a very profitable business. Today, Dutch bulbs are grown in huge fields and are exported around the world. Tulips are easy to grow. Many people design artistic, colourful layouts for the blooms.

How to grow tulips
1 Buy the finest quality bulbs. Buying 'cheap' tulip bulbs can result in inferior blooms. In general, the larger the bulb, the larger the bloom. There are early-, mid-, and late-blooming varieties.
2 Select a location for planting. Tulips will bloom in almost any soil, almost anywhere. There can be difficulties is in wet soils, as the bulbs tend to rot.
3 Prepare the soil by working it well, removing rocks and weeds. Add plenty of organic material and fertilizer. Special bulb formulas and bone meal work well.
4 Plant the bulbs any time in autumn. If directions are not available from the supplier, plant the bulbs 15 cm apart, at a depth of 10 cm.
5 After blooming, it is important to let the plant continue to grow until it dies off. After flowering, the plant is sending energy to the bulb to store for use next spring.
Tulip bulbs should be stored in cool, well-ventilated areas—not in hot garages or sheds, as they dry out.

7 According to the text which fact about tulips is correct? Tulips
   A are difficult to grow.   B flower in August.   C are multi-coloured.   D are only grown in Holland.

8 Which statement about tulips is correct?
   A Good blooms can come from bulbs of any size.
   B Bulbs are best stored in cool, ventilated places.
   C Once the flower has died, the bulb should be removed from the soil.
   D Tulips flower for a short period each year.

9 The word 'avid' could be aptly replaced by which **two** words?
   | keen | agile | excited | adventurous | enthusiastic |
   | A | B | C | D | E |

10 'Tulipmania' suggests that people
   A got sick from tulips.   B pulled out all their tulips.
   C became insane growing tulips.   D would do anything to get tulip bulbs.

11 Tulips do not grow well in
   A sandy soil.   B garden soil.   C wet soil.   D stony soil.

12 Some tulip beds are masterpieces in design. This suggests that tulip growers
   A make a lot of money from their tulips.   B are creative in their tulip gardens.
   C open their gardens to the public.   D paint pictures of their gardens.

**It would be a good idea to check your answers to questions
1 to 12 before moving on to the other questions.**

☞ Answers and explanations on page 184

Look at and read the cartoon. Then answer questions 13 to 16.

13 The cartoon is called Comprehension because
A Jim doesn't understand his father's comment.
B Grandpa doesn't know how to ride the motorbike.
C Jim hopes his Grandpa will use training wheels.
D Jim's father thinks he is too young for a motorbike.

14 The look on Grandpa's face suggests
A shock and horror.   B wicked delight.   C amazement.   D confusion.

15 The cloud-like bubble is used to indicate
A that Jim is too shocked to talk.
B the speed Jim thinks Grandpa should be going.
C how Jim remembers Grandpa using training wheels.
D the thoughts Jim is having about his father's comment.

16 You are going to compare the texts *Growing tulips* (page 112) and *Comprehension* (above).
For what purposes were these texts written? Tick **two** options for each text.

	Growing tulips	*Comprehension*
to explain	A ☐	A ☐
to encourage	B ☐	B ☐
to instruct	C ☐	C ☐
to entertain	D ☐	D ☐

☞ **Answers and explanations on page 185**

Read *As if I would* by Elaine Horsfield and answer questions 17 to 22.

As if I would

Grown ups are always telling me
The things I mustn't do.
Like, when I leave for school -
'Don't miss the bus!'
And if I have to buy my lunch
Mum calls out as I go,
'Now, Sue, don't spend the change!'
As if I would!

When I'm in the kitchen
There's so much I mustn't do.
'Don't burn yourself!'
If I go near the stove.
'That knife is sharp. Don't cut yourself!'
Or 'Don't you spill that milk!'
'Don't drop that plate!' I mean,
As if I would!

On Friday when I get my pay
And head off to the mall,
Mum says, 'Don't lose it now,
And don't buy junk.'
Dad says, 'Save some for later on,
Don't spend it all at once.
Don't throw it all away.'
As if I would!
When I go to my mate's, Dad says,
'Now don't stay there all day!'
And 'Don't fall off those
Skateboards at the park!'
Mum says, 'Don't get run over
When you go across the road!'
I wonder, do they really
Think I would?

17 Where does Sue ride her skateboard? Write your answer on the line.

_____

18 Sue's parents could be described as being
   A fussy.   **B** meddling.   **C** worried.   **D** protective.

19 Sue's parents are **not** worried that she might
   A waste money.   **B** get lost.   **C** be injured   **D** miss school.

20 The warnings Sue's parents offer are
   A meant as a joke.   **B** sensible suggestions.
   C unnecessary advice.   **D** helpful instructions.

21 You are going to compare the texts *As if I would* (above) and *Night of the Muttonbirds* (page 115). For what purposes were these texts written? Tick **two** options for each text.

	As if I would	*Night of the Muttonbirds*
to engage the reader	A ☐	A ☐
to recount a fictional event	B ☐	B ☐
to question an attitude	C ☐	C ☐

22 When Sue goes to her friend's place, her father is worried she will
   A stay there all day.   **B** spend too much money.   **C** miss the bus.   **D** drop a plate.

**It would be a good idea to check your answers to questions
13 to 22 before moving on to the other questions.**

☞ **Answers and explanations on page 185**

Read the extract from *Night of the Muttonbirds* by Mary Small and answer questions 23 to 28.

Extract: Night of the Muttonbirds

Matthew looked at his new school clothes laid out neatly on his chair. Reluctantly, he started to dress then stopped to finger his collection of shells spread out along the top of the chest of drawers. How beautiful they were: all sorts of shapes and colours. It was no wonder Clinton always wanted to play with them. His pride were his nautiluses, delicate brittle white shells of various sizes that resembled bizarre yet beautiful helmets. He picked up the biggest, his favourite. It always amazed him that its frail paper thinness could survive the storms and the temper of the Bass Strait waters. How easy it would be to crush it in his hand and destroy it. Gently he put it back with the others and continued dressing, throwing his clean shirt aside and putting on shorts and a T-shirt. Later, only when he had to, he would put on his clothes for school.

Barefooted, Matthew trod softly out to the kitchen. His mother was still asleep. He could hear her snoring. Being Saturday, all of the family could rest comfortable; all of them except Matthew. On top of the stove the kettle was sighing from the heat of the water inside. Matthew lifted the lid of the large black stockpot and warm steam rose from the chicken bones still simmering. The wood stove never went out. In it, his mother cooked all the meals; the roasts and the stew, the cakes and the scones. Matthew wondered with a sinking heart what the food would be like at the school in Launceston.

A cluster of jars overbrimming with jam crowded one corner of the kitchen table. Mathew felt one. It was still slightly warm. He ran his finger round the rim then licked it. The jam was deliciously sweet.

'I don't want to leave', whispered Matthew. 'I wish I could stay but how can I tell them?'

23 What event was Matthew preparing for?
   A shell collecting   **B** a fishing trip   **C** getting breakfast   **D** starting school

24 Draw a line to match the object or article with its location.

1 kettle	**2** new clothes	**3** shells	**4** jam jars
A chair	**B** stove	**C** table top	**D** chest top

25 What is Matthew experiencing in the passage?
   A reluctance   **B** frustration   **C** excitement   **D** distress

26 Life in Matthew's household could be described as
   A depressing.   **B** busy.   **C** grand.   **D** hostile.

27 Write the numbers 1 to 5 in the boxes to show the order of events in the text.
The first one (☐1) has been done for you.

	Matthew walked to the kitchen
1	Matthew saw his school clothes on a chair.
	Matthew licked jam off his finger.
	Matthew checked out the contents of the stockpot.
	Matthew stopped getting dressed to look at his shells.

28 The kettle was 'sighing'. This means the kettle was
   A about to boil.   **B** leaking.   **C** almost empty.   **D** bubbling furiously.

☞ **Answers and explanations on pages 185-186**

Read the instructions for making a hovercraft and answer questions 29 to 34.

CD balloon hovercraft
You will need: • an old CD   • a plastic pop-top drink bottle lid   • craft adhesive   • a balloon
What to do:
1 Remove and close the pop-top lid and then glue the base to the CD so the lid is centred over the hole in the CD.
2 Blow up a balloon and pinch the neck so that no air can escape.
3 Stretch the neck of the balloon over the closed pop-top.
4 Place the CD hovercraft on a flat surface, such as a table, and open the pop-top.
5 Quickly give your hovercraft a gentle push.
This hovercraft will glide across a smooth, flat surface until it runs out of air.

Note: Using a pop-top lid, you can transport your hovercraft to a number of different surfaces to test a variety of 'terrains'.

What is happening?
When the pop-top lid is opened (and the balloon is attached), air flows out of the balloon, down through the pop-top and under the CD. The CD is evenly weighted and has a very flat surface so the air lifts the entire CD off the surface of the table. The layer of air between the tabletop and the CD greatly reduces the friction between the two surfaces so the CD hovercraft can glide easily across a flat surface after being given a gentle push.

Experiment with your hovercraft over different surfaces – cement, carpet, floor tiles, brick path—even water! Under what conditions does the hovercraft perform the best?

---

29 What is an 'adhesive'?
   A   a sticking agent   B   a music CD   C   an adaptor   D   a drink bottle top

30 'Terrain' as used in the passage is meant to imply
   A   rocky ground.   B   an outside location.
   C   military grounds.   D   other textured surfaces.

31 The push of the CD balloon hovercraft is done quickly so that it
   A   rises off the surface.   B   doesn't spin on the spot.
   C   starts gliding before all the air is lost.   D   doesn't go backwards.

32 It is suggested that a CD balloon hovercraft be tested on a flat surface. Why? Write your answer on the lines.

_____

_____

33 The CD balloon hovercraft will not lift off the table if
   A   it is not given a gentle push.   B   the tabletop is narrow.
   C   the pop-top is closed.   D   the CD is new.

34 The CD balloon hovercraft would be useful in a science experiment on
   A   sound.   B   speed.   C   expansion.   D   friction.

☞ **Answers and explanations on page 186**

Read the interview and answer questions 35 to 39.

Interview with Brian McWilliam (November 2008)

Interviewer: How long have you been interested in model trains?

Brian: It started when I was about eight years old.

Interviewer: I see you have quite a collection in this room where you have set up your model railway. Is there anything that you are really proud of or that is special in some way?

Brian: The making of scenery and scale buildings for my track layout as well as constructing the locos.

Interviewer: Are you a member of a train group? You might like to tell me about it. What do they do?

Brian: There is a group of about fourteen train enthusiasts in Townsville. We have home meetings once a week. Each member has a track layout and we all use identical control equipment so that we can all run our trains on any home layout.

Interviewer: Where do you get your model trains from?

Brian: Retail hobby shops using suppliers in NSW. I use the internet to purchase some of my models.

Interviewer: What is actually involved in improving the model trains that you collect?

Brian: I repaint my models to give them a 'weathered' look. I like them to look like real working models. I add detail and sound decoders to give the trains an authentic sound as they circuit the track.

Interviewer: Do you have any other hobbies or interests?

Brian: Yes, flying radio-controlled model aircraft. I play sport – golf and bicycle riding. At high school I played basketball and as a young adult I raced bicycles on road and track. I also like to visit train museums and take photographs of trains to assist in my modelling. I was once a keen member of a photography club in Young, NSW.

Interviewer: Have you ever been on any special train trips? Where? When?

Brian: I rode on a steam train from Sydney to Dubbo in the 1960s. Recently, when I was in Europe I rode on some of their very fast trains.

Interviewer: What advice would you give anyone who was interested in model trains as a hobby?

Brian: Visit a club or a model railway exhibition. Seek advice from modellers and purchase copies of the Australian Model Railways Magazine.

---

35 What interest does Brian have other than model trains?

A playing computer games B flying radio-controlled model planes

C writing articles for a model railway magazine D racing model cars

36 Where was Brian when he was a keen member of a

photography club? Write your answer in the box.

37 What does Brian enjoy about his modelling?

A photographing his models B making scenery to scale

C collecting overseas model trains D racing his trains

38 When Brian paints his model trains, he

A wants them to look brand new. B adds striking colours.

C makes them look like working trains. D copies designs from European trains.

39 If someone was interested in the hobby of model trains, the first thing they should do is

A get advice from people with model trains. B take a trip on a real train.

C take photographs of trains. D buy a clockwork train.

☞ **Answers and explanations on page 186**

1 Which of the following correctly completes this sentence?

Malcolm was ▮▮▮▮▮ to school after his accident.

drive	drove	droven	driven
A	**B**	**C**	**D**

2 Which of the following correctly completes this sentence?

The wind is cold ▮▮▮▮▮ we have a warm house.

because	whether	however	so
A	**B**	**C**	**D**

3 Choose the word or words that are not required in this sentence.

Did you ask the policeman the question about the dangerous dog?

ask	the question	about	dangerous
A	**B**	**C**	**D**

4 Choose the word in this sentence that is a pronoun.

Both girls knew the time but they didn't make an effort to catch the bus. Write your answer in the box.

5 Which of the following correctly completes this sentence?

▮▮▮▮▮ you study tonight or you study on Saturday morning.

Neither	If	Either	Whether
A	**B**	**C**	**D**

6 Shade a bubble to show where the missing apostrophe (') should go.

Ⓐ   Ⓑ   Ⓒ   Ⓓ

Chris ▾ knew it was Peter▾s old bus ▾ pass but the inspector▾s did not check it.

7 Which verb best completes this sentence? Write your answer in the box.

Bruno is about to have his race and it ▭ still his dream to get a medal.

Read the text *Play With Me*. The text has some gaps.
Choose the best option to fill each gap.

Play With Me

Everyone was too busy to play with me.
"Want to play hide and ▮▮▮▮▮ I asked

8

seek,"	seek"?	seek?"	seek.
A	**B**	**C**	**D**

my brother ▮▮▮▮▮ was watching TV.

9

who	what	that	which
A	**B**	**C**	**D**

"Sorry Tessa," he said without ▮▮▮▮▮

10

takes	took	taken	taking
A	**B**	**C**	**D**

☞ **Answers and explanations on pages 186-188**

his eyes off the screen. " ▢▢▢ busy."

That was the end of that, ▢▢▢ so I

thought, but I was wrong. ▢▢▢ brother

suddenly turned the TV off!

11

i'm	Im	I'm	I'am
A	**B**	**C**	**D**

12

but	or	and	while
A	**B**	**C**	**D**

13

My	me	A	my
A	**B**	**C**	**D**

14 Which sentence has the correct punctuation?
   A Jackie asked, 'her friend to slow down?'
   B Jackie asked her friend to, 'slow down.'
   C Jackie asked her friend, 'to slow down.'
   D Jackie asked her friend to slow down.

15 Which sentence has the correct punctuation?
   A If it's not yours then it must be Sharon's turn.
   B If it's not your's then it must be Sharon's turn.
   C If its not yours then it must be Sharon's turn.
   D If it's not your's then it must be Sharon's turn.

16 Which of the following correctly completes the sentence?

After her operation Kate felt ▢▢▢ .

real good	much good	better	more better	best
A	**B**	**C**	**D**	**E**

17 Which of the following correctly completes the sentence?

Most days this week there ▢▢▢ no winds but Monday was different.

is	was	were	are
A	**B**	**C**	**D**

18 Shade the bubbles to show where the missing commas (,) should go.

The new driver ▲ Ms Peters ▲ found the school ▲ run along the main street ▲ very tiring.
   Ⓐ   Ⓑ   Ⓒ   Ⓓ

19 Which sentence has the correct punctuation?
   A our neighbours, Ted and Jan Tsang, have just bought a new Holden utility.
   B Our neighbours, Ted and Jan Tsang, have just bought a new Holden utility.
   C Our neighbours, Ted and Jan Tsang, have just bought a new Holden Utility.
   D Our neighbours, Ted and Jan tsang, have just bought a New Holden Utility.

20 Read this sentence.

Four noisy parrots fought over the fruit that were almost ripe on the plum tree.

Write any adjectives from the sentences in the boxes. Use as many boxes as you need.

☞ **Answers and explanations on pages 186-188**

21 Which sentence is correct?

  A Millie will bring the damp clothes inside and dried them in the drier.

  B Millie will brought the damp clothes inside and dries them in the drier.

  C Millie will bring the damp clothes inside and dry them in the drier.

  D Millie will brang the damp clothes inside and dried them in the drier.

22 Brackets **( )** are required in this sentence. Which part of the sentence needs brackets?

The male Australian emu *Dromaius novaehollandiae* builds a nest on the ground to incubate the eggs laid by the female.

male	*Dromaius novaehollandiae*	on the ground	incubate
A	B	C	D

23 Shade two bubbles to show where the missing speech marks (" ") should go.

   Ⓐ   Ⓑ Ⓒ   Ⓓ

"Look ▼ over here ▼ Janis, ▼ called Tanya. ▼ There's a crack in the glass."

24 Which of the following correctly completes this sentence?

When you _____ up you will see more of the parade.

stood	stand	stands	standing
A	B	C	D

25 Which of the following correctly completes this sentence?

There was a _____ of cars coming in from the airport.

fleet	bunch	group	heap
A	B	C	D

It would be a good idea to check your answers to questions
1 to 25 before moving on to the other questions.

To the student

Ask your teacher or parent to read the spelling words for you. The words are listed on page 202. Write the spelling words on the lines below.

26 _____

27 _____

28 _____

29 _____

30 _____

31 _____

32 _____

33 _____

34 _____

35 _____

36 _____

37 _____

38 _____

39 _____

40 _____

☞ **Answers and explanations on pages 186-188**

Read *Amanda's discovery* below. The spelling mistakes have been underlined.
Write the correct spelling of each word in the box.

Amanda's discovery

41 In the corner was a heap of lawn <u>clipings</u> and rubbish.

42 Amanda pushed the rubbish <u>asside</u> and began digging.

43 There, in the damp soil, were <u>dozons</u> of brown worms

44 all wriggling to escape a <u>possable</u> attack. The attack

45 would not come from <u>hungary</u> birds. These worms

were for fresh bait!

Read the text *Cable Beach*.

Each line has a word that is incorrect. Write the correct spelling of the word in the box.

Cable Beach

46 Cable Beach is the main beach fore the town of Broome.

47 It is twenty kilometers long. This white, sandy beach

48 with its boarder of sand dunes, was so named because

49 it was the end of the underwarter cable that linked Australia

50 to Java in Indonesia. The cable was a telegraf line.

☞ **Answers and explanations on pages 186-188**
Excel Revise in a Month Year 5 NAPLAN*-style Tests
121

Circle the correct answer.

1 Cameron placed a toy truck and a toy car along his ruler.

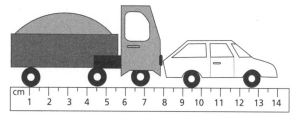

How long is the toy car?

A 6 cm   B 8 cm

C 12 cm   D 14 cm

2 Hannah and her friends watched a movie which started at 12:30 and finished at 2:15. How long was the movie?

A 1 hour 45 minutes

B 2 hour 15 minutes

C 2 hour 35 minutes

D 2 hour 45 minutes

3 On a map of Australia, Richard located some places.

Richard is in Leigh Creek. In which direction is Mackay?

A south-east

B south-west

C north-east

D north-west

4 Carl was playing with these six wooden blocks.

When he finished he packed them away into a box. Which box contains all the blocks?

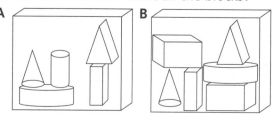

5 Demi checked her emails.

Date	From	Subject	Size
Thu 7:45	Yasmin	Youth Group info	6 kb
Thu 11:35	Jay	Hi	3 kb
Thu 17:13	Yasmin	re:re: Youth Group info	11 kb

She had received three emails: one from Jay and two from Yasmin. Which clock below shows the time she had received Jay's email?

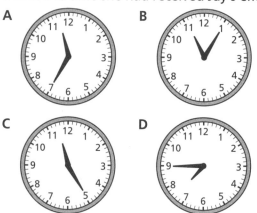

6 Charlie rewrote the number 3405 in words. Which is the correct number?

A Three thousand four hundred and five

B Three thousand four hundred and fifty

C Three thousand four hundred and forty five

D Three thousand and forty five

7 Which of these has the same value as 17 × 9? Select **all** the possible answers.

A 17 × 10 − 9   **B** 17 × 10 − 17

C 20 × 9 − 27   **D** 20 × 9 − 3

8 A shop had DVDs on sale. What is the largest number of DVDs that Cameron can buy for $50.00?

DVD SALE
3 for $25

A 2   **B** 6   **C** 8   **D** 75

9 The grid shows squares which have areas of 1 square unit. Olive estimated the shaded area.

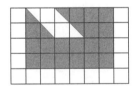

What is the closest estimate of the area, in square units?

A 20   **B** 21   **C** 22   **D** 24

10 Which of these pairs of numbers have a difference of 18? Select **all** the possible answers.

A 27 and 11

B 23 and 5

C 34 and 16

D 40 and 18

11 What number is 43 less than 310?

12 Kate surveyed her classmates to find their favourite takeaway meal. The graph shows the results of her survey.

Thai was the most popular meal.

Pizza was more popular than Indian.

Mexican was less popular than Indian.

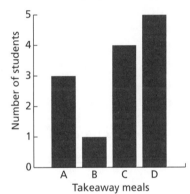

Which column represents Pizza?

A   **B**   **C**   **D**

13 Ben has $4.65 and his grandpa gives him another $3.85. He wants to buy a magazine that costs $10.

How much more money does Ben need?

$ [   ]

14 Kara is collecting shells. She has 84 shells and she puts them in groups of 4.

How many groups of shells does Kara have?

[   ]

It would be a good idea to check your answers to questions 1 to 14 before moving on to the other questions.

☞ **Answers and explanations on pages 189-191**

15 The homes of five classmates have been located on the grid.

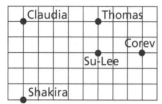

Thomas and Su-Lee live 80 metres apart. What is the shortest distance between Claudia and Shakira?

A 50 metres

B 80 metres

C 160 metre

D 200 metres

16 What is the perimeter of this shape?

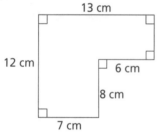

A 35 cm **B** 42 cm **C** 46 cm **D** 50 cm

17 Jonathon arranges 12 discs in lines.

He counts four red discs and two yellow discs. The remainder of the discs are white. What fraction of the discs are white?

A $\frac{1}{6}$ **B** $\frac{1}{3}$ **C** $\frac{1}{2}$ **D** $\frac{2}{3}$

18 A hexagon has 6 sides. Mario used 2 hexagons and rectangles to make a hexagonal prism.

How many rectangles did he use?

19 Here is a map of the school.

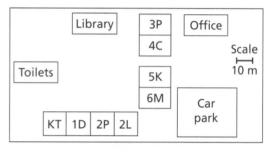

David is in class 5K. The distance from David's classroom to the toilets is closest to

A 5 m.

B 50 m.

C 500 m.

D 5000 m.

20 What number is missing?

A 4 **B** 5 **C** 6 **D** 7

21 Alfie divided 2515 by 5.

2515 ÷ 5 = ☐

What is the answer?

A 53 **B** 503 **C** 530 **D** 5030

☞ **Answers and explanations on pages 189-191**

22 Before he went to school Ravi checked his thermometer. It measured 18 degrees. The diagram shows the thermometer when he arrived home. How much has the temperature increased?

A 4 degrees
B 12 degrees
C 14 degrees
D 16 degrees

23 Hung found the answer to the question $2^2 + 3^2 + 4^2$

What was Hung's answer?
A 29   B 18
C 2   D 81

24 These eight cards have either a heart (♥), diamond (♦), club (♣) or spade (♠).

The cards are turned over and mixed up. If one card is chosen, what is the chance that the card is a diamond (♦) ?
A 1 out of 4
B 1 out of 3
C 1 out of 2
D 2 out of 5

25 Mia writes the number that is the same as

4 thousands + 2 tens + 6 tenths.

What number did she write? ☐

26 Isabella used these four cards to make a four-digit number.

0 7 5 6

Write the largest possible odd number in the box. ☐

27 Jacqueline bought a pencil and a ruler.

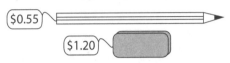

How much change will she receive from a $5 note?

Change = $ ☐

28 Which spinners show an equal chance of landing on each letter? Select **all** the possible answers.

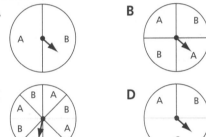

It would be a good idea to check your answers to questions 15 to 28 before moving on to the other questions.

---

29 Add one hundred and fifty on to 953. What is the answer? ☐

30 The table shows two world record times for the 100 metres sprint.

100 m Sprint world records (seconds)		
Men's	Usain Bolt	9.58
Women's	Florence Griffith Joyner	10.49

What is the difference in seconds between the men's record and the women's record?
A 0.91 seconds
B 1.09 seconds
C 1.11 seconds
D 1.91 seconds

☞ **Answers and explanations on pages 189-191**

31 Su-Li has a $5 note. She buys a bottle of milk for $3.65. What change could Su-Li receive?

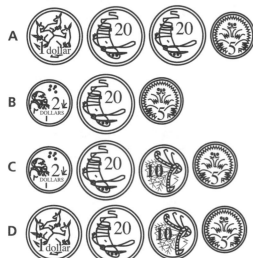

A
B
C
D

32 A whole number is multiplied by 5. Which of these numbers could be the answer? Select **all** the possible answers.

A 45   **B** 53   **C** 60   **D** 85

33 Mario uses this net to form a cube.

		12	8
4	6	10	
2			

When the cube is formed, each pair of opposite faces adds up to the same total. What is this total?

A 8   **B** 10   **C** 12   **D** 14

34 What number is placed in the box to make the number sentence true?

3 4 5 + ☐ 7 = 4 0 2

A 5   **B** 6   **C** 7   **D** 8

35 The diagram shows the lengths of four rectangles: P, Q, R and S.

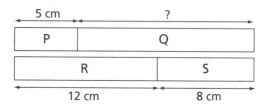

What is the length of rectangle Q?
A 10 cm
B 15 cm
C 18 cm
D 20 cm

36 Cameron wrote these numbers on cards.

| 8 | 22 | 18 | 28 | 34 |

He wrote down the factors of each number. How many of the numbers has 4 as one of its factors? Write your answer in the box.

37 Klaus divided 748 by a number.

His answer was 74.8.

$748 \div$ ☐ $= 74.8$

What is the missing number?
A 10   **B** 100   **C** 1000   **D** 10 000

38 The cooking time for a turkey is 30 minutes for each kilogram. How many minutes will it take to cook a 2.5 kg turkey?

☐ minutes

☞ **Answers and explanations on pages 189–191**

39 Theon ate half the grapes on a bunch. His friend Gemma then ate two of the remaining grapes. If there were still six grapes remaining on the bunch, how many grapes were on the bunch at the start?

40 Which angle is closest in size to 60°?

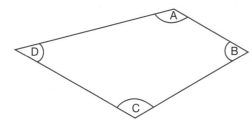

A A   **B** B   **C** C   **D** D

41 This table shows the distance from Adelaide to Perth is 2690 km.

Distance between cities (km)				
	Adelaide	Brisbane	Melbourne	Perth
Brisbane	2055			
Melbourne	725	1660		
Perth	2690	4340	3410	
Sydney	1385	955	875	3910

What is the distance from Sydney to Perth?
A 1385 km
B 955 km
C 875 km
D 3910 km

42 Mike has saved $300.

Marg has saved $200 and plans to save another $20 each week.

After how many more weeks will Marg have the same amount of money as Mike?

☞ **Answers and explanations on pages 189-191**

A recount tells about events that have happened to you or other people. It is usually a record of events as they have happened. Events are told in order. A recount can conclude with a personal opinion of the event. Write your recount as a report; that is, tell what happened but don't write it in the first person.

Choose one of the following topics for your recount.
- A special meal
- A visit to a circus or rodeo or country show
- You may like to check out Tips for Writing Recounts on page 51 before you start.

Start writing here or type your answer on a tablet or computer.

_____

_____

_____

_____

_____

_____

_____

_____

_____

_____

_____

_____

_____

_____

_____

_____

_____

_____

_____

_____

_____

_____

_____

_____

_____

☞ **Marking guide on pages 191-192**

Read the extract from *The Rats of Wolfe Island* by Alan Horsfield and answer questions 1 to 6.

Extract from The Rats of Wolfe Island

The next morning was humid as Kingy and I set off for Buka Buka Village, Kingy leading, and me more or less tagging along. We used Kingy's boat to cross the lagoon, then sat in the shade of a raintree to wait for the bus or someone willing to give us a ride.

After half an hour I grumbled, 'Hope you got the day right!'

He slapped his forehead in mock dismay. 'It's Thursday isn't it?'

'Wednesday!' I corrected.

'Oh, thank God for that! There's no bus on Thursday!' he laughed. 'Unless it's gone Eddie, it should be along in half an hour!'

The bus came down the road about three-quarters of an hour later.

'Not bad,' said Kingy. He nodded his head with satisfaction as we climbed on board just before the dust settled, but I could sense that his mood was changing. He was becoming more introspective. It was nothing obvious, just that he was a little less outgoing.

The trip to Buka Buka Village turn-off was short and bumpy, but much too far to walk under such humid conditions. Hats were a necessity.

After alighting, we headed down the puddle-studded track, Kingy swinging his precious documents in an old plastic shopping bag. We both carried a bottle of water.

The village was a bit of a surprise. All of a sudden the jungle thinned out and there it was. It was on a long, narrow peninsula with good views of the sea on both sides.

There was quite a collection of houses, but there seemed to be no order in their location. There were no streets. Some houses were close together. Others were set some distance from their neighbours. Most had replaced the thatched roofs of tourist brochures with corrugated iron.

1 The bus that Eddie and Kingy caught was
  A a Thursday bus.
  B on time.
  C three-quarters of an hour late.
  D a quarter of an hour late.

2 During the trip to Buka Buka village, Kingy was
  A subdued.
  B excited.
  C tense.
  D morbid.

3 The village surprised Eddie because
  A it was in the jungle.
  B they came upon it unexpectedly.
  C it was along walk off the main road.
  D the sea was close by.

4 What was Kingy taking to Buka Buka village?
Write your answer in the box.

5 Write the numbers 1 to 5 in the boxes to show the order of events in the text.

	Kingy and the narrator arrived at a village with thatched roofs.
	Kingy and the narrator waited by the road in the shade of a tree.
1	Kingy and the narrator set off across the lagoon in a boat.
	The bus let passengers off at the Buka Buka turn-off.
	A bus arrived in a cloud of dust.

6 A good title for the passage would be
  A Village Visit.
  B Humid Days.
  C Muddy Roads.
  D Bus Stop.

☞ **Answers and explanations on page 192**

Read *The Smile* and answer questions 7 to 11.

The Smile
Smiling is infectious,
You catch it like the flu,
When someone smiled at me today
I started smiling too.
I passed around the corner
and someone saw my grin,
when he smiled, I realised
I'd passed it on to him.
I thought about that smile
and then I realised its worth,
A single smile like mine
could travel around the Earth.
If you feel a smile begin,
don't leave it undetected
Let's start an epidemic quick,
and get the world infected.

Anonymous

7 How does a smile travel around the world?
  A by physical contact
  B through infections
  C passed on from person to person
  D sent out secretly

8 What should a person do if they feel like smiling?
  A conceal it   **B** suppress it   **C** enjoy it   **D** share it

9 The poet was first seen smiling
  A in a hospital.
  B at a corner.
  C at a medical clinic.
  D while travelling the world.

10 To compare a smile to an epidemic suggests that
  A everyone will be affected.   **B** it is dangerous.
  C it goes undetected.   **D** it quickly becomes out of control.

11 The poem conveys a feeling of
  A fatigue.   **B** suspense.
  C friendliness.   **D** disappointment.

**It would be a good idea to check your answers to questions
1 to 11 before moving on to the other questions.**

☞ **Answers and explanations on pages 192-193**

Look at the diagram and answer questions 12 to 16.

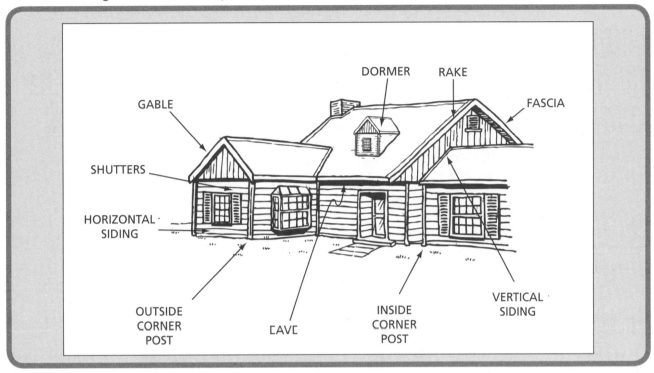

12 This diagram would be useful as it
  A shows that houses are complex buildings.
  B avoids confusion when discussing parts of a house.
  C would help builders understand what they are doing.
  D makes it simple to design a home.

13 The arrow to the eave is 'hooked'. This is to show that the eave
  A has a curve in it. 　　　　　　　**B** is not necessary in a house plan.
  C cannot be seen in the diagram. 　**D** is the under the roof overhang.

14 How many shutters are shown in the diagram?
Write a number in the box.

15 The fascia is
  A a flat board covering the ends of the roof. **B** an outside corner.
  C the highest part of a house. 　　　　　　 **D** the front wall of a house.

16 Look at *The Smile* (page 130) and the *House diagram* (above) again.
For what purposes were these two texts written? Tick two boxes for each text.

	The Smile	*House diagram*
to explore a topic through language	A ☐	A ☐
to encourage a behaviour	B ☐	B ☐
to inform through graphics	C ☐	C ☐
to educate and portray	D ☐	D ☐

☞ **Answers and explanations on page 193**

Read the recipe and answer questions 17 to 22.

Delicious chicken dragon sandwich

Want to give oomph to an ordinary old chicken sandwich?

Try chicken with tarragon. But what is tarragon?

Tarragon (or dragon's-wort) is a herb that grows to about 1.5 metres. The common term for the plant is 'dragon herb'. Tarragon is one of the four fine herbs of French cooking, and is particularly suitable for chicken, fish and egg dishes. French tarragon has a small slender leaf with a mild aniseed or liquorice flavour. Of course, you can substitute chives, parsley, marjoram or basil if you prefer – or have difficulty obtaining tarragon.

For four serves, you will need:

1 roast chicken	1 tablespoon of chopped tarragon
1 tablespoon of wholegrain mustard	2 sticks of finely chopped celery
small bag of mixed lettuce leaves	6 tablespoons of mayonnaise
8 slices of wholemeal bread	freshly ground white pepper and salt to taste

Preparation

Remove the chicken flesh from the carcass and shred. Mix in a bowl with the other ingredients (except bread and lettuce leaves!). Spread the chicken mixture onto four slices of bread. Add the lettuce leaves and then the top slices of bread. Cut into diagonal halves. Serve with fruit juice for a refreshing lunch. Taste that oomph!

17 Why does the writer suggest trying a chicken dragon sandwich?
   A It is cheaper than most chicken sandwiches.   **B** The ingredients are readily available.
   C Most chicken sandwiches are not very interesting.   **D** It's a good way to use up bread.

18 What is the common name for tarragon?
Write your answer in the box.

19 When are the lettuce leaves included in the recipe?
   A after the chicken mixture has been spread on the bread
   B while mixing the other ingredients in a bowl
   C on the sandwich as decoration after cutting the sandwiches in half
   D before the flesh is removed from the chicken carcass

20 How many roast chickens are needed for four serves of chicken dragon sandwich?
   A half   **B** one   **C** two   **D** four

21 Which ingredient is added depending on taste?
   A dragon's wort   **B** liquorice   **C** salt   **D** ground white pepper

22 It is suggested that the chicken dragon sandwich is served
   A with a glass of juice.   **B** in a bag of mixed lettuce leaves.
   C on a bed of lettuce.   **D** with four fine French herbs.

**It would be a good idea to check your answers to questions
12 to 22 before moving on to the other questions.**

☞ **Answers and explanations on page 193**

Read *Living rocks* and answer questions 23 to 28.

Living rocks

Stromatolites are called 'living rocks' because they are rock-like structures built by micro-organisms. Lake Clifton, south of Perth, in Western Australia is one of the few places in the world where the stromatolites grow. The shallow lake is also one of only two sites known where such 'rocks' occur in water less salty than sea water. The lake contains the largest stromatolite reef in the southern hemisphere. It is over 6 km long and in parts, 120 m wide. Stromatolite 'rocks' reach heights of up to 1.3 m. Stromatolites are formed when micro-organisms photosynthesise – the same process green plants use to take energy from sunlight. During this process, calcium from the lime-enriched lake waters forms the rock-like structures. Lake Clifton has an abundance of fresh ground water, which is high in calcium, providing an ideal environment.

How it all began

Millions of years ago there was hardly any oxygen in the atmosphere and no protective ozone layer. Scientists believe that things began changing when tiny organisms began to appear (where from, no one knows). These tiny organisms lived in water and produced oxygen, which entered the atmosphere and over time created the air we live in today. This didn't happen overnight, or even over a hundred years. The organisms had to produce large quantities of oxygen over a very long period before earth could sustain life. One of the descendants of these tiny organisms is algae: tiny aquatic plants. Stromatolites developed from algae and represent the earliest forms of tiny animals on earth.

23 What is the source of energy for Stromatolites?
Write your answer in the box.

24 Millions of years ago
 A there was no ozone layer.
 B Lake Clifton was dry.
 C stromatolites grew to 120 cm high.
 D the world was much smaller.

25 At Lake Clifton, stromatolites grow
 A six kilometres off the coast.
 B in the open sea.
 C in water 120 m deep.
 D in shallow water.

26 Lake Clifton is important because it
 A has the largest stromatolite reef in the world.
 B is the largest lake in Western Australia.
 C has the largest stromatolite reef in the southern hemisphere.
 D holds more fresh water than salt water.

27 Where does the calcium needed to form stromatolites come from?
 A Perth
 B the atmosphere
 C fresh underground water
 D tiny aquatic plants

28 Who would be especially interested in going to Lake Clifton?
 A swimmers   B gardeners   C bricklayers   D geologists

☞ **Answers and explanations on pages 193-194**

Read the letter and answer questions 29 to 33.

Dear Councillors
Blue Bay Council

I am writing to express my disapproval at the plans to construct a new council road through an important conservation area near the lake at Pacific Palms, just to allow a boat-hiring shed to be built.

This conservation area is home to much wildlife, including possums, parrots, tree snakes, a number of threatened birds and rare bats. Bats are very territorial and if they are forced out, the colony will die out. It is appreciated that the road is important to the business but surely the boatshed could be sold land near the old wharf. This small tract of wilderness is the last for over fifty kilometres along this part of the coastline.

Many tourists enjoy hiking in through the area on the well maintained tracks. Tourism is an important industry in this area. School classes make regular visits as part of their practical, environment studies. Why should a wide road corridor be pushed through this native bushland? Everyone involved understands that the road will be a danger to hikers but more importantly it will be a greater danger to wildlife. Road-kill in the area is bound to increase.

A boatshed may seem important to local council; however, without developing a whole new wildlife sanctuary, we would lose endangered wildlife that only exists in a few places around the country.

The loss of just one species is a loss for all future generations, long after any boatshed has gone.

The loss of this pocket of native bush would be bad for the environment, locals, tourists, schoolchildren and a range of endangered wildlife species.

Yours sincerely
Ms PA Turner
Pacific Palms

29 What is Ms Turner's main objection in her letter to the council? Write your answer on the line.

_____

30 Who will be responsible for building the road to the boatshed?
   A boatshed owners   **B** conservation people **C** council   **D** tourists

31 The conservation area is called a pocket of native bush. This is because it
   A is surrounded by bush.   **B** is small.
   C can be difficult to get into.   **D** has one entrance.

32 If the road is built, what animals may never return to the area?
   wading bird   possums   tree snakes   bats   kangaroos
      A   **B**   **C**   **D**   **E**

33 Look at *Living rocks* (page 133) and the *Letter to council* (above) again.
   For what purposes were these two texts written? Tick two boxes for each text

	Living rocks	*Letter to council*
to fascinate	A ☐	A ☐
to persuade	B ☐	B ☐
to inform	C ☐	C ☐

☞ **Answers and explanations on page 194**

Read the poster and answer questions 34 to 39.

Keeping Fit Keeping Healthy Keeping Strong

Here are some healthy food ideas for feeling good:

☺ Eat a healthy breakfast every day that includes cereal, bread and fruit. In winter, porridge and fruit is a good choice.

☺ Eat fruit for snacks—not chips

☺ Drink lots of water. Not sweet drinks like fizzy drinks and cordials.

☺ Use lots of vegetables in main meals. Vegetables go well in stews or curries with a little bit of meat.

☺ Eat less fat, sugar and salt foods. When cooking, instead of frying in fat, try barbecuing or steaming.

☺ Cut fat off meat before it's cooked.

☺ Choose healthy take-away food not fried fatty foods.

Sometimes Food

34 Which two foods make a good winter breakfast?

Write your answers in the boxes. [ ] and [ ]

35 Vegetables go well
A in curries.　　B with fruit.　　C with chips.　　D for snacks.

36 This poster is likely to be displayed at a
A railway station.　B fast-food cafe.　C birthday party.　D health food store.

37 What are the two foods people should eat to stay healthy? Write your answer on the lines.

_____

_____

38 The poster is persuading the reader to choose certain foods to
A save money.　　　　　　　　B enjoy feeling good.
C have a healthy diet.　　　　　D enjoy snacks more often.

39 What is a good reason for having the 'sad' face in red?
A The foods in 'Sometimes Food', can lead to poor health.
B Many of the snack foods contain red colouring.
C Red means stop and people should stop eating so much 'Sometimes Food'.
D Many snack food packets have red warnings on them.

☞ **Answers and explanations on page 194**

1 Which of the following correctly completes this sentence?

The truck was _____ to pay for a new tractor.

sold	sell	solled	sells
A	B	C	D

2 Which word best starts this sentence? Write your answer in the box.

_____ you nor Aldo have the speed to win the race but do your best.

3 Choose the word that is not required in this sentence.

The farmer raised a closed fist at the parrots as they flew off.

closed	fist	flew	off
A	B	C	D

4 Which of the following correctly completes this sentence?

At school, the teachers _____ turns to run a video every Friday.

taked	takes	take	tooks
A	B	C	D

5 Which word in this sentence is a pronoun?

Jack knew he was right but was too afraid to say so.

he	right	afraid	so
A	B	C	D

6 Shade a bubble to show where the missing full stops (.) should go.

'What do you want?' asked Jill as she stood up 'I can get you something'
     (A)   (B)   (C)   (D)

7 Which of the following correctly completes this sentence?

Later the dog should walk _____ across the stage.

slow	slowest	slowed	slowly
A	B	C	D

Read the text *Ever played Oztag?* The text has some gaps.
Choose the best option to fill each gap.

Ever played Oztag?

Oztag football is the latest non-contact sports craze.

It is a non-tackling game played _____

half a field. Eight players in each team _____

on the field at any one time. _____ wear

8

on	in	onto	over
A	B	C	D

9

am	are	is	were
A	B	C	D

10

player	Player	players	Players
A	B	C	D

☞ **Answers and explanations on pages 195–197**

shorts with side Velcro patches. _____ cloth

strip, attached to the Velcro, is the _____

Any player _____ has the ball must pass

it if the tag is removed.

⑪	a	The	an	A
	A	**B**	**C**	**D**

⑫	tag,	Tag	tag.	tag?
	A	**B**	**C**	**D**

⑬	who	what	that	which
	A	**B**	**C**	**D**

⑭ Which sentence has the correct punctuation?
   A The boss explained, "to the workers the safety rules."
   B The boss explained to the workers the safety rules.
   C The boss explained to the workers, "the safety rules."
   D The boss explained to the workers, "The safety rules."

⑮ Read this sentence.

Two days later the actors quickly and quietly removed all the items from the stage.
Write any adverbs from the sentence in the boxes. Use as many boxes as you need.

⑯ Choose the sentence that is a command.
   A Can you get it for me?   **B** Take your medicine before food.
   C Dad always says the weirdest things.   **D** Pat was told to behave herself.

⑰ Which of the following correctly completes the sentence?

Both red and green _____ suitable team colours.

are	was	is	wasn't
A	**B**	**C**	**D**

⑱ Shade **two** bubbles to show where the missing commas (,) should go.

Mary looked at the flowers. There were splashes ˬ of red ˬ pink ˬ yellow ˬ and white.
                                              Ⓐ   Ⓑ   Ⓒ   Ⓓ

⑲ Which sentence has the correct punctuation?
   A These books aren't mine and its not my mess!
   B These books are'nt mine and it's not my mess!
   C These book's aren't mine and it's not my mess!
   D These books aren't mine and it's not my mess!

⑳ Choose the **two** words that can be both singular and plural.

sheep	postmen	geese	fungus	deer
A	**B**	**C**	**D**	**E**

㉑ In which sentence is the word *head* used as an adjective?
   A He has no hair on his head.
   B Tina had a head start in her race.
   C The girls head for the waterfall.
   D Ben can head a ball into a net.

☞ **Answers and explanations on pages 195-197**

22 Which word best completes this sentence? Write your answer in the box.

Comparing the five puppies' sizes, they are

all very small but that one is definitely the [   ].

23 Which sentence has the correct punctuation?
A The babies clothes aren't in the basket.
B The baby's clothes aren't in the basket.
C The baby's clothes ain't in the basket.
D The babys clothes aren't in the basket.

24 Read this text.

When Natalie found the ball she had kicked into the long grass she also found a broken bottle that had been smashed the last time the grass had been mown.

The first thing that happened was
A Natalie found her ball.
B someone had broken a bottle.
C the grass had been mown.
D Natalie kicked her ball.

25 Which of the following correctly completes this sentence?

The eagle soared from the cliff top [   ] the valley below.

onto   at   into   beneath
A   B   C   D

It would be a good idea to check your answers to questions 1 to 25 before moving on to the other questions.

To the student
Ask your teacher or parent to read the spelling words for you. The words are listed on page 202. Write the spelling words on the lines below.

26 _____ **34** _____

27 _____ **35** _____

28 _____ **36** _____

29 _____ **37** _____

30 _____ **38** _____

31 _____ **39** _____

32 _____ **40** _____

33 _____

☞ **Answers and explanations on pages 195-197**

Read *Festival of the Winds* below. The spelling mistakes have been underlined.
Write the correct spelling of each word in the box.

Festival of the Winds

41 The Bondi Beach Festival of the Winds is held <u>annualy</u>,

42 in September when the <u>breazes</u> can be quite strong.

43 The skies come <u>allive</u> with kites of all shapes and sizes.

44 <u>Locale</u> and international kite makers and

45 fliers take part in Australia's most <u>populer</u> competition.

Read the text *Dune Bashing in Dubai*. Each line has a word that is incorrect.
Write the correct spelling of the word in the box.

Dune Bashing in Dubai

46 This is a challenging journey through the jiant sand dunes

47 of Dubai desert, riding a quad bike and trying to compleat all

48 the levels. Dune bashing is an action sport were you have to

49 ride your quad bike through the dangrous desert landscape.

50 You must maintain your balance untill you reach the finish.

☞ **Answers and explanations on pages 195-197**

1 Nathan folded a sheet of paper in half. From the folded edge, he cut out a shape.

What did his paper look like when he unfolded it?

A

B

C

D

2 Amy multiplies 204 by 6.

Write the correct answer in the box.

204 × 6 = [ ]

3 Which of these pairs of numbers have a sum of 25? Select **all** the possible answers.

A 18 and 7
B 11 and 13
C 16 and 11
D 6 and 19

4 Andrew spins the arrow on the wheel. The arrow points to the winning colour: R = red, Y = yellow, B = blue, G = green. Which colour has the smallest chance of winning?

A yellow
B blue
C green
D red

5 Juliet rotated the square a quarter of a turn in a clockwise direction. Which of these is the new square?

A   B

C   D

6 Five cousins recorded the year of their birth in the table.

Name	Year of Birth
Maxine	1975
Nicole	1992
Jarryd	1993
Jessica	1990
Stacey	1981

Who is the second youngest cousin?

A Maxine   B Nicole
C Jarryd   D Jessica
E Stacey

7 What number does the [?] represent?   [ ]

42   54   [?]

8 This clock on the kitchen wall is showing the wrong time. It is 25 minutes slow. What is the correct time?

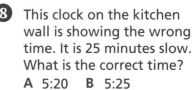

A 5:20   B 5:25
C 6:10   D 6:15

9 Write a number in the box to make the subtraction true.

☞ **Answers and explanations on pages 197–200**

10 This scale is balanced.

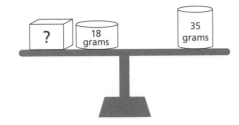

What is the weight of the block?

	grams

11 385 + ☐ ? + 11 = 673.

What is the missing number?

12 represents $\frac{3}{5}$.

Which of these represents one whole?

A

B

C

D

13 Jackson has some identical cubes. When he makes a stack of 3 cubes it is 12 cm tall.

What will be the height of 5 cubes?

A 8 cm   B 17 cm
C 18 cm   D 20 cm

14 Sam is baking cookies for the school fair. She sells the cookies in bags of 5. What is the maximum number of bags she can sell if she bakes 64 cookies?

10	12	16	20	13
A	B	C	D	E

It would be a good idea to check your answers to questions 1 to 14 before moving on to the other questions.

---

15 This is a map of Noah's town.

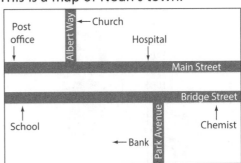

He knows that the shortest distance from the Post Office to the Hospital is about 200 metres. What is the best estimate for the shortest distance from the School to the Chemist?

A 100 m   B 150 m
C 250 m   D 500 m

16 This graph shows the number of goals scored in soccer games.

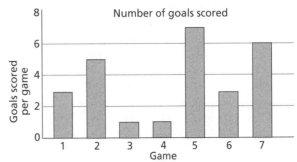

Which of these statements is true? Select **all** possible answers.

A The same number of goals were scored in Game 1 and Game 7.

B There was a total of 26 goals scored.

C There were 3 games where at least 4 goals were scored.

D There were 5 games where there was less than 5 goals scored.

E The most goals were scored in Game 7.

☞ **Answers and explanations on pages 197–200**

17 The chart shows the heights of Josh and Emily.

Simon's height is halfway between Josh and Emily. What is Simon's height?

A 60 cm **B** 100 cm **C** 110 cm **D** 120 cm

18 This graph shows the number of students in different classes at a school who own mobile phones.

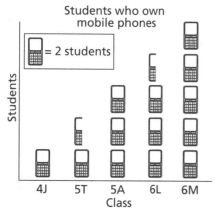

How many more students in Class 6M had mobile phones than students in Class 5T?

A 3 **B** 4 **C** 5 **D** 7

19 Connor needs to catch a train to Juniper Valley. He arrives at the railway station 20 minutes before the train will leave.

Train departs at	Train Destination
3:29	Mount Carmel
3:39	Laurence
3:43	Juniper Valley
3:55	Barton Ridge

At what time does Connor arrive at the railway station?

20 The shape is made from 24 tiles.

What fraction of the shape is shaded?

A $\frac{1}{6}$ **B** $\frac{1}{4}$ **C** $\frac{1}{3}$ **D** $\frac{1}{2}$

21 Nina asked her classmates where their parents were born. The results are shown in the table.

	Country of birth	
	Australian	Overseas
Fathers	12	14
Mothers	18	8

How many parents were born in Australia?

A 12 **B** 20 **C** 30 **D** 52

22 Paul opens a 1-kg packet of sugar. He pours 350 g of sugar into a measuring bowl.

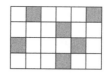

What is the mass of sugar left in the packet?

A 350 g **B** 650 g
C 700 g **D** 750 g

23 $120 \div 4 = \boxed{} \times 6$

What is the missing number?

A 4 **B** 5 **C** 6 **D** 8

☞ **Answers and explanations on pages 197–200**

24 Fiona buys a ball of string which is 4 metres in length. For a craft activity Fiona needs pieces of string which are 5 cm long. How many pieces of string can she cut from a ball of string which is 4 metres long?

25 Which of these number sentences equals 4.75? Select **all** the possible answers.

A 0.4 + 0.7 + 0.5

B 4 + 0.7 + 0.5

C 4 + 0.7 + 0.05

D 4.0 + 0.07 + 0.05

E 4.7 + 0.05

26 Baby Gus is 6 days old and baby Henry is exactly 4 weeks old. How many days older is Henry than Gus?

27 The sign below is located at the start of Monkey Face Trail and shows the distances from the sign to different points of interest along the trail.

Monkey Face Trail	
Gap Creek Falls	1.3 km
Cedar Brush	2.0 km
Pines Picnic Area	2.7 km
Moirs Lookout	3.5 km

Chris walked from the start of the trail to Moirs Lookout. She then walked back to the Pines Picnic Area for lunch. What was the total distance in kilometres that she walked?

 km

28 Emilee divides a large square into four smaller squares. She then divides one of these smaller squares into four very small squares. She shades two of the squares.

What fraction of the original square is shaded?

A one-quarter

B one-eighth

C five-twelfths

D five-sixteenths

It would be a good idea to check your answers to questions 15 to 28 before moving on to the other questions.

---

29 The diagram shows a hundred chart with a section covered by a rectangle. Cassie placed 20 small discs in a counting pattern starting at 3.

1	2	●	4	5	●	7	8	●	10
11	●	13	14	●	16	17	●	19	20
●	22	23	●	25	26	●	28	29	●
31	32	●	34	35	●	37	38	●	40

On what number will Cassie place the sixteenth disc?

A 45   B 47

C 48   D 55

☞ **Answers and explanations on pages 197–200**

Advanced level

30 The grid is a map showing the location of six towns.

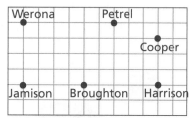

The shortest distance from Jamison to Broughton is 20 km. Which two towns are about 30 km apart?

A Werona and Jamison

B Werona and Petrel

C Cooper and Harrison

D Broughton and Harrison

31 Ella made a spinner with 3 colours. When she spins the arrow on her spinner:

- it is three times as likely to spin a green than a blue
- it is twice as likely to spin a red than a blue.

Which of these could be Ella's spinner?

A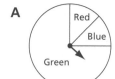

B

C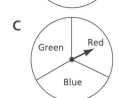

D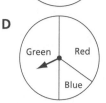

32 Small boxes are to be packed into a large box.

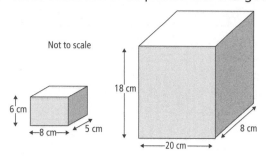

What is the **greatest** number of small boxes that will fit in the large box?

33 Josef used one half of a square to paint the letter R. Before the paint could dry, he folded the square along the dotted line. Which diagram shows Josef's square?

A B

C D

34 Mia and Jack are standing in a line to buy lunch.

- There are 6 people between Jack and Mia.
- There are 11 people in front of Jack including Mia.
- There are 9 people behind Mia including Jack.

How many people are in the line?

35 A new skateboard costs $240. Shani has saved $85.

Which of these number sentences can be used to find the amount of money she needs to buy the skateboard? Select **all** the possible answers.

A $240 − $85 =

B $240 − ? = $85

C $85 + ? = $240

D ? − $240 = $85

36 A shop has a '$\frac{1}{3}$ off all products' sale.

What will Grace pay for a toaster originally priced at $48?

$

☞ **Answers and explanations on pages 197–200**

144   *Excel* Revise in a Month Year 5 NAPLAN*-style Tests

37 Gordon had four lengths of wood measuring 320 cm, 3095 mm, 3800 mm and 0.35 metres.

Rearrange the lengths from shortest to longest.

shortest ─────────────────→ longest

38 A bucket contains lots of coloured balls. The balls are either coloured red, green, blue or yellow. A ball is selected at random from the bucket. Which of these could be the probability that it is green? Select **all** the possible answers.

A $\frac{1}{3}$ **B** 0.25   **C** 1.4   **D** $\frac{3}{8}$

39 The usual price of a coffee machine is $650. The machine is on sale for 10% off its usual price. What is the sale price of the coffee machine?

$ [   ]

40 What is the missing number?

$\boxed{?} - 16 + 11 = 45$

[   ]

41 In a game, a white disc is worth twice as many points as a black disc.

 = 24 points

What will be the value of 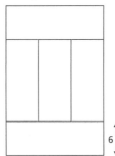 ?

42 Tara has 5 identical rectangular cards which each have a width of 6 cm.

When placed together they form a larger rectangle.

6 cm

What is the area of the larger rectangle in square centimetres?

[   ] square centimetres

☞ **Answers and explanations on pages 197–200**

WEEK 1

NUMBER AND ALGEBRA (Test Your Skills)
Whole numbers   Page 2

Test 1

1 5 thousands

2 2034 + 100 = 2134

3 2020 − 1 = 2019

4 54 + 76 = 130; 130 ÷ 2 = 65

5 1335: Odd numbers end in 1, 3, 5, 7 or 9 regardless of all other digits in the number.

6 One hundred and two thousand, five hundred and seven

7 64 is greater than (>) 45

8 1526 rounds to 2000.

9 2178 + 5 = 2183

Test 2

1 5000 + 600 + 7 = 5607

2 Factors of 12: 1, 2, 3, 4, 6, 12. There are 6 factors of 12.

3 2006 + 20 = 2026

4 61 is closest to 60 as it is only 1 away.

5 364 is closer to 400 than 300. 1364 rounds (up) to 1400.

6 The **face** value of 5 is 5 but its **place** value is 500. The difference is 500 − 5 = 495.

7 1200 is 12 hundred, or 1 thousand 2 hundred.

8 odd + even = odd

9 102 is less than 110. This means 102 < 110.

NUMBER AND ALGEBRA (Real Test)
Whole numbers   Page 4

1 A **2** 499, 706, 998, 1021, 1100 **3** C **4** A, B, C, E
5 C **6** D **7** A **8** A **9** C **10** C **11** B **12** C **13** C **14** 3
15 A, D **16** 975

EXPLANATIONS

1 Eight thousand three hundred and nine
= 8 × 1000 + 3 × 100 + 9 × 1
= 8 × 1000 + 3 × 100 + 0 × 10 + 9 × 1
= 8309

2 From smallest to largest the order is 499, 706, 998, 1021, 1100.

3 The arrow points to 64.

4 The factors of 18 are 1, 2, 3, 6, 9, 18. From the list the answer is 2, 3, 6, 18.

5 4007 = 4 × 1000 + 7 × 1
= 4 × 1000 + 0 × 100 + 0 × 10 + 7 × 1
= four thousand and seven

6 From smallest to largest: 34 89 287 541

7 32 400 = 3 × 10 000 + 2 × 1000 + 4 × 100

8 5430 becomes 543 when the zero is removed. This new number is 10 times smaller than 5430.

9 Consider each of the choices:
7: is 63 from 70
64: is 6 away from 70
69: is 1 away from 70
73: is 3 away from 70
The closest to 70 is 69.

10 There are 34 shaded squares.

11 In 23 547, the 3 represents 3000. This means the value is 3 thousands.

12 There are 4 rows of 10 and another row which is one less than a complete row.
This means 4 × 10 + 9 = 40 + 9 = 49

13 The middle number is the average:
$$\text{Average} = \frac{12+18}{2}$$
$$= \frac{30}{2}$$
$$= 15$$

14 Here is the line of students:
x x Samuel x x x Bronson x
This means that there are 3 students between Samuel and Bronson.

15 The symbols are greater than (>) and less than (<).
The true statements are 25 > 9 (25 is greater than 9) and 8 < 11 (8 is less than 11).

16 The largest possible number uses the three largest digits, commencing with the largest digit. The correct answer is 975.

NUMBER AND ALGEBRA (Test Your Skills)
Addition and subtraction   Page 5

Addition

1 7 + 8 + 5 + 6 = 26

2 No trading is necessary. Simply add each column starting with the right-hand column (units).

3 Add the units (10), put down the 0 and 'carry' the 1 tens to the middle column. Then add the tens column (9). Then the hundreds column (6). Total = 690.

4 You can use trial-and-error approach or you may subtract the known numbers from the total. 204 − 149 = 55. The missing digit is 5.

5 8300 + 82 = 8382

6 Add each column as in Question 3, keeping the cents and dollars in their columns and the decimal point under the decimal point.

7 Use the subtraction method. 73 − 37 = 36

Subtraction

1 25 − 8 − 5 − 2 = 25 − 5 − 8 − 2
         = 20 − 8 − 2
         = 10

2 Simply subtract starting on the right. There is no trading. 4 − 2 = 2; 9 − 0 = 9; 7 − 6 = 1 (192)

3 Subtract starting on the right (9 − 7 = 2). In the tens column, because the 3 is less than the 4, take 1 from the 5 (making it 4) and the 3 becomes 13 (13 − 4 = 9). In the hundreds column there is nothing to take from the 4 (492).
Set out it would look like this: $^4\cancel{5}^13\ 9$
                                              $-\ \ 4\ 7$
                                              $\overline{4\ 9\ 2}$

4 Subtract the answer from 256 (256 − 167 = 89). The missing digit = 9.

---

5 Working: 6 − 8 becomes 16 − 8 (= 8). The 8 becomes 7.
7 − 6 = 1, then 4 − 0 = 4 (418).

6 Work subtraction of money as normal subtraction, trading as required. Remember to keep the numbers in their columns and the decimal point always goes under the decimal point.

7 Use the subtraction method (81 − 47 = 34)

NUMBER AND ALGEBRA (Real Test)
Addition and subtraction   Page 7

1 B **2** C **3** C **4** D **5** D **6** C **7** A, B, D **8** D **9** B
10 C **11** 35 **12** 5 **13** B, C **14** A **15** C **16** 21

EXPLANATIONS

1 4 + 8 + 2 + 6 + 1 = 4 + 6 + 8 + 2 + 1
                      = 10 + 10 + 1
                      = 21

2 Half of 24 is 12 and twice 13 is 26. This means 12 + 26 = 38

3 45 and 'what number' is 67?
We can find the number using subtraction: 67 − 45 = 22
The missing number is 22.

4 Smallest = 21 and largest = 76
21 + 76 = 97

5 326 + 7 + 23 = 356
826 + 7 + 23 = ____
Since 826 is 500 more than 326, then answer will be 500 more than 356.
The answer is 356 + 500 = 856

6 Age = 11 + 59
        = 11 + 60 − 1
        = 70

7 6 + 6 + 6 + 6 + 6 = 5 × 6 = 30
7 + 7 + 7 + 7 = 4 × 7 = 28
8 + 8 + 8 = 3 × 8 = 24
9 + 9 + 9 = 3 × 9 = 27
30, 28 and 27 are between 25 and 35.

8   684
      + 253
      ‾‾‾‾‾‾‾
        937   This means that X = 9 and Y = 7

9 20 − 6 = 14

10 Lollypops = 24 − 4 − 6
= 20 − 6
= 14

11 Change = 100 − 65
= 100 − 60 − 5
= 40 − 5
= 35
Joanne receives $35 change.

12
```
   95
 − 42
   53
```
The missing number is 5.

13 Next number = 104 − 19
= 104 − 20 + 1
= 84 + 1
= 85

Following number = 85 − 19
= 85 − 20 + 1
= 65 + 1
= 66

The possible numbers are 85 and 66.

14 42 − 24 = 42 − 22 − 2
= 20 − 2
= 18

15 Difference between four 18s and five 18s is one 18. This means the difference is 18.

16 Number of DVDs = 80 − 16 − 43
rated M = 80 − 10 − 6 − 43
= 70 − 6 − 43
= 64 − 43
= 64 − 40 − 3
= 24 − 3
= 21
Here is another method:
We could have first
added 16 and 43:
```
    16
  + 43
    59
```
Now use subtraction:
```
    80
  − 59
    21
```
This means that there are 21 DVDs rated M.

NUMBER AND ALGEBRA (Test Your Skills)
Multiplication and division   Page 8

Multiplication

1 There are 4 lots of 13. The answer is 4 × 13.

2 Start with the units (right). 7 × 3 = 21.
Put down the 1 and 'carry' the 2. 7 × 2 = 14, then add the 2 (14 + 2 = 16).
The answer is 161.

3 Suggested method: Cross off the zero.
Put it in the units column of the answer.
Then simply multiply from the tens position.
```
    205
  ×  40
   8200
```

4 Use trial and error approach
(2 × 35 = 70; 4 × 35 = 140; 6 × 35 = 210).

5
```
    51
  ×  3
   153
```

6 Multiply in the usual way, remembering to put the decimal point under the decimal point.

7 Use the division method. 108 ÷ 12 = 9

8 7^2 = 7 × 7 = 49

Division

1 6 goes into 9 once with 3 'left over'. 6 goes into 36 six times. The answer is 16.

2 Division by 10 short cut. Just drop the zero in the number being divided (360 ÷ 10 = 36).

3 The factors of 24 are 1, 2, 3, 4, 6, 8, 12, 24.
The highest factors are 8 and 12 (not including 24).

4 See how many 7s in 2 (0). Then see how many 7s in 21 (= 3). See how many 7s in 3 (= 0) but the three is 'carried' to the next digit.
See how many 7s in 35 (= 5).
The answer is 0305 or simply 305.
```
       305
  7)2135
```

5 This is simply another way of asking a 'division' question. Use the method shown above.

6 12 × 9 = 108. The remainder is 2 (110 − 108 = 2).

7 You could use trial and error. Another method is 7 × 117 = 819. Add 1 (the remainder) = 820. The missing digit is zero (0).

8 Divide as if for straight short division, remembering to put a decimal point above the decimal point.

9 To find an average add all the given numbers (or items) and then divide by the number of items added. 5 + 9 + 4 = 18; 18 ÷ 3 = 6

NUMBER AND ALGEBRA (Real Test)
Multiplication and division Page 11

1 12 **2** D **3** B **4** D **5** D **6** C **7** C **8** D **9** B
10 A, C **11** A **12** A **13** A, C, E **14** 5 **15** 1 **16** 5

EXPLANATIONS

1 4 plates with 3 biscuits each:
Total = 4 × 3
= 12
The answer is 12 biscuits.

2 Elephant: 4 legs and Monkey = 2 legs
Total = 2 × 4 + 3 × 2
= 8 + 6
= 14

3 Age of Aziz's uncle = 7 × 8
= 56
This means Aziz's uncle is 56 years old.

4 As 10 ÷ 2 = 5, Rachael can buy 5 bags of oranges.
This means number of oranges = 5 × 6
= 30
Rachael can buy 30 oranges.

5 Multiplying a whole number by 100 means that we write two zeros on the end of the number: 35 × 100 = 3500

6 6 rows of 8 dots: Total = 6 × 8
= 48
There are 48 dots.

7
$$\begin{array}{r} 87 \\ \times\ 4 \\ \hline 348 \end{array}$$

This means the missing digit is 4.

8 5515 ÷ 5:
$$\begin{array}{r} 1103 \\ 5\overline{)5515} \end{array}$$

We say: 5 into 5 is 1
5 into 5 is 1
5 into 1 is 0 with remainder 1
5 into 15 is 3
This means the answer is 1103.

9 4 rows of 6 cards means 4 × 6 = 24.
Now the 24 cards are arranged in 3 rows:
Number in each row = 24 ÷ 3
= 8
Sophie has 8 cards in each row.

10 The answer will be even. As even numbers end in 0, 2, 4, 6, or 8 the numbers are 310 and 11 372.

11 Number in each group = 19 ÷ 6
= 3 remainder 1
This means that there is 1 left over.

12 Number of pizzas = 20 ÷ 6
= 3 remainder 2
This means that Courtney could order 3 pizzas (with $2 change).

13 As 368 can be divided by 4, then the last digit must be divisible by 4 if the whole 4-digit number is divisible by 4. The last digit could be 0, 4 or 8.

14
Average $= \dfrac{2 + 6 + 7}{3}$
$= \dfrac{15}{3}$
$= 5$

The answer is 5.

15
$$\begin{array}{r} 71 \\ 6\overline{)426} \end{array}$$

We say: 6 into 4 will not go
6 into 42 is 7
6 into 6 is 1
The answer is 71.
This means the missing number is 1.

16 A dozen is 12.
Cost of each cupcake = 60 ÷ 12
= 5
This means each cupcake costs $5.

SPELLING (Real Test)
Common misspellings Page 13

1 addresses

2 fabric

3 brushes

4 escaping

5 carpenter

6 shoulder

7 deputies

8 raspberry

9 lighthouse

10 horizon

11 dune

12 wooden

13 pearling

14 spent

15 trudging

16 being

17 contents

18 depended

GRAMMAR AND PUNCTUATION (Real Test)
Types of sentences and articles Pages 15–16

1 D **2** C **3** A **4** B **5** D **6** B **7** C **8** A **9** B **10** A
11 C **12** D **13** group, tourists, way, Bondi, beach
14 D **15** B **16** was **17** D **18** B
EXPLANATIONS

1 This is a grammar question. The correct word is the definite article *the*.
Tip: *The* is used because it refers to a particular dog—*my pet dog*.

2 This is a grammar question. The correct word is *better*.
Tip: Remember *good*, *better* and *best* when describing items. *Good* is used when describing one item. *Better* is used when comparing two items. *Best* is used when judging more than two items. 'More better' is incorrect. 'Gooder' is not a word.

3 This is a grammar question. The correct word is *wept*.
Tip: *Wept* is an irregular verb. Most verbs in English form their past tenses by adding *ed* (e.g. *he walked*). There are a number of irregular verbs when this doesn't happen. We say *wept* instead of 'weeped'. 'Weept' is not a real word.

4 This is a grammar question. The correct word is the conjunction *because*.
Tip: Conjunctions join single words or ideas. Think of the sentence as: *You didn't make a mistake because you listened to the instructions! Because* provides the reason.

5 This is a grammar question. The correct words are *had left*.
Tip: *Left* is the past tense of *leave*. With the verb *left* you need a 'helper'—another verb to 'help' it. *Have*, *has* and *had* can be helping verbs. *Had* is also past tense. The helping verb is always close to the verb it is helping.

6 This is a grammar question. The correct word is the preposition *onto*.
Tip: Prepositions put events in position, in time or place. Use *onto* to indicate that the cat is moving towards a position to be on it.

7 This is a grammar question. The correct word is the adverb *very*.
Tip: Adverbs modify meaning. *Very* is used to emphasise just how poisonous it is.

8 This is a grammar question. The correct word is the pronoun *which*.
Tip: *Which* is a common pronoun used to refer to animals or things (an event). *Who* is used to refer to people. *What* is most often used to ask a question.

9 This is a grammar question. The correct word is the verb *has*.
Tip: Basic rule: singular subjects (nouns) need singular verbs; plural subjects (nouns) need plural verbs. In this case *has* must be used because there is one type of fungi—*Death Cap*.

10 This is a grammar question. The correct word is the conjunction *and*.
Tip: Conjunctions join single words or ideas. *And* is used to join things that are similar or go together.

11 This is a punctuation question. *If* is used (with a capital) to start a new sentence.
Tip: The word *ring* is the last word of the previous sentence. It is followed by a full stop. *However* is incorrect as it would suggest some form of contrasting condition.

12 This is a punctuation question. The correct sentence is: *There is no cure.* (with a full stop).
Tip: Statements end with a full stop. *Cure* is not a proper noun so no capital letter is required.

13 This is a grammar question. Nouns are naming words. There are four types of nouns: group (collective), tourists, way, beach (common), Bondi (proper). There are no abstract nouns.

14 This is a punctuation question. The correct sentence is: *Most days this week there were no westerly winds but Monday was different.*
Tip: *Monday* is the only proper noun in this sentence.

15 This is a grammar question. The unnecessary words are *at a time*.
Tip: *When* provides the necessary indication of time. The words *at a time* are redundant. No meaning is lost by omitting *at a time*.

16 This is a grammar question. The correct word is the verb *was*.
Tip: Basic rule: Singular subjects (nouns) need singular verbs; plural subjects (nouns) need plural verbs. In this case *was* must be used because there is one dog (even though there are many frogs).

17 This is a grammar question. The correct sentence is: *They sold their old car to pay for the new TV screen.*

Tip: *Sold* is the past tense of *sell*. *Sold* is an irregular verb. Most verbs in English form their past tenses by adding *ed* (e.g. *he walked*). There are a number of irregular verbs when this doesn't happen. We say *sold* instead of 'selled'. *As a result of having sold the car they could pay for a TV screen.*

18 This is a punctuation question. The correct sentence is: *Jessie had to buy new shoes, bag and books after the sudden storm.*
Tip: Use a comma to separate the items in a series—three or more things—or for a pause. There is no comma where *and* is used in the series: *new shoes, bag and books.*

READING (Test Your Skills)
Understanding narratives   Page 17

The Rats of Wolfe Island
1 B **2** D **3** A, E **4** C **5** B **6** D

EXPLANATIONS

1 The extract is most likely from a mystery novel. The reader is not told a lot as the scene opens. The other options are not entirely likely. It is certainly not a fable or legend. There are no clues that it is a historical novel.

2 'Ajar' means slightly open. This lets the narrator listen to possible sounds from inside.

3 'Uneasy' and 'cautious' are the best terms. He is not sure what has happened.

4 The narrator was suddenly worried about Kingy's whereabouts and then he had a sinking feeling that he might be dead.

5 The word 'lab' (laboratory) suggests scientific work.

6 'Gusto' implies enthusiasm. The narrator called out with more enthusiasm than he felt.

READING (Real Test)
Understanding narratives — Page 18

Spooked
1 in Gerry's bedroom **2** C **3** A **4** D **5** D **6** C **7** C

EXPLANATIONS

1 The boys are staying *in Gerry's bedroom*. Henk jumped out of bed to hurry home.

2 With questions like this one you have to work out the answer from clues in the text. Henk's eyes were wide open (popping out of his head!). The movement in the wardrobe spooked him (terrified him).

3 Henk rushed from the room because he was so scared he couldn't face what might be in the wardrobe.

4 The rattling doors made the boys' scalps prickle.

5 The boys kept talking to conceal their feelings of the fear of the unknown.

6 If you don't know the meaning of a word, its context will give some indication of its meaning. It was like a faint sigh or a whisper.

7 The incident took place a little after midnight (1:28). The boys were too scared to go to sleep. They knew there was something in the wardrobe.

READING (Real Test)
Understanding narratives — Page 19

Cadaver Dog
1 A **2** B **3** A **4** overgrown **5** D **6** B **7** C

EXPLANATIONS

1 Shane was lonely and a bit bored. He was trying to find something to do, something to occupy his mind.

2 The setting is an isolated one. It's kilometres from the last store. It is not barren as there is bush around the site. Shane doesn't find it exciting.

3 A wry smile is a smile that is a result of an unfunny (private) joke. It is usually crooked.

4 A track that is hardly ever used will become overgrown by vegetation.

5 Shane was looking for something to do. He would have preferred to have someone to talk to but he was not sure about the girl with the pram.

6 There would be people at the grocery store —someone to talk to.

7 The 'new farm' is mentioned in paragraph three.

READING (Real Test)
Understanding narratives — Page 20

The Incredible Experience of Megan Kingsley
1 5 **2** B **3** B **4** C **5** A **6** C **7** B **8** A

EXPLANATIONS

1 Five people: the captain, Patrick and Annabel, their mother, Megan.

2 The group will leave the boat to go to the house where they are to have lunch.

3 She feels concerned about Megan. She frowns.

4 They saw a cove that appeared to be cut out of a cliff.

5 A stony silence implies hostility (I don't want to talk to anyone!).

6 The clue is in the words 'clambered down'. A hatch is a hole in the deck.

7 The seas are choppy so the boat bounced (bobbed) up and down.

8 The cabin is below, or at, water level. The boat is not sinking.

READING (Real Test)
Understanding explanations — Page 21

Kites
1 B **2** C **3** A **4** C **5** *Incredible Experience* A, D; *Kites* B, C **6** written response **7** C

EXPLANATIONS

1 The extract would be found in a craft book as it gives information on making a kite. The information is not precise enough to be in a manual. It is not part of a story (novel). It is not news.

2 To master a skill means to become skilled in that activity.

3 String is required to guide the kite in wind. Without string the kite would either blow away or not fly at all.

4 'Timber yeards' are mentioned in paragraph three.

5 *The Incredible Experience* text is intended to be read for enjoyment—to **entertain** the reader. In a lesser way, it **recounts** a fictional incident. The *Kites* text **instructs** people on how to make a kite. It also **explains** some facts about a kite's features.

6 Possible answer:

Strong winds can tear the kite covering so reinforcing tape will be required.

7 Kite flying is not dangerous. This information is implied in the passage. As kites can be made from 'scraps' new materials are not necessary. As scraps are cheap (or worthless) kite making is not costly.

WRITING (Real Test)
Persuasive text 1   Page 26

Tick each correct point.
Read the student's work through once to get an overall view of their response.

Focus on general points
☐ Did it make sense?
☐ Did it flow? Were the arguments logical and relevant?
☐ Did the opinions expressed arouse any feelings/reactions?
☐ Was the body of the writing mainly in the third person?
☐ Did you want to read on to understand/ appreciate the writer's point of view?
☐ Were the arguments convincing?
☐ Has the writer been assertive (e.g. the use of *is* rather than a less definite term)?
☐ Was the handwriting readable?
☐ Was the writing style suitable for a persuasive text (objective; not casual or dismissive)?

Now focus on the detail. Read each of the following points and find out whether the student's work has these features.

Focus on content
☐ Did the opening sentence(s) focus on the topic?
☐ Was the writer's point of view established early in the writing?
☐ Did the writer include any evidence to support his or her opinion?
☐ Did the writer include information relevant to his or her experiences?
☐ Were the points/arguments raised by the writer easy to follow?
☐ Did the writing follow the format with an introduction, the body of the text and a conclusion?
☐ Were personal opinions included?
☐ Was the concluding paragraph relevant to the topic?

Focus on structure, vocabulary, grammar, spelling, punctuation
☐ Was there a variety of sentence lengths, types and beginnings?
☐ Was a new paragraph started for each additional argument or point?
☐ Has the writer used any similes (e.g. *as clear as crystal*) to stress a point raised?
☐ Did the writer avoid approximations such as *probably, perhaps* and *maybe*?
☐ Did the writer use such phrases as *I know …* and *It is important to …*?
☐ Did the writer refer to the question in the points raised (A good way to do this is to use the key words from the question or the introduction.)?
☐ Has the writer used any less common words correctly?
☐ Was indirect speech used correctly?
☐ Were adjectives used to improve descriptions (e.g. *expensive* buildings)?
☐ Were adverbs used effectively (e.g. *firstly*)?
☐ Were capital letters used correctly?
☐ Was punctuation used correctly?
☐ Was the spelling of words correct?

Marker's suggestions (optional)

Tick each correct point.
Read the student's work through once to get an overall view of their response.

Focus on general points
☐ Did it make sense?
☐ Did it flow? Were the arguments logical and relevant?
☐ Did the opinions expressed arouse any feelings/reactions?
☐ Was the body of the writing mainly in the third person?
☐ Did you want to read on to understand/appreciate the writer's point of view?
☐ Were the arguments convincing?
☐ Has the writer been assertive (e.g. the use of *is* rather than a less definite term)?
☐ Was the handwriting readable?
☐ Was the writing style suitable for a persuasive text (objective; not casual or dismissive)?

Now focus on the detail. Read each of the following points and find out whether the student's work has these features.

Focus on content
☐ Did the opening sentence(s) focus on the topic?
☐ Was the writer's point of view established early in the writing?
☐ Did the writer include any evidence to support his or her opinion?
☐ Did the writer include information relevant to his or her experiences?
☐ Were the points/arguments raised by the writer easy to follow?
☐ Did the writing follow the format with an introduction, the body of the text and a conclusion?
☐ Were personal opinions included?
☐ Was the concluding paragraph relevant to the topic?

Focus on structure, vocabulary, grammar, spelling, punctuation
☐ Was there a variety of sentence lengths, types and beginnings?

☐ Was a new paragraph started for each additional argument or point?
☐ Has the writer used any similes (e.g. *as clear as crystal*) to stress a point raised?
☐ Did the writer avoid approximations such as *probably, perhaps* and *maybe*?
☐ Did the writer use such phrases as *I know …* and *It is important to …*?
☐ Did the writer refer to the question in the points raised (A good way to do this is to use the key words from the question or the introduction.)?
☐ Has the writer used any less common words correctly?
☐ Was indirect speech used correctly?
☐ Were adjectives used to improve descriptions (e.g. <u>expensive</u> *buildings*)?
☐ Were adverbs used effectively (e.g. *firstly*)?
☐ Were capital letters used correctly?
☐ Was punctuation used correctly?
☐ Was the spelling of words correct?

Marker's suggestions (optional)

Tick each correct point.
Read the student's work through once to get an overall view of the student's response.

Focus on general points
☐ Did it make sense?
☐ Did it flow?
☐ Did the story arouse any feeling?
☐ Did you want to read on? Did the story create any suspense?
☐ Was the handwriting readable?

Now focus on the detail. Read the following points and find out whether the student's work has these features.

Focus on content
☐ Did the opening sentence(s) 'grab' your interest?
☐ Was the setting established (i.e. when and where the action took place)?

- ☐ Was the reader told when the action takes place?
- ☐ Was it apparent who the main character(s) is? (It can be the narrator, using *I*.)
- ☐ Was there a 'problem' to be 'solved' early in the writing?
- ☐ Was a complication or unusual event introduced?
- ☐ Did descriptions make reference to any of the senses (e.g. *cold nose, warm coat*)?
- ☐ Was there a climax (a more exciting part near the end)?
- ☐ Was there a conclusion (resolution of the problem) and was it 'believable'?

Focus on structure, vocabulary, grammar, spelling, punctuation
- ☐ Was there variation in sentence length and beginnings?
- ☐ Was a new paragraph started for changes in time, place or action?
- ☐ In conversations or speaking were there separate paragraphs for each change of speaker? Were speech marks used correctly?
- ☐ Were adjectives used to improve descriptions (e.g. <u>careful</u> *movements*)?
- ☐ Were adverbs used to make 'actions' more interesting (e.g. *tail wagged* <u>*joyfully*</u>)?
- ☐ Were capital letters where they should have been?
- ☐ Was punctuation correct?
- ☐ Was the spelling of words correct?

Marker's suggestions (optional)

WRITING (Real Test)
Narrative text 2   Page 30

Tick each correct point.
Read the student's work through once to get an overall view of their response.

Focus on general points
- ☐ Did it make sense?
- ☐ Did it flow?
- ☐ Did the story arouse any feeling?

- ☐ Did you want to read on? Did the story create any suspense?
- ☐ Was the handwriting readable?

Now focus on the detail. Read the following points and find out whether the student's work has these features.

Focus on content
- ☐ Did the opening sentence(s) 'grab' your interest?
- ☐ Was the setting established (i.e. when and where the action took place)?
- ☐ Was the reader told when the action takes place?
- ☐ Was it apparent who the main character(s) is? (It can be the narrator, using *I*.)
- ☐ Was there a 'problem' to be 'solved' early in the writing?
- ☐ Was a complication or unusual event introduced?
- ☐ Did descriptions make reference to any of the senses (e.g. *pink sky, cool breeze*)?
- ☐ Was there a climax (a more exciting part near the end)?
- ☐ Was there a conclusion (resolution of the problem) and was it 'believable'?

Focus on structure, vocabulary, grammar, spelling, punctuation
- ☐ Was there variation in sentence length and beginnings?
- ☐ Was a new paragraph started for changes in time, place or action?
- ☐ In conversations or speaking were there separate paragraphs for each change of speaker?
- ☐ Were adjectives used to improve descriptions (e.g. <u>hollow</u> *sound*)?
- ☐ Were adverbs used to make 'actions' more interesting (e.g. *listened* <u>*carefully*</u>)?
- ☐ Were capital letters where they should have been?
- ☐ Was punctuation correct?
- ☐ Was the spelling of words correct?

Marker's suggestions (optional).

WEEK 2

NUMBER AND ALGEBRA (Test Your Skills)
Fractions, decimals and percentages   Page 32

1 This number starts with the whole number 12. The digits after the decimal point represent tenths, hundredths and thousandths in that order.

2 Two thirds is not the same as half, but $\frac{2}{4} = \frac{4}{8} = \frac{3}{6} = \frac{1}{2}$

3 $\frac{1}{3} + \frac{1}{3} = \frac{2}{3}$

4 To simply a fraction divide the top number (numerator) and bottom number (denominator) by the **same** number.
Both 8 and 12 can be divided by 4 ($\frac{2}{3}$).

5 $1\frac{1}{2} + 1\frac{1}{2} = 2 + \frac{1}{2} + \frac{1}{2}$
$= 3$

6 There are 4 quarters in 1 whole. This means 8 quarters in 2 wholes.

7 $6 \times 0.3 = 1.8$

8 10 parts are shaded out of 25 parts $= \frac{10}{25}$
or $\frac{2}{5}$. It can also be seen as 2 columns shaded out of five columns. $\frac{2}{5} = 0.4$

9 Add vertically in the normal fashion keeping all the decimals in line.
```
0.5
1.2
0.3
1.1
───
3.1
```

10 Rewrite some of the decimals: 0.09 = 0.090; 0.7 = 0.700; 0.62 = 0.620; 1.088
Easy to see the smallest is 0.090 or 0.09

11 A quarter is 0.25, as a half was 0.5, or 0.50

12 Total mark = 100%.
Mary needed 100% − 65% = 35%.

13
```
  1.60
+ 0.23
──────
  1.83
```

14 3.25 is closer to 3 than 4.

15 Treat as a normal subtraction, remembering to keep the decimal points in line.

16 Treat as a normal multiplication. There will be one number behind the decimal point as there is only one number behind the decimal that is being multiplied.

17
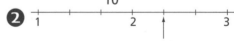
The arrow points to 3.6

18 There are 10 tenths in 1 whole. This means there are 20 tenths in 2 wholes.

19 A half is bigger than a quarter.
This means $\frac{1}{2} > \frac{1}{4}$

NUMBER AND ALGEBRA (Real Test)
Fractions, decimals and percentages   Page 34

1 C **2** C **3** A **4** D **5** C **6** $\frac{1}{10}, \frac{1}{5}, \frac{1}{4}, \frac{1}{3}$ **7** A **8** D **9** B
10 A **11** A **12** B **13** C **14** B, D **15** 2.75 **16** 37

EXPLANATIONS

1 Counting unshaded shapes: 7 out of 10
This means $\frac{7}{10}$ is not shaded.

2

The arrow points to $2\frac{1}{3}$.

3
About a quarter is not shaded.

4 Fraction removed = 6 out of 8
$= \frac{6}{8}$
$= \frac{3}{4}$

5 Half of $10 = \frac{1}{2} \times \$10$
$= \$5$
This means Laura paid $5 for the magazine.

6 For these fractions, the larger the number in the denominator, the smaller the fraction.

The correct order is $\frac{1}{10}, \frac{1}{5}, \frac{1}{4}, \frac{1}{3}$

7 In 23.051, the 5 is 5 hundredths.

8

0	0.2	0.4	0.6	0.8	1

The arrow is pointing to 0.6.

9 Compare the decimals by rewriting as 0.27, 0.70, 0.63, 0.08. This means the decimals from smallest to largest is 0.08, 0.27, 0.63, 0.70. The largest decimal is 0.7.

10 As $1.74 - 1.68 = 0.06$, the pattern is adding on 0.06. This means the new number is $1.74 + 0.06$
The missing number is 1.80 or 1.8.

$$\begin{array}{r} 1.74 \\ + 0.06 \\ \hline 1.80 \end{array}$$

11 $107.03 = 1 \times 100 + 7 \times 1 + 3 \times \frac{1}{100}$

$= 1$ hundred $+ 7$ units $+ 3$ hundredths

12 Change $= \$5.00 - \$3.25$

$$\begin{array}{r} 5.00 \\ - 3.25 \\ \hline 1.75 \end{array}$$

Sarah received $1.75 in change.

13 Change $6.50 to 650 cents

Cost $= 650 \div 10$

Each can costs 65 cents or $0.65.

$$10\overline{)650} = 65$$

14 Take care with the place values:
$0.3 + 0.5 + 0.2 = 1$ and $0.7 + 0.2 + 0.1 = 1$.

15 Money required $= \$10 - \$7.25$
Riann needs another $2.75.

$$\begin{array}{r} 10.00 \\ - 7.25 \\ \hline 2.75 \end{array}$$

16 By counting, 37 out of 100 squares are shaded. This means $\frac{37}{100}$ or 37% shaded.

**MEASUREMENT AND GEOMETRY
(Test Your Skills)**
2D shapes and position   Page 35

1 is a pentagon.

2 has parallel lines.

3 Obtuse angle:

4 A right angle has 90°.

5 A perpendicular line is always at right angles to the given line regardless of the slope of the given line.

6 An isosceles triangle has 2 equal sides and 2 equal angles.

7 Diagonals are lines that join corners, not just the opposite corners. They cannot be sides of the pentagon.

8 From the petrol station the bank is north-west.

9

10 : the triangle tessellates.

11 Five single triangles, 4 doubles (overlapping). Total = 9.

MEASUREMENT AND GEOMETRY (Real Test)
2D shapes and position   Page 37

1 C **2** A **3** D **4** C, E **5** C **6** D **7** C **8** C **9** C
10 A **11** B **12** D **13** B **14** B3 **15** C1 **16** C

EXPLANATIONS

1 pentagon

2 There are no axes of symmetry.

3 Square has 4 sides. As $12 - 4 = 8$, the missing shape has 8 sides, which is an octagon.

4 H and M have a pair of parallel lines.

5 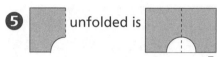 unfolded is

6 The smallest angle is

7 Here are the rectangles:

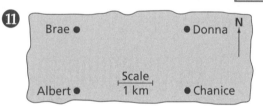

There are 5 rectangles.

8 The letter F is turned a quarter of a circle: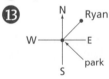

9 A hexagon has 6 sides:

10 The paper will look like this:

11

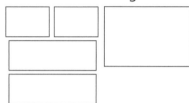

Chanice lives south of Donna.

12 By estimation Brae is 3 km from Donna.

13

The park is south-west of Ryan.

14 The coin is in column B, row 3.
This means the coin is in B3.

15 The coin is now at C1.

16 The arrow is pointing north-west.

MEASUREMENT AND GEOMETRY
(Test Your Skills) *3D shapes*   Page 38

1 Rectangular prism.

2 Triangular prism.

3 6 on front layer, 5 on back layer: 11 cubes

4 4 triangular faces: triangular pyramid

5 From the top, view is a rectangle and a square.

6 Cross-section will be a rectangle.

7 6 edges + 6 edges + 6 edges = 18 edges

8 Cylinder

9 $3 \times 2 \times 4 = 24$

10 6 faces + 1 face = 7 faces

MEASUREMENT AND GEOMETRY (Real Test)
3D shapes   Page 40

1 C **2** B **3** D **4** A **5** A **6** A **7** D **8** A **9** A **10** B
11 B **12** C **13** C **14** 8 **15** 12 **16** A

EXPLANATIONS

1 The rectangular prism has 6 faces.

2 B is on the opposite face to E.

3 D is on the opposite face to F.

4 The sphere is not a prism.

5 This is a cylinder

6 This is the net of a cylinder:

7 This net will not form a cube:

8 This is a triangular prism.
It is made of 2 triangles
and 3 rectangles.

9 This is the top view of
the rectangular pyramid.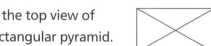

10 When the cylinder is cut, the two faces will look like:

11 Tin of tomatoes:
The shape is a cylinder

12 This is the top view:

13 This is the view from the left:

14 The two bases join together:
The new shape has 8 faces.

15 The new shape has 12 edges.

16

cone   cylinder   sphere   cube

Dhama did not make a cone.

SPELLING (Real Test)
Common misspellings   Page 42

1 discover
2 allowed
3 wonder
4 elastic
5 assembly
6 garage
7 worried
8 hurdles
9 hiking
10 ankle
11 sole
12 steel
13 colour
14 usually
15 blooded
16 forest
17 spines
18 protection

GRAMMAR AND PUNCTUATION (Real Test)
Tenses, contractions and punctuation   Pages 44–45

1 D **2** B **3** C **4** A **5** C **6** A **7** C **8** C **9** D **10** B
11 A **12** D **13** B **14** C **15** B **16** D **17** A
18 *Of* and *French*

EXPLANATIONS

1 This is a grammar question. The correct word is the verb *had done*.
Tip: *Had* is the past tense of *has* or *have*. *Had* is an irregular verb. Most verbs form their past tenses by adding *ed* (e.g. *he walked*). There are a number of irregular verbs when this doesn't happen. We say *had* instead of 'haved'. With the verb *done* you need a 'helper'—another verb to 'help' it. *Have*, *has* and *had* can be helping verbs—*Jackie and Joyce had done* ... The helping verb is always close to the verb it is helping.

2 This is a grammar question. The correct word is *should've*.
Tip: Learn to pronounce words correctly. *Should've* is short for *should have*.

3 This is a grammar question. The correct sentence is: "There are bins in every room but the new boys have left their wrappers on the floor!".
Tip: *Their* is a pronoun showing ownership. *There* is often used to indicate a place.

4 This is a grammar question. The correct word is the abstract noun *anger*.
Tip: *Angry* and *angered* can be used as verbs. *Angry* can also be an adjective. *Angrily* is an adverb. *Anger* is a noun following *The*.

5 This is a grammar question. *Free* is unnecessary.
Tip: *Free* is a redundant word as it carries the same meaning as *gift*. A gift is free; otherwise it is not a gift.

6 This is a grammar question. The correct word is *much*.
Tip: *Much* and *many* are used to show how much of something. *Many* is used with things that can be counted, e.g. *many birds*.

Much is use with things that are not counted, e.g. *much sand*. Coins and notes are counted. *Money* refers to a mixture of currency.

7 This is a grammar question. The correct word is the verb *drawn*.
Tip: *Drawn* is an irregular verb. Most verbs in English form their past tenses by adding *ed* (e.g. *he walked*). There are a number of irregular verbs when this doesn't happen. We say *drawn* instead of 'drewed'. *Had* is the past tense of *has* or *have*. With the verb *drawn* you need a 'helper'—another verb to 'help' it. *Have*, *has* and *had* can be helping verbs—*Peta has drawn* ... The helping verb is always close to the verb it is helping.

8 This is a grammar question. The correct word is the verb *made*.
Tip: Basic rule: Singular subjects (nouns) need singular verbs; plural subjects (nouns) need plural verbs. In this case *made* must be used because *Peta* is one person and the action happened in the past.

9 This is a grammar question. The correct word is the definite article *the*.
Tip: *The* is used because it refers to a particular person—*the cricket captain*.

10 This is a grammar question. The correct word is the verb *seen*.
Tip: *Seen* is an irregular verb. Most verbs in English form their past tenses by adding *ed* (e.g. *he walked*). There are a number of irregular verbs when this doesn't happen. We say *seen* instead of 'sawed'. With the verb *seen* you need a 'helper'—another verb to 'help' it. *Were* and *was* can be helping verbs —*he was seen* ... The helping verb is always close to the verb it is helping.

11 This is a grammar question. The correct word is the preposition *on*.
Tip: A preposition describes a relationship between other words in a sentence. Prepositions put events in position in time or place. We use *on* to show just where the captain was ... *on the field*. It is usual to use *on* in this situation.

12 This is a punctuation question. The correct sentence is: *He won't do that again!* (with an exclamation mark).
Tip: The word *again* is the last word in an exclamation sentence and ends with an exclamation mark and without a capital letter.

13 This is a punctuation question. The correct sentence is: *'Take your time,' Dad warned.*
Tip: The inverted commas (quotation marks) enclose the actual words that are spoken: *'Take your time,'* (a comma is added after time as this is not the end of a longer sentence).

14 This is a punctuation question. The correct sentence is: *Horses, cows and sheep need more care than cats and dogs.*
Tip: Use a comma to separate the items in a series—three or more things—or for a pause. There is no comma where *and* is used in the series: *Horses, cows and sheep.*

15 This is a grammar question. The correct word is *shiver*.
Tip: This is a situation where you have to know the differences in meaning of words that look or sound similar.

16 This is a grammar question. The correct sentence is: *May James and I give out the pencils?*
Tip: When you speak about yourself doing something you say *I*. *May I give out the pencils?* Think of the sentence as two sentences joined together: *May James give out the pencils?* and *May I give out the pencils?* You don't say: *Me give out the pencils.*

17 This is a grammar question. The correct sentence is: *'That's mine!' exclaimed Reg as he dashed across the room.*
Tip: The exclamation mark goes inside the inverted commas. It tells how Reg spoke.

18 This is a punctuation question. The correct word are *Of* and *French*.
Tip: *French* is a proper adjective describing a person from France and so has a capital letter. *Of* is the first word in a sentence.

READING (Test Your Skills)
Understanding poetry   Page 46

Stray Dog
1 B **2** D, E **3** B **4** D **5** B **6** A

EXPLANATIONS

1 The poem portrays one small incident—when a stranger meets a stray dog.

2 A wary animal would be a suspicious and distrusting animal.

3 The stranger was trying to win the dog's trust. He bent down to it and called softly to it.

4 A tentative bark is a cautious bark. The dog was not sure if it should trust the stranger.

5 The dog had been hurt earlier by strangers. It is implied by the line 'She'd been hurt before'.

6 The stranger was trying to put the dog at ease. He had 'bent down'.

READING (Real Test)
Understanding poetry   Page 47

Rain
1 B **2** C **3** A **4** A **5** B **6** C **7** D **8** A

EXPLANATIONS

1 The poem paints a word picture that reveals the poet's feelings about the rain.

2 Drooping means to sag (bend over).

3 The rain makes the poet feel sad. Words that contribute to this are 'disturbing', 'grey' and 'drooping'. The type of words used gives the poem a certain slowness/heaviness.

4 A leaden sky is one that is grey like lead (the metal) and looks heavy with clouds or rain.

5 The last line suggests that the poet's mood will continue as long as it rains.

6 A trickle is a flow of a very small amount of water—a dribble.

7 The raindrops are like cars in heavy traffic, starting and stopping a lot.

8 It has been raining for quite a while and the poet would probably like a break from the rain.

READING (Test Your Skills)
Interpreting notices   Page 48

Cockatoo School Fete
1 C **2** B **3** C **4** D **5** selling cold drinks **6** A

EXPLANATIONS

1 The word 'annual' means yearly. An annual meeting is a once a year meeting.

2 On the school oval. Most of the events are on the school oval as they include a soccer match and tug-of-war.

3 The stars make the event seem likely to be a sparkling (fun) event. The visit by a star author helps convey this sense.

4 A hamper is a food basket (picnic hamper).

5 This is a 'search and find question'. Year 6 students are selling cold drinks.

6 This is another 'search and find question'. The lucky dip is for pre-school children.

READING (Real Test)
Interpreting notices   Page 49

Betty's Big Spaghetti
1 D **2** soup **3** A **4** C **5** C **6** B **7** $10

EXPLANATIONS

1 The word 'rich' has many meanings. In this case it means 'full of flavour'.

2 This is a 'search and find' question. The cheapest item is 'Soup of the day' ($4).

3 The answer for this is not given in the ad. You have to work it out. Most likely the arrows are meant to draw your eyes to the name.

4 Marinara is a pasta dish that uses seafood (tuna, clams, mussels, prawns).

5 The important word in this question is LEAST. The impression the ad gives of Betty's Big Spaghetti is **not** of 'expensive dining'.

6 This is a 'search and find' question. Napoli has 'extra garlic'.

7 Greek salad costs $8 + $2 (delivery) = $10.

Check Your Answers

READING (Real Test)
Following a procedure   Page 50

Crunchy Apple Balls
1 A **2** 2, 3, 1, 4 **3** D **4** D **5** A **6** B
7 written response

SELECTED EXPLANATIONS

❶ Steps would be the best word to replace Method.

❸ 'Bland' and 'plain' both mean without much taste. The ingredients are not bitter. They are sweet.

❹ 'Set' in the recipe means to harden (or become firm).

❺ The pot is required to warm the jam (Method Point 4).

❻ The tablespoon of cooking oil.

❼ Possible answer:
The hole is required to hold the jam and melted chocolate before stirring (mixing).

WRITING (Real Test)
Recount 1   Page 52

Tick each correct point.
Read the student's work through once to get an overall view of their response.

Focus on general points
☐ Did it make sense?
☐ Did it flow?
☐ Did the events arouse any feeling?
☐ Did you want to read on? (Were the events interesting?)
☐ Was the handwriting readable?

Now focus on the detail. Read the following points and find out whether the student's work has these features.

Focus on content
☐ Did the opening sentence(s) introduce the subject of the recount?
☐ Was the setting established (i.e. when and where the action took place)?
☐ Was the reader told when the action takes place?

☐ Was it apparent who the main character(s) is?
☐ Have personal pronouns been used (e.g. *I, we, our*)?
☐ Were the events recorded in chronological (time) order?
☐ Was the recount in past tense?
☐ Did the writing include some personal comments on the events (feeling hot, disappointed)?
☐ Did descriptions make reference to any of the senses (e.g. *loud commentary, blue water*)?
☐ Were interesting details included?
☐ Did the conclusion have a satisfactory summing-up comment?

Focus on structure, vocabulary, grammar, spelling and punctuation.
☐ Was there variation in sentence length and beginnings?
☐ Was there a new paragraph started for changes in time, place or action?
☐ Were subheadings used? (optional)
☐ Were adjectives used to improve descriptions (e.g. <u>neat</u> dive)?
☐ Were adverbs used to make 'actions' more interesting (e.g. *swam <u>bravely</u>*)?
☐ Are time words used for time changes (e.g. *later, soon, then*)?
☐ Were capital letters where they should have been?
☐ Was punctuation correct?
☐ Was the spelling of words correct?

Marker's suggestions (optional).

WRITING (Real Test)
Recount 2   Page 53

Tick each correct point.
Read the student's work through once to get
an overall view of their response.

Focus on general points
☐ Did it make sense?
☐ Did it flow?
☐ Did the events arouse any feeling?
☐ Did you want to read on? (Were the events
   interesting?)
☐ Was the handwriting readable?

Now focus on the detail. Read the following
points and find out whether the student's
work has these features.

Focus on content
☐ Did the opening sentence(s) introduce the
   subject of the recount?
☐ Was the setting established (i.e. when and
   where the action took place)?
☐ Was the reader told when the action takes
   place?
☐ Was it apparent who the main character(s) is?
☐ Have personal pronouns been used (e.g. *I,
   we, our*)?
☐ Were the events recorded in chronological
   (time) order?
☐ Was the recount in past tense?
☐ Did the writing include some personal
   comments on the events (feeling hot,
   disappointed)?
☐ Did descriptions make reference to any of the
   senses (e.g. *loud commentary, blue water*)?
☐ Were interesting details included?
☐ Did the conclusion have a satisfactory
   summing-up comment?

Focus on structure, vocabulary, grammar,
spelling and punctuation.
☐ Was there variation in sentence length and
   beginnings?
☐ Was there a new paragraph started for
   changes in time, place or action?
☐ Were subheadings used? (optional)
☐ Were adjectives used to improve
   descriptions (e.g. *neat* dive)?

☐ Were adverbs used to make 'actions' more
   interesting (e.g. swam *bravely*)?
☐ Are time words used for time changes
   (e.g. *later, soon, then*)?
☐ Were capital letters where they should
   have been?
☐ Was punctuation correct?
☐ Was the spelling of words correct?

Marker's suggestions (optional)

WRITING (Real Test)
Recount 3   Page 54

Tick each correct point.
Read the student's work through once to get an
overall view of their response.

Focus on general points
☐ Did it make sense?
☐ Did it flow?
☐ Did the events arouse any feeling?
☐ Did you want to read on? (Were the events
   interesting?)
☐ Was the handwriting readable?

Now focus on the detail. Read the following
points and find out whether the student's
work has these features.

Focus on content
☐ Did the opening sentence(s) introduce the
   subject of the recount?
☐ Was the setting established (i.e. when and
   where the action took place)?
☐ Was the reader told when the action takes
   place?
☐ Was it apparent who the main character(s)
   is?
☐ Have personal pronouns been used
   (e.g. *I, we, our*)?
☐ Were the events recorded in chronological
   (time) order?
☐ Was the recount in past tense?

☐ Did the writing include some personal comments on the events (feeling hot, disappointed)?

☐ Did descriptions make reference to any of the senses (e.g. *loud commentary, blue water*)?

☐ Were interesting details included?

☐ Did the conclusion have a satisfactory summing-up comment?

Focus on structure, vocabulary, grammar, spelling and punctuation.

☐ Was there variation in sentence length and beginnings?

☐ Was there a new paragraph started for changes in time, place or action?

☐ Were subheadings used? (optional)

☐ Were adjectives used to improve descriptions (e.g. _neat_ dive)?

☐ Were adverbs used to make 'actions' more interesting (e.g. swam _bravely_)?

☐ Are time words used for time changes (e.g. *later, soon, then*)?

☐ Were capital letters where they should have been?

☐ Was punctuation correct?

☐ Was the spelling of words correct?

Marker's suggestions (optional)

WRITING (Real Test)
Recount 4   Page 55

Tick each correct point.
Read the student's work through once to get an overall view of their response.

Focus on general points

☐ Did it make sense?

☐ Did it flow?

☐ Did the events arouse any feeling?

☐ Did you want to read on? (Were the events interesting?)

☐ Was the handwriting readable?

Now focus on the detail. Read the following points and find out whether the student's work has these features.

Focus on content

☐ Did the opening sentence(s) introduce the subject of the recount?

☐ Was the setting established (i.e. when and where the action took place)?

☐ Was the reader told when the action takes place?

☐ Was it apparent who the main character(s) is?

☐ Have personal pronouns been used (e.g. *I, we, our*)?

☐ Were the events recorded in chronological (time) order?

☐ Was the recount in past tense?

☐ Did the writing include some personal comments on the events (feeling hot, disappointed)?

☐ Did descriptions make reference to any of the senses (e.g. *loud commentary, blue water*)?

☐ Were interesting details included?

☐ Did the conclusion have a satisfactory summing-up comment?

Focus on structure, vocabulary, grammar, spelling and punctuation.

☐ Was there variation in sentence length and beginnings?

☐ Was there a new paragraph started for changes in time, place or action?

☐ Were subheadings used? (optional)

☐ Were adjectives used to improve descriptions (e.g. _neat_ dive)?

☐ Were adverbs used to make 'actions' more interesting (e.g. swam _bravely_)?

☐ Are time words used for time changes (e.g. *later, soon, then*)?

☐ Were capital letters where they should have been?

☐ Was punctuation correct?

☐ Was the spelling of words correct?

Marker's suggestions (optional)

WEEK 3

1 A hen's egg is closest to 60 g.

2 Door about 2 m.

3 3 × 100) + 50 = 350

4 Perimeter is the distance around a shape (4 × 8 = 32).

5 (5 + 13) × 2 = 36

6

4 cm
6 cm
10 cm
8 cm
4 cm
12 cm

Perimeter = 10 + 12 + 4 + 8 + 6 + 4
= 44
This means a perimeter of 44 cm.

7 If one side is 6 m the opposite side is 6 m. The remaining two sides are (36 − 12) ÷ 2 = 12.

8 As 36 ÷ 3 = 12, each side is 12 cm.

9 Total mass of spheres = 24 kg.
24 kg ÷ 4 = 6 kg

10 Trundle wheel.

11 5 (cm) × 2 km = 10 km

12 By estimation, about 15 cm.

1 6 **2** A **3** C **4** B **5** 12 **6** D **7** C **8** B **9** D
10 C **11** D **12** D **13** C **14** 90 g, 600 g, 1.7 kg 0.5 t
15 650 **16** C

EXPLANATIONS

1 The pencil is 6 cm

2 The eraser starts at 2.5 cm on the ruler and finishes at 5 cm. By subtraction, the length of the eraser is 2.5 cm or 25 mm.

3 Use a ruler to measure your own handspan. It will be about 10 cm.

4 Each step for Sebastian is likely to be a little less than 1 metre. This means that he would have walked a distance a little less than 7000 metres. As 6 km = 6000 metres, 6 km would be the best estimate for the distance he walked.

5 The perimeter is the distance around the outside of the shape.
Perimeter = 4 + 2 + 4 + 2
= 12
The answer is 12 units.

6 From the grid we can see that the length of the bottom side of the triangle is 5 units This means that each side is 5 units
Perimeter = 5 + 5 + 5
= 15
The perimeter is 15 units.

7 Distance = 600 × 5
= 3000
Ivan ran 3000 metres, or 3 km.

8 This book is about 30 cm long.

9 Using 1 metre = 100 cm, we need to multiply 50 by 100.
Number of centimetres = 50 × 100
= 5000
There are 5000 cm in 50 metres.

10

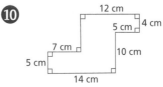

12 cm
5 cm
4 cm
7 cm
10 cm
5 cm
14 cm

The missing side is 9 cm, as 14 − 5 = 9.
Perimeter = 12 + 4 + 5 + 10 + 14 + 5 + 7 + 9
= 66
This means the perimeter is 66 cm.

11 Using the information in the question, 2 units = 12 km. This is a scale of 1 unit = 6 km. On the map, from Elderslie to Glendon is 4 units.
This means distance = 4 × 6
= 24
Elderslie and Glendon are 24 km apart.

12 The distance from Elderslie to Glendon is 24 km (from question 11). The distance from Stanhope to Glendon will be more than 24 km. This means the distance will be 27 km.

Check Your Answers

13

Removing a cylinder from both sides means that the cylinder balances 3 blocks.

This means ⬭ = ▨▨▨

14 The four masses are 500 kg (500 000 g), 600 g, 1700 g and 90 g. The order from lightest to heaviest is 90 g, 600 g, 1.7 kg and 0.5 t.

15 As 1 kg = 1000 grams, we use subtraction: 1000 – 350   There is 650 grams remaining in the bag.

$$\begin{array}{r} 1000 \\ -\ 350 \\ \hline 650 \end{array}$$

16 As 715 is close to 700, 280 is close to 300 and 985 is close to 1000, this means 700 + 300 + 1000 = 2000 g or 2 kg.

MEASUREMENT AND GEOMETRY (Test Your Skills)
Area, volume and capacity   Page 61

1 3 × 7 = 21, the area is 21 cm².

2 By counting, 7 cm².

3 Shape is 6 squares and 2 half squares. This means an area of 7 square units.

4
$$\begin{array}{r} 1000 \\ -\ 350 \\ \hline 650 \end{array}$$
There is 650 mL remaining.

5 Solution: 3 × 3 × 3 = 27, the volume is 27 cm³.

6 A normal bucket holds 10 litres.

7 By counting, the shape with an area of 6 square units is: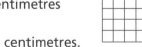

8 Area is 16 square centimetres by counting, or 4 × 4 = 16 square centimetres.

9 By counting, volume is 9 cubic units.

10 A cup would be measured in millilitres.

MEASUREMENT AND GEOMETRY (Real Test)
Area, volume and capacity   Page 63

1 C **2** B **3** C **4** B **5** A **6** 4 **7** D **8** D **9** A **10** C
11 B **12** D **13** A **14** 60 **15** 8 **16** 350

EXPLANATIONS

1 The shape covers 10 squares. This means the area is 10 square units.

2 Number = 260 ÷ 20
= 26 ÷ 2
= 13
13 squares are needed to cover 260 square metres.

3 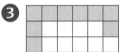 Belinda needs another 9 squares to completely cover the rectangle.

4 Counting the squares:
10 squares and 4 half squares.
This means 10 + 2 = 12
The area is 12 square units.

5 By counting, the area of 2 is 8 square units and the area of 3 is 9 square units. As difference is subtraction, 9 – 8 = 1

6  4 more stickers are needed.

7 By counting the number of squares, the smallest area is 6 squares: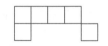

8

The original rectangle had dimensions of 3 units by 2 units. If the lengths are doubled, the new rectangle will be 6 units by 4 units. By counting, the area has changed from 6 squares to 24 squares. This means the area has multiplied by 4.

9 In the large rectangle there are 24 squares. This means that Tiffany needs 12 shaded. By counting, she already has 10 shaded. She needs another 2 shaded.

10 By counting, the volume is 8 cubic units.

11 By counting, the volume is 20 cubic units.

12 There are 1000 millilitres in 1 litre. In half a litre, there will be half of 1000. This means 500 mL in 1 L.

13 In a teaspoon there are about 5 millilitres.

14 Andrew uses 30 L to raise the level from half full to full. This means that there must have already been 30 L in the tank before he started. As 30 + 30 = 60, the tank holds 60 L when full.

15 As 1 cup = 250 mL, 2 cups = 500 mL, 4 cups = 1000 mL, 8 cups = 2000 mL
Now, 2000 mL = 2 L, it takes 8 cups.

16 As 1 litre = 1000 mL, we need to subtract 650 from 1000:
This means there is still 350 mL remaining in the carton.

$$\begin{array}{r} 1000 \\ -\ 650 \\ \hline 350 \end{array}$$

MEASUREMENT AND GEOMETRY (Test Your Skills)
Time   Page 64

1 65 minutes is 1 hour, 5 minutes later.

2 Digital times are stated in hours and minutes later. 20 to 11 would be 10:40.

3 At 'a quarter to six' it is 5:45

4 November has 30 days. Three weeks = 21 days. There are 20 days left in November. The 1st of December is 3 weeks later.

5 1857 to 1900 is 43 years. Now 78 − 43 = 35. Mr Ryan died in 1935.

6 Since 2.5 minutes means $2\frac{1}{2}$ minutes, there are 60 + 60 + 30 seconds. This means 150 seconds

7 Solution: 100 (century) − 13 = 87

8 Solution: 256 (minutes) ÷ 60 = 4 h 6 min.

9 Consider the Thursdays after 25th July: 1st August (1 week), 8th August (2 weeks), 15th August (3 weeks), 22nd August (4 weeks).

10 Determine if 2026 is a leap year by dividing by 4 (2026 ÷ 4 = 506 r 2). As it doesn't divide evenly it is not a leap year. February that year had 28 days.

11 The clock is showing 6:15. Adding 10 minutes gives 6:25

12 From 1998 count forward 50:
1998 + 50 = 1998 + 2 + 48
           = 2048

MEASUREMENT AND GEOMETRY (Real Test)
Time   Page 66

1 D   **2** A   **3** C   **4** D   **5** A   **6** C   **7** D   **8** C   **9** D
10 D   **11** 7   **12** 14   **13** C   **14** C   **15** A

EXPLANATIONS

1 As 60 minutes in one hour,
Number = 60 × 2
          = 120
There are 120 minutes in one hour.

2 The time on the clock is 7:55, or 5 to 8.

3 Cedric's bedroom clock is 10 minutes ahead of 7:55. This means 7:55 plus 5 minutes is 8:00 and another 5 minutes gives 8:05.

4 After 20 minutes the big hand moves from the 4 to the 8.

5 From 4:30 we add 2 hours. This means the closing time is 6:30.

6 Consider each of the choices:
7 days in 1 week   Yes!
24 hours in 1 day   Yes!
60 seconds in 1 hour   No!
– there are 60 seconds in 1 minute
31 days in March   Yes!

7 From 4:15 add 1 hour to reach 5:15, then half an hour, or 30 minutes, to reach 5:45. This means that training finishes at 5:45.

8 From 8:28 pm adding hour means that the display will be 9:28 pm.

9 From 5:35 add on 2 hours to reach 7:35 and then another 20 minutes reaches 7:55.

10 First, we find the number of 30 seconds in 2 minutes:
2 lots of 30 seconds = 1 minute
4 lots of 30 seconds = 2 minutes.
This means that Bree will be charged 4 lots of 25 cents.
Cost = 25 × 4
       = 100
Bree will be charged 100 cents, or $1.00.

11 Age difference is found using subtraction:
Age difference = 18 – 11
               = 7
This means Manu's sister was 7 years old when he was born.

12 Number of days = 17 – 3
                    = 14
There are 14 days until Lucas's birthday.

13

			JULY			
S	M	T	W	T	F	S
	1	2	3	4	5	6
7	8	9	10	11	12	13
14	15	16	17	18	19	20
21	22	23	24	25	26	27
28	29	30	31	1	2	3
4						

This means that 4th August is a Sunday.

14 The Sundays in July are 7th, 14th, 21st and 28th. This means the third Sunday is 21st July.

15 From the calendar, 5th July is a Friday. This means tomorrow is a Saturday and the day after tomorrow is a Sunday.

SPELLING (Real Test)
Common misspellings Page 68

1 attach
2 conflict
3 hospital
4 various
5 drowsy
6 vowel

7 quality
8 governor
9 barber
10 comb
11 scissors
12 chair
13 Later
14 powerful
15 towed
16 felt
17 baited
18 gently

GRAMMAR AND PUNCTUATION (Real Test)
Verbs using 'of', 'have' and 'off' Pages 70–71

1 A **2** B **3** B, C **4** D **5** B **6** A **7** A **8** B **9** D
10 D **11** C **12** A **13** B **14** When, Mt, Victoria, Lithgow **15** C **16** A **17** B **18** C

EXPLANATIONS

1 This is a grammar question. The correct word is the verb *shops*.
Tip: Basic rule: Singular subjects (nouns) need singular verbs; plural subjects (nouns) need plural verbs. In this case *shops* must be used because there only one Wong family.

2 This is a grammar question. *Advance* is unnecessary.
Tip: *Advance* is a redundant word as it carries the same timing as *warning*. A warning is always in advance of an event; otherwise it is not a warning.

3 This is a punctuation question. The correct sentence is: *I went to see Batman 4, the new movie, at the Star Cinema.*
Tip: The words *the new movie* explain what *Batman 4* is. Commas are used to separate parts of the sentence and to make the meaning clear. Commas are also added to show pauses.

4 This is a grammar question. The correct word is the preposition *in*.
Tip: A preposition describes a relationship between other words in a sentence. Prepositions put events in position in time or place. We use *in* to show just where Kevin's interests lie … *in collecting model cars*. It is usual to use *in* in this situation.

5 This is a grammar question. The correct word is the verb *done*.
Tip: *Done* is an irregular verb. Most verbs in English form their past tenses by adding *ed* (e.g. *he walked*). There are a number of irregular verbs when this doesn't happen. We say *done* instead of 'dided'. With the verb *done* you need a 'helper'—another verb to 'help' it. *Have*, *has* and *had* can be helping verbs—*Has Sandra done* … The helping verb is always close to the verb it is helping.

6 This is a grammar question. The correct word is *uglier*.
Tip: Only use *est* words (*ugliest*) when comparing more than two items. When comparing two items, use words ending in *er* (*uglier*). For short words you can add *er*: *brighter*, *faster*. Only use *more* with longer words (e.g. *beautiful*—*more beautiful*). 'More brighter' is incorrect.

7 This is a grammar question. The correct word is the conjunction *and*.
Tip: The conjunction *and* joins together things that are similar—*fast and rowdy game and as exciting as the outdoor game*.

8 This is a punctuation question. The correct sentence is: *It is as fast and rowdy a game and as exciting as the outdoor game, but much safer.*
Tip: The comma indicates a pause in the sentence. It is not the end of a sentence. The next word does not start with a capital letter.

9 This is a grammar question. The correct word is *so*.
Tip: *So* is used in this situation to emphasise just how safe the game is. *Also* is incorrect, meaning 'in the same or similar way'.

10 This is a grammar question. The correct word is the adverb *between*.
Tip: *Between* is used when two people or objects are involved, e.g. *two players*. *Among* is used when the number is greater than two.

11 This is a grammar question. The correct word is the definite article *the*.
Tip: *The* is used because it refers to a particular position—*the centre of the board*.

12 This is a grammar question. The correct word is the verb *gives*.
Tip: Basic rule: Singular subjects (nouns) need singular verbs; plural subjects (nouns) need plural verbs. In this case *gives* must be used because there only one person—*the referee*.

13 This is a punctuation question. The correct sentence is: *Ask Casey for a hand. She's not doing anything.*
Tip: As no actual words are spoken (they are the reported words) inverted commas are not required. There is no actual question asked—just the report that a question was asked.

14 This is a punctuation question. Four words require capital letters. The correct words are *When*, *Mt*, *Victoria* and *Lithgow*.
Tip: *When* is the first word in a sentence. *Mt Victoria* and *Lithgow* are proper nouns— the names of places.

15 This is a grammar question. The correct word is *shining*.
Tip: This is a situation where you have to know the differences in meaning of words that have similar meanings. *Flickering* and *sparkling* are incorrect as the water is still. *Glowing* suggests giving off light (like a fire) rather than reflecting it.

16 This is a grammar question. The correct word is the adverb *slowly*.
Tip: *Slowly* describes how the team walked. Many adverbs end with *ly*. *Slow* is often used as an adjective.

17 This is a grammar question. The correct sentence is: *My brother and I are in the school choir.*

Tip: When you speak about yourself doing something you say *I. I am in the school choir.* Think of the sentence as two sentences joined together: *My brother is in the school choir and I am in the school choir.* You don't say: *Me am in the school choir.* The verb *are* is used because two people are involved. It is common practice to place yourself (*I*) last when including other people: *My brother and I.*

18 This is a punctuation question. The dates of the voyage should be in brackets (1772–1775). Tip: Writers use brackets to add information to a sentence without changing the meaning of the sentence. The information in brackets provides quick additional information for the reader without adding unnecessary text.

READING (Test Your Skills)
Understanding recounts   Page 72

The Face on Mars
1 A **2** D **3** members of NASA **4** A **5** B **6** C **7** B

EXPLANATIONS

1 Dr Hoagland is a space scientist working with NASA.

2 Dr Hoagland thought he had found a city. The space photographs had earlier shown a face.

3 *They* is a pronoun standing for more than one person. *They* refers to members of NASA as in the previous sentence. Do not confuse it with Martians, astronauts or Mars Project scientists.

4 The complex refers to the 'buildings' of the 'city'—a complex is made up of connected parts.

5 The term refers to a false impression—something that seems to be what it is not.

6 As most of Dr Hoagland's 'discoveries' have been shown to be false, it calls his conclusions (work) into doubt (question).

7 The probe Mars Observer took photos to get more information about Mars—gather information.

READING (Real Test)
Understanding recounts   Page 73

As The Wind Blows
1 D **2** B **3** 1978 **4** B **5** D **6** A **7** 1B, 2C, 3A

EXPLANATIONS

1 The festival was born out of John Silk's father (a school teacher) trying to get a kite to fly.

2 The second last sentence tells who the present organisers are.

3 In the last paragraph you read that the first Festival poster was dated September 1978.

4 Bondi Beach.

5 A defunct event is one that is no longer produced.

6 People usually pay tribute only to those they respect.

7 Read the text carefully to discover the connections: Hargrave/box kite designer, John Silk/founder of the kite festival, Peter Travis/creator of kite sculptures.

READING (Test Your Skills)
Understanding explanations   Page 74

Olympic Games
1 B **2** A **3** D **4** A **5** D **6** D **7** B

EXPLANATIONS

1 The word 'prior' means that which has gone before (the same as 'previous'). 'Foregoing' means just mentioned or stated.

2 This is a 'search and find' type of question. Swimming was not an original Olympic sport.

3 The winner received a wreath and had poems sung about their deeds.

4 A wreath (garland) was placed on the winner's head.

5 Wars between states ceased (halted).

6 This question requires an understanding of the intent or purpose of the passage. It is about the origins of the Olympics in Greece.

7 The ancient Greeks valued physical fitness in their youth (young people). It was part of the students' education.

READING (Real Test)
Understanding explanations   Page 75

What a Waste!
1 A **2** C **3** food scraps **4** C **5** D **6** A **7** B

EXPLANATIONS

1 The extract is to inform readers of the dangers (hazards) of waste disposal.

2 Waste gases are the hardest to dispose of. They often go straight into the air.

3 This is a 'search and find' question. Food scraps are not mentioned as they are organic wastes and can be composted without difficulty.

4 In the passage industry would include factories.

5 If something is incinerated it is burnt.

6 Infectious wastes cause diseases. Hospitals have infectious waste. Poisonous wastes from factories can cause sickness and disabilities (and sometimes disease).

7 This question expects you to draw a conclusion. The medical and scientific usefulness of the passage is limited. It is too vague to be a safety manual. It is meant to make readers aware of environmental issues.

READING (Real Test)
Understanding narratives   Page 76

Show Off
1 A **2** the most imaginative creature **3** B **4** D **5** D **6** C **7** A

SELECTED EXPLANATIONS

1 The events take place in a school classroom as it is Grade 5 getting ready to put entries in a show. Mrs Black treats all the children in the class as her children.

2 Amanda's entry was a 'most imaginative creature'. The narrator had entered a lop-sided mug. The reader is not told who entered the monster mask or knitted squares.

3 Mrs Black fumbled for the pen because she couldn't see all that well. She had lost her glasses.

4 The best word to replace 'piled' is 'heaped'. 'Covered' and 'topped' do not indicate an excess of entries. Tables are covered, not filled, which is usually used for holes.

5 The toothpicks were put in a pineapple to make a model echidna.

6 The answer can be found in Mrs Black's words in paragraph five.

7 The extract is most likely from an amusing (humorous) story. It is not the right style for a myth or legend. It is not a news report.

WRITING (Real Test)
Description of a scene   Page 78

Tick each correct point.
Read the student's work through once to get an overall view of their response.

Focus on general points
- ☐ Did it make sense?
- ☐ Did it flow?
- ☐ Did it arouse your interest?
- ☐ Did you want to read on to understand more about the scene?
- ☐ Was the handwriting readable?

Now focus on the detail. Read the following points and find out whether the student's work has these features.

Focus on content
- ☐ Is the general scene and basic location clearly stated?
- ☐ Has the writer provided some physical general description of scene, landscape?
- ☐ Is the description broken up into parts (e.g. house, tree, pond)?
- ☐ Does the writer try to put the scene in a time frame (e.g. late autumn day)? (optional)
- ☐ Is relevant detail included (e.g. long verandah)?
- ☐ Does the language create clear pictures?
- ☐ Does the writer make reference to reactions to the scene through several senses (e.g. *cool water*)?

☐ Does the writer convey any feelings created by the scene?

☐ Is there a concluding comment, opinion or reaction to the scene?

Focus on structure, vocabulary, grammar, spelling, punctuation

☐ Is the description in the present tense?

☐ Was there variation in sentence length and beginnings?

☐ Are there paragraphs separating different aspects of the scene?

☐ Has the writer used any similes   (e.g. *reflected as if in a mirror*)?

☐ Is there a generous use of adjectives to enhance the writing (e.g. *cool, shady* lawns)?

☐ Are adverbs used effectively (e.g. *sitting snugly by ...*)?

☐ Were capital letters where they should have been?

☐ Was punctuation correct?

☐ Was the spelling of words correct?

Practical suggestion: ask yourself if you can visualise the scene.

Marker's suggestions (optional)

WRITING (Real Test)
Description of a person   Page 79

Tick each correct point.
Read the student's work through once to get an overall view of their response.

Focus on general points
☐ Did it make sense?
☐ Did it flow?
☐ Did it arouse your interest?
☐ Did you want to read on to understand more about the person?
☐ Was the handwriting readable?

Now focus on the detail. Read the following points and find out whether the student's work has these features.

Focus on content

☐ Has the character to be described been established?

☐ Has the writer provided some general physical description of the person?

☐ Is the description broken up into parts (e.g. appearance, mannerisms, age, interests)?

☐ Does the writer try to put the scene in a time frame (e.g. late autumn day)? (optional)

☐ Is relevant detail included (e.g. hair colour)?

☐ Does the language create clear pictures?

☐ Does the writer make reference to reactions to the person through several senses (e.g. *wiry* hair, *soft* skin)?

☐ Does the writer convey any feelings towards the character?

☐ Is there a concluding comment, opinion or reaction to the person? (It can be reflective.)

Focus on structure, vocabulary, grammar, spelling, punctuation

☐ Is the description in the present tense?

☐ Was there variation in sentence length and beginnings?

☐ Are there paragraphs separating different aspects of the character?

☐ Has the writer used any similes (e.g. *bent like an old stick*)?

☐ Is there a generous use of adjectives to enhance the writing (e.g. *long, bony* fingers)?

☐ Are adverbs used effectively (e.g. *smiled happily*)?

☐ Were capital letters where they should have been?

☐ Was punctuation correct?

☐ Was the spelling of words correct?

Practical suggestion: ask yourself if you can visualise the person described.

Marker's suggestions (optional)

WRITING (Real Test)
Book review   Page 80

Tick each correct point.
Read the student's work through once to get an overall view of their response.

Focus on general points
☐ Did it make sense?
☐ Did it flow?
☐ Did the review arouse your interest?
☐ Did you want to read on to understand more about the book?
☐ Was the handwriting readable?

Now focus on the detail. Read the following points and find out whether the student's work has these features.

Focus on content
☐ Has the title been stated correctly?
☐ Do the introductory sentences identify book and author? (Giving cost is optional.)
☐ Is the type of book stated (e.g. fantasy, comedy)?
☐ Do you have some idea what the book is about?
☐ Is there a short description of the main characters and events (e.g. evil stepmother)?
☐ Does the writer suggest who would like the book?
☐ Are there short statements of the book's strengths?
☐ Are there short statements of the book's weaknesses (if any)?
☐ Is there information on where the book is available? (optional)
☐ Does the writer comment on the author's style (e.g. *lively paced story full of humorous incidents*)?
☐ Does the writer give a concluding comment, opinion or personal judgement of the book?

Focus on structure, vocabulary, grammar, spelling, punctuation
☐ Is the review in the past tense?
☐ Was there variation in sentence length and beginnings?
☐ Are the review sections broken up into clear paragraphs?

☐ Are adjectives used to enhance the writing (e.g. *long* descriptions)?
☐ Were capital letters where they should have been?
☐ Was punctuation correct?
☐ Was the spelling of words correct?

Practical suggestion: ask yourself if this review provides enough information for you to make a decision whether or not to read the book.

Marker's suggestions (optional)

WRITING (Real Test)
Review of a production   Page 81

Tick each correct point.
Read the student's work through once to get an overall view of their response.

Focus on general points
☐ Did it make sense?
☐ Did it flow?
☐ Did the review arouse your interest?
☐ Did you want to read on to understand more about the show?
☐ Was the handwriting readable?

Now focus on the detail. Read the following points and find out whether the student's work has these features.

Focus on content
☐ Has the show's title been stated correctly?
☐ Do the introductory sentences identify the show and performers? (Giving the cost is optional.)
☐ Is the type of show described (e.g. concert, play)?
☐ Do you have some idea what the show is about?
☐ Is there a short description of the show's main features (e.g. acting, singing)?
☐ Does the writer suggest who would enjoy the show?

□ Are there short statements of the show's strengths?

□ Are there short statements of the show's weaknesses (if any)?

□ Is there information on where the show can be seen? (optional)

□ Does the writer comment on the show's style (e.g. *lively paced, amateur*)?

□ Does the writer give a concluding comment, opinion or personal judgement of the show?

Focus on structure, vocabulary, grammar, spelling, punctuation

□ Is the review in the past tense?

□ Was there variation in sentence length and beginnings?

□ Are the review sections broken up into clear paragraphs?

□ Are adjectives used to enhance the writing (e.g. *colourful* costumes)?

□ Were capital letters where they should have been?

□ Was punctuation correct?

□ Was the spelling of words correct?

Practical suggestion: ask yourself if this review provides enough information for you to make a decision whether or not to see the show.

Marker's suggestions (optional)

WEEK 4

NUMBER AND ALGEBRA (Test Your Skills)
Patterns   Page 84

1 $5 \times 8 = 40$, $2 \times 20 = 40$.

2 Doubling is multiplying by 2.

3 Multiplication and division are opposite (inverse) operations.

4 The terms increase by 0.8, so $5.1 + 0.8 = 5.9$

5 The terms increase by 7. Four terms are given. $55 + 7 + 7 + 7 + 7 + 7 + 7 = 97$.

6 Solution: $(16 + 25) - 29 = 12$.

7 There are five 29s.

8 $8 + 7 \times 9 = 9 \times 7 + 8$

9 The terms are decreasing by 12. The first term must be $89 + 12$ ($= 101$).

10 Solution: $13 + 9 = 22$, $28 - 6 = 22$

11 3 add 3 is 6, double is 12, add 3 is 15, double is 30, and so on.

12 Rule: double + 2 ($13 + 13 + 2 = 28$).

13 Top line is divided by 3 to get bottom line ($3 \div 3 = 1$).

NUMBER AND ALGEBRA (Real Test)
Patterns   Page 86

1 B **2** C **3** A **4** B **5** B **6** 64 **7** D **8** C **9** D **10** D
11 B, E **12** B **13** D **14** C **15** 1.1 **16** 85

EXPLANATIONS

1 Adding 11 to each number:
Next number $= 39 + 11$
$= 39 + 10 + 1$
$= 49 + 1$
$= 50$
The next number is 50.

2 The numbers are counting backwards by 9.
Next number $= 58 - 9$
$= 58 - 8 - 1$
$= 50 - 1$
$= 49$
The next number is 49.

3 'What number' times by 3 = 24.
The number is 8 as $8 \times 3 = 24$.

4 The numbers are the multiples of 3. The number is $7 \times 3 = 21$. The seventh number is 21.

5 From the top row to the bottom row you multiply by 6. This means the missing number is $4 \times 6 = 24$.

6 The number pattern is dividing each number by 2 to get the following number. This means 'what number' divided by 2 gives 32. Or we could double 32 and get 64.
The answer is 64.

7 Consider each of the choices:
11, 21, 31, 41 is counting forward by 10
6, 16, 116, 1116 is placing the digit 1 in front
20, 31, 43, 57 is adding different numbers
3, 14, 25, 36 is counting forward by 11

8 $12 \times 3 = 36$.
This means 4 times 'what number' is 36?
The missing number is 9, as $4 \times 9 = 36$

9 Complete this pattern:
$30 - 12 = 18$
$40 - 12 = 28$
$50 - 12 = 38$
$80 - 12 = 68$
In the first part of the question, 50 is increased by 30 to become 80. This means that 30 can be added on to the answer 38 to get the new answer 68.

10  ?

The final diagram has
$5 + 4 + 3 + 2 + 1 = 15$ squares

11 The pattern is counting backwards by 8.
First number $= 66 - 8$
$= 66 - 6 - 2$
$= 60 - 2$
$= 58$
Second number $= 50 - 8$
$= 42$
The numbers are 58 and 42.

12 The triangle △ $= 6$, as $6 + 6 = 12$
For the 2nd line, $6 -$ 'what number' $= 4$
This means the circle ◯ $= 2$, as $6 - 2 = 4$

13 As $20 + 5 = 25$; $20 - 5 = 15$; $20 \times 5 = 100$ and $20 \div 4 = 5$
The missing symbol is $\div$.

14 The pattern is counting forward by 3. This means that the eighth number is found by multiplying 8 and 3:
Number $= 8 \times 3$
$= 24$

15 The pattern is counting forward by 0.2.
Next number $= 0.9 + 0.2$
The answer is 1.1

$$\begin{array}{r} 0.9 \\ + 0.2 \\ \hline 1.1 \end{array}$$

16 Arpita called these numbers:
100, 95, 90, 85
This means the fourth number she called out was 85.

STATISTICS AND PROBABILITY (Test Your Skills)
Graphs, tables and data Page 87

1 $5 + 5 + 3 = 13$

2 Solution: $(6 + 8 + 9 + 5 + 7) \div 5 = 7$

3 Solution: To get an average of 12 her total has to be 60 ($5 \times 12 = 60$). She has a total of 44 so she will need 16 ($60 - 44$).

4 One quarter of $80 = $20.

5 Each symbol = 2 ski lifts ($2 \times 14 = 28$)

6 25 paintings sold.

7 Add Raffle 1 to Raffle 2 to get totals. Select highest.

8 All the bottom row ($18 + 14 + 26 + 15 = 73$)

9 Golf is about 3 out of 24: 3 h

STATISTICS AND PROBABILITY (Real Test)
Graphs, tables and data Page 89

1 B **2** B **3** B **4** C **5** B **6** D **7** B **8** A **9** B
10 C **11** C **12** 10 **13** 66 **14** A **15** 2 **16** 4.75

EXPLANATIONS

1 For year 5, the graph shows 4 symbols.
This means $4 \times 10 = 40$
Year 5 sold 40 pies.

2 As 45 pies $= 4\frac{1}{2}$ symbols, the graph shows two year groups who have sold more than 45 pies.

3 As $40 - 25 = 15$, there were 15 more pies sold by Year 5.

4 Count the number of symbols in the graph
Symbols $= 5 + 2\frac{1}{2} + 4 + 5\frac{1}{2}$
$= 17$
Number of pies $= 17 \times 10$
$= 170$
The school sold 170 pies.

5 As 75 ÷ 3 = 25, Year 4 made $75 profit from their 25 pies.

6 The largest section of the graph represents netball. This means the students' favourite sport was netball.

7 Basketball is a quarter of the graph:

$\frac{1}{4}$ of 120 = 30 students

8 The part of the graph that represents soccer is less than a $\frac{1}{4}$ of the circle. This

means that less than $\frac{1}{4}$ of 120 like soccer.

As $\frac{1}{4}$ of 120 is 30, then an estimate for

those who chose soccer is 20.

9 From the table, ten 11-year-olds attended camp.

10 From the table: 5 + 8 +11 + 14 + 10 + 2 = 50
There were 50 students at the camp.

11 More than 10 years old means 11-year-olds and 12-year-olds.
Number over 10 years old = 10 + 2
= 12

12 We add the numbers already in the table:
Total for 4 days = 10 + 8 + 12 + 10
= 10 + 20 + 10
= 40
If total for 5 days was 50, then sit-ups for
Wednesday = 50 − 40
= 10

13 As 2 × 8 = 16, Shayne completed 16 sit-ups on the Saturday. As 50 + 16 = 66, then the total number of sit-ups was 66.

14 Comparing the four amounts, the largest is $3.30 by Josie.

15 The amounts that were at least $2 are Josie $3.30 and Angie $2.90.
This means 2 students. The answer is 2.

16 Total = $2.90 + $1.85
= $2.90 + $0.10 + $1.75
= $3.00 + $1.75
= $4.75

STATISTICS AND PROBABILITY
(Test Your Skills)
Probability   Page 90

1 There is only **one** five out of the six numbers.

2 Most likely to have warm days in Spring.

3 There are 2 possibilities: head or tail. The chance of a tail is 1 out of 2.

4 There are 12 blocks in the bag. The chance of Tim taking a red block is 4 out of 12 ($\frac{4}{12}$) or 1 in 3.

5 There is one 3 in the six cards. This means the probability is 1 out of 6.

6 Red, because 2 of the 6 sections are red, which is more than any other colour.

7 As there are 2 black balls, there must be 4 white balls. This means the chance it is white is 4 out of 6, which means that it is likely.

8 A baby can be either a boy or a girl so there is 1 chance in 2 or fifty(%)/fifty(%) chance.

9 'Fifty-fifty' means a chance of 1 out of 2. Jo will have to buy 10 out of the 20 tickets if the chance she wins is 'fifty-fifty'. [$\frac{10}{20} = \frac{1}{2}$]

10 Less than 4 is 1, 2 or 3. As there are 3 numbers less than 4, the chance is 3 in 6, which is the same as 1 in 2 because $\frac{3}{6} = \frac{1}{2}$.

11 There are more Mazdas going past so a Mazda is most likely to be the next car.

STATISTICS AND PROBABILITY (Real Test)
Probability   Page 92

1 D   **2** A   **3** B   **4** B   **5** D   **6** D   **7** C   **8** D   **9** C
10 5   **11** C   **12** A   **13** C   **14** A   **15** 3   **16** A

EXPLANATIONS

1 The sun will certainly rise tomorrow. This means the chance is certain.

2 If the chance is likely but not certain, this means the majority of the balls are white, but not all the balls.

3 As the shaded section is less than half of the circle, the chance of the spinner landing on that section is called unlikely.

4 In the bag were green (G) cards and yellow (Y) cards.
G G G Y Y Y
The chance of a yellow card selected is 3 out of 6, or 1 out of 2, or 'an equal chance'.

5 On a dice, the six faces are numbered 1 to 6. There is one face with the number 4. This means the chance of rolling a 4 is $\frac{1}{6}$, or 1 chance in 6.

6 The chance has not changed: The chance is still 1 chance in 6.

7 There are four possibilities:
A head, followed by a head
A head, followed by a tail
A tail, followed by a head
A tail, followed by a tail.
It is impossible to get a head, tail then a head.

8 For every 3 red balls there is 1 blue ball. The chance of a red ball being selected is 3 in 4.

9 As there are 3 yellow sections, 2 red sections and 1 blue section, it is most likely that Hayden will spin a yellow.

10 As 12 + 3 = 15, and 20 − 15 = 5, there must be 5 green jelly beans on the bag. The answer is 5.

11 There are 3 red jelly beans out of 20 jelly beans in the bag. This means the chance is 3 in 20.

12 There is only one 5 in the twelve cards. This means that the chance of selecting a 5 is $\frac{1}{12}$.

13 There are three 4s in the twelve cards. This means that the chance of selecting a 4 is $\frac{3}{12}$, which is the same as $\frac{1}{4}$.

14 The numbers less than 3 are:
2 1 2 1 0 2
There are 6 cards that are less than 3. This means that the chance of selecting a card less than 3 is $\frac{6}{12}$, which is the same as $\frac{1}{2}$.

15 The chance of a red ball is 1 out of 3 which can be written as $\frac{1}{3}$ or $\frac{3}{9}$. As there are 9 balls, there are 3 red balls. The answer is 3 red balls.

16 The balls are only either red or blue. If the chance of a red ball is 1 out of 3, then the chance of a blue ball must be 2 out of 3.

SPELLING (Real Test)
Common misspellings   Page 94

1 achieve
2 knapsack
3 blanket
4 single
5 gloated
6 whirlpool
7 blur
8 fortieth
9 bow
10 outboard
11 propeller
12 hull
13 stranded
14 locate
15 difficult
16 fresh
17 campsite
18 level

GRAMMAR AND PUNCTUATION (Real Test)
Pronouns, prepositions and punctuation   Pages 96–97

1 B **2** A **3** D **4** B **5** C **6** A **7** D **8** C **9** B **10** D
11 A **12** D **13** C **14** B **15** B **16** B **17** D **18** B, C

EXPLANATIONS

❶ This is a grammar question. The correct word is the pronoun *that*.
Tip: *That* is used here to identify a particular man—*the man behind the car*.

❷ This is a grammar question. The correct word is *so*.
Tip: *So* is used to connect two related clauses. It carries the meaning of *therefore*.

❸ This is a grammar question. The correct word is *stole*.
Tip: *Stole* is an irregular verb. Most verbs in English form their past tenses by adding *ed* (e.g. *he walked*). There are a number of irregular verbs when this doesn't happen. We say *stole* instead of 'stealed' (or 'stealt', which is not a real word).

❹ This is a grammar question. The correct word is the preposition *on*.
Tip: A preposition describes a relationship between other words in a sentence. Prepositions put events in position in time or place. We use *on* to show when Bev's party will be held … *on the weekend*. It is usual to use *on* in this situation.

❺ This is a grammar question. The verb is *carried*.

Tip: Verbs are often called doing words or action words. The action being undertaken in this sentence is established by *carried*.

❻ This is a punctuation question. The correct sentence is: *Mum, Pat and Kim crossed Lake Louise in a kayak.*
Tip: The proper nouns are *Mum*, *Pat*, *Kim* and *Lake Louise*. The word *kayak* is a common noun.

❼ This is a grammar question. The correct word is the verb *said*.

Tip: *Said* is an irregular verb. Most verbs in English form their past tenses by adding *ed* (e.g. *he walked*). There are a number of irregular verbs when this doesn't happen. We say *said* instead of 'sayed'.

❽ This is a grammar question. The correct word is the verb *begun*.
Tip: *Begun* is past tense. With the verb *begun* you need a 'helper'—another verb to 'help' it. *Have*, *has* and *had* can be helping verbs—*April Fool's Day is said to have begun* … The helping verb is always close to the verb it is helping. 'Beginned' is not a real word.

❾ This is a grammar question. The correct word is the verb *was*.
Tip: Basic rule: Singular subjects (nouns) need singular verbs; plural subjects (nouns) need plural verbs. In this case *was* must be used because there was one decision—referred to as it: *It was decided*.

❿ This is a grammar question. The correct word is the definite article *The*, with a capital because it begins the sentence.
Tip: *The* is used because it refers to a particular decision—*the decision to change the calendar*.

⓫ This is a grammar question. The correct word is the preposition *to*.
Tip: Prepositions put events in position in time or place. We use *to* in order to show movement toward a place—*to the first day in January.*

⓬ This is a punctuation question. The correct sentence is: *The new calendar moved New Year to the first day in January from March.*
Tip: *March* is a proper noun and at the end of a statement and requires a full stop.

⓭ This is a punctuation question. The correct sentences are: *I heard you knock. What do you want? I am very busy right now.*
Tip: The passage is made up of three short sentences. The question starts with *What* and ends with the question mark after *want*.

⓮ This is a punctuation question. The correct sentence is: *'How far are you going?' asked Jason.*

Tip: The inverted commas (quotation marks) enclose the actual words that are spoken: *'How far are you going?'* A question mark is added after *going* as this is the end of the question.

15 This is a grammar question. The correct sentence is: *I could <u>either</u> pump up my bike <u>or</u> walk to the beach.*
Tip: *Either–or* indicates that the speaker was limited to two choices. Some conjunctions combine with other words to form what are called correlative conjunctions, e.g. *either–or*. They always travel in pairs.

16 This is a grammar question. The correct word is *thick*.
Tip: This is a situation where you have to know the differences in how word meanings are applied. It is appropriate to refer to toast by its thickness—*thick* or *thin*.

17 This is a grammar question. The correct sentence is: *He and his brother work in Richmond.*
Tip: *He's* is short for *he is* and is incorrect usage. Split the sentence into two shorter sentences. You say: *He works in Richmond* and *His brother works in Richmond*. The verb *works* is used because two brothers are involved.

18 This is a punctuation question. The correct sentence is: *The new coach for our team, from Newcastle, was late for his first meeting.*
Tip: The words *from Newcastle* explain where the new coach came from. Commas are used to separate parts of the sentence and to make the meaning clear. Commas are also added to show pauses.

READING (Test Your Skills)
Following procedures   Page 98

Captain Hook Hand
1 C **2** scissors **3** A **4** D **5** C **6** B **7** B, E

EXPLANATIONS

1 The instructions in procedures can be called steps. There are six steps.

2 The maker of the Captain Hook hand needs scissors to cut the end off a plastic bottle.

3 'Embed' means to set in or insert. The handle should be set in the plaster.

4 As the plastic bottle extends up the arm that part should be hidden under a sleeve.

5 In Point 4 the maker is told to wait for the plaster to dry.

6 In this question you have to draw a conclusion. A hook hand would be of little use rowing a boat, not much use in bed and pointless at a football match. It would be fun to wear to a fancy dress party if you went as a pirate.

7 This is a 'search and find' question. You have to find what was *not* used. No wood or string are used to make the hand.

READING (Real Test)
Following procedures   Page 99

Worm farm
1 C **2** B **3** B **4** point 2 **5** D **6** A **7** A

EXPLANATIONS

1 Point 2 tells the reader to keep a terrarium (glass case) in a shady place.

2 The word 'eventually' has a similar meaning to 'finally'.

3 The worms get used to their surroundings and start 'working'.

4 Point 2 explains how to start the worm farm.

5 The plastic sheet is used when the contents of the terrarium are poured out and the 'compost' (dirt) is separated from the worms.

6 A terrarium is a glass 'cage' like a fish tank.

7 The 'soil' from the worm farm is rich and so fertiliser is not a necessity. The plastic bag is used to store the worm 'soil'. The jar is used to store the worms while the new dirt is added to the terrarium. The watering can is used to dampen the soil in the terrarium.

READING (Test Your Skills)
Understanding a book review Page 100

Disturbing Discoveries
1 D 2 C 3 A 4 B 5 D 6 C 7 D

EXPLANATIONS

1 The writer's name is at the end of the writing: M Gilroy.

2 The review does not praise the writing. It is a negative (bad) review.

3 Leaving the sentence unfinished implies that the reviewer had doubts about the book.

4 The reviewer liked the cover (but not much else).

5 The reviewer states that the book had 'one saving factor and that is the detailed descriptions of school grounds and council parks'.

6 You have to make a judgement here. It is most likely the author would be unhappy, as the review is critical.

7 The reviewer was disappointed. The reviewer expected more than descriptions of everyday places.

READING (Real Test)
Understanding a table of contents Page 101

Table of Contents for *What a Waste!*
1 page 25 2 B 3 A 4 D 5 B 6 C 7 C

EXPLANATIONS

1 It would be on page 25, which tells how to 'dispose of solid and liquid waste'.

2 This question requires knowledge of the parts of a reference book. The Glossary would give the meaning of the word.

3 'Waste through the ages' would give a history of waste. History is a record of events through the ages.

4 The Pronunciation guide would show how to say words used in the book.

5 A throw-away society buys goods that are replaced with new goods and not repaired or reused.

6 The book is not scientific enough for scientists. It has general information useful for the home owner.

7 This is a 'search and find' type of question (and requires a little mathematics). The Chapter on 'Difficult wastes' starts on page 30 and finishes on page 31. It is one page long (31 – 30 = 1).

READING (Real Test)
Understanding poetry Page 102

Washing the Car
1 D 2 A 3 B 4 D 5 written response 6 A, E 7 D

SELECTED EXPLANATIONS

1 The children are going to enjoy cleaning the car and are likely to splash water around. The best word is eager or keen. They will probably be careful but they expect to spill some water.

2 'Impatient' implies that the children may be a bit annoyed. The word 'frenzied' suggests being out of control.

3 If the water is swished around, it is stirred quickly and noisily.

4 The children should first shut the windows so that water doesn't get into the car.

5 Possible answer:
Dad inspects to see how well the car has been cleaned.

6 Say the words softly to yourself to find the ones that rhyme with 'done'. The spelling is not always a clue.

7 To answer this question you have to use your imagination—the children are going to have fun and probably spill some of the suds.

WRITING (Real Test)
Procedure Page 104

Tick each correct point.
Read the student's work through once to get an overall view of their response.

Focus on general points
☐ Did it make sense?
☐ Did it flow?

☐ Did the procedure seem clear?
☐ Was the handwriting readable?

Now focus on the detail. Read the following points and find out whether the student's work has these features.

Focus on content
☐ Does the title clearly advise the reader of the topic?
☐ Is the goal/aim of the writing clearly presented in the first sentences?
☐ Is the equipment to be used listed and/or briefly described?
☐ Is there some advice on what NOT to do? (optional)
☐ Is there some advice on the topic chosen?
☐ Are the steps listed in sequence (can be numbered) and each one on a new line?
☐ Is the instruction in each step clear?
☐ Are the main sections readily defined or spaced and do any headings stand out?
☐ Have helpful tips or suggestions been included?
☐ Has a last comment or suggestion been included?
☐ Were interesting details included?
☐ Did the conclusion have a satisfactory summing-up comment?

Focus on structure, vocabulary, grammar, spelling, punctuation
☐ Are sentences short and clear?
☐ Were subheadings used? (optional)
☐ Are action verbs used to start most steps (e.g. *make, lift, speak*)?
☐ Were adverbs used to describe how to carry out actions (e.g. *talk clearly*)?
☐ Were capital letters where they should have been?
☐ Was punctuation correct?
☐ Was the spelling of words correct?

Practical suggestion: follow the steps as written and see if the explanation really works.

Marker's suggestions (optional)

WRITING (Real Test)
Explanation   Page 105

Tick each correct point.
Read the student's work through once to get an overall view of their response.

Focus on general points
☐ Did it make sense?
☐ Did it flow?
☐ Did the writing and subject arouse your interest?
☐ Did you want to read on?
☐ Was the handwriting readable?

Now focus on the detail. Read the following points and find out whether the student's work has these features.

Focus on content
☐ Has the subject been clearly identified?
☐ Do the introductory sentences clearly identify (and define) the subject?
☐ Are the features of the subject precisely described (e.g. colour, size, shape)?
☐ Does the information sound factual and informed?
☐ Are the uses of the subject explained?
☐ Is there any information explaining specific or unusual instances of use? (optional)
☐ Does the writer suggest who would use the object?
☐ Does the writer give a concluding comment, opinion or personal judgement of the subject?

Focus on structure, vocabulary, grammar, spelling, punctuation
☐ Was there variation in sentence length and beginnings?
☐ Have 'longer' sentences been used (sentences with clauses beginning with words such as *so, because, when, if*)?
☐ Are the sections broken up into clear paragraphs?
☐ Are the paragraphs based on single topics (e.g. shape, use, how to operate)?
☐ Have subheadings been used? (optional)
☐ Have technical or scientific words been used?
☐ Do some sentences begin with such words as *because, if* and *when*?

□ Is the explanation in present tense?
□ Are adjectives used to enhance the writing (e.g. *strong* cord)?
□ Were capital letters where they should have been?
□ Was punctuation correct?
□ Was the spelling of words correct?

Practical suggestion: ask yourself if this explanation provides enough information for you to use the object.

Marker's suggestions (optional)

WRITING (Real Test)
Report from an outline   Page 106

Tick each correct point.
Read the student's work through once to get an overall view of their response.

Focus on general points
□ Did it make sense?
□ Did it flow?
□ Did the writing and subject arouse your interest?
□ Did you want to read on?
□ Was the handwriting readable?

Now focus on the detail. Read the following points and find out whether the student's work has these features.

Focus on content
□ Has the title been stated and does it suggest the subject matter?
□ Do the introductory sentences clearly identify time and place?
□ Are the events in chronological (time) order?
□ Does the information sound factual or informed?
□ Is surf swimming briefly explained? (optional)

□ Have personal comments or responses been added (usually only a single or a few words, e.g. *foolishly*)?
□ Does the writer give a concluding comment, opinion or personal judgement of the subject?

Focus on structure, vocabulary, grammar, spelling, punctuation
□ Are the facts presented in full sentences?
□ Was there a variation in sentence length and beginnings?
□ Do some sentences begin with adverbs of time (e.g. *later, after a while*)?
□ Are the sections broken up into clear paragraphs?
□ Is some information expanded to make short paragraphs?
□ Have some explanations of terms been used (e.g. flagged area, transported)?
□ Do some sentences begin with such words as *because, if* and *when*?
□ Is the explanation in the past tense?
□ Are adjectives used to enhance the writing (e.g. *rough* surf)?
□ Were capital letters where they should have been?
□ Was punctuation correct?
□ Was the spelling of words correct?

Marker's suggestions (optional)

WRITING (Real Test)
Response to a picture   Page 107

Tick each correct point.
Read the student's work through once to get an overall view of their response.

Focus on general points
□ Did it make sense?
□ Did it flow?
□ Did the writing and subject arouse your interest?

☐ Did you want to read on?
☐ Was the handwriting readable?

Now focus on the detail. Read the following points and find out whether the student's work has these features.

Focus on content
☐ Do the introductory sentences clearly identify time and place?
☐ Is there a brief description of the picture and its possible origins?
☐ Does the response relate to a real or imagined event?
☐ Does the response sound informed?
☐ Has the writer included some personal feelings?
☐ Does the writer predict an outcome of the incident in the picture (e.g. what may have happened next)?
☐ Have personal comments or responses been added (usually only a single or a few words, e.g. *sorry*)?
☐ Does the writer give a concluding comment, opinion or personal judgement of the subject?

Focus on structure, vocabulary, grammar, spelling, punctuation
☐ Was there variation in sentence length and beginnings?
☐ Do some sentences begin with adverbs of time (e.g. *later, after a while*)?
☐ Does the writer include adjectives and adverbs as emotive words (e.g. *sad eyes*)?
☐ Do descriptive sentences make reference to several senses (e.g. *warm fur, soft purring*)?
☐ Are different aspects of the scene in different paragraphs?
☐ Is the explanation in the past tense?
☐ Were capital letters where they should have been?
☐ Was punctuation correct?
☐ Was the spelling of words correct?

Marker's suggestions (optional)

SAMPLE TEST PAPERS
SAMPLE TEST PAPER 1

LITERACY – WRITING Page 110

Persuasive text

Tick each correct point.
Read the student's work through once to get an overall view of their response.

Focus on general points
☐ Did it make sense?
☐ Did it flow? Were the arguments logical and relevant?
☐ Did the opinions expressed arouse any feelings/reactions?
☐ Was the body of the writing mainly in the third person?
☐ Did you want to read on to understand/ appreciate the writer's point of view?
☐ Were the arguments convincing?
☐ Has the writer been assertive (e.g. the use of *is* rather than a less definite term)?
☐ Was the handwriting readable?
☐ Was the writing style suitable for a persuasive text (objective; not casual or dismissive)?

Now focus on the detail. Read each of the following points and find out whether the student's work has these features.

Focus on content
☐ Did the opening sentence(s) focus on the topic?
☐ Was the writer's point of view established early in the writing?
☐ Did the writer include any evidence to support his or her opinion?
☐ Did the writer include information relevant to his or her experiences?
☐ Were the points/arguments raised by the writer easy to follow?
☐ Did the writing follow the format with an introduction, the body of the text and a conclusion?
☐ Were personal opinions included?
☐ Was the concluding paragraph relevant to the topic?

Focus on structure, vocabulary, grammar, spelling, punctuation

☐ Was there a variety of sentence lengths, types and beginnings?

☐ Was a new paragraph started for each additional argument or point?

☐ Has the writer used any similes (e.g. *as clear as crystal*) to stress a point raised?

☐ Did the writer avoid approximations such as *probably, perhaps* and *maybe*?

☐ Did the writer use such phrases as *I know …* and *It is important to …*?

☐ Did the writer refer to the question in the points raised (A good way to do this is to use the key words from the question or the introduction.)?

☐ Has the writer used any less common words correctly?

☐ Was indirect speech used correctly?

☐ Were adjectives used to improve descriptions (e.g. <u>expensive</u> *buildings*)?

☐ Were adverbs used effectively (e.g. *firstly*)?

☐ Were capital letters used correctly?

☐ Was punctuation used correctly?

☐ Was the spelling of words correct?

Marker's suggestions (optional)

LITERACY – READING   **Pages 111–117**

Bush Stone-Curlew

1 A **2** C **3** B **4** D **5** A **6** D

EXPLANATIONS

1 Bush Stone-Curlews are found Australia wide. The distribution map shows this fact.

2 The curlew's main method of survival is using camouflage tactics.

3 The curlew is a meat eater (carnivore). They specialise in hunting small grassland animals: frogs, spiders, insects, molluscs, crustaceans, snakes, lizards and small mammals.

4 Foxes are a threat to curlews because foxes hunt by scent. Camouflage doesn't cover scent.

5 Curlews are nocturnal animals; that is, they are night hunters. During the day the tend to remain inactive.

6 You have to be able to recognise different types of writing. This is an information report. An information report gives a factual description of a thing or animal.

Growing tulips

7 C **8** B **9** A, E **10** D **11** C **12** B

EXPLANATIONS

7 Tulips are multi-coloured. Multi-coloured means many coloured. This information is in the text and implied in the picture.

8 You have to read through the whole passage to determine which statement is correct. Bulbs are best stored in cool, ventilated places.

9 This is an inferring type of question because you have to 'read between the lines' when you read the passage. Avid means keen and enthusiastic. Tulip growers 'create works of art in planting their tulip beds'.

10 'Tulipmania' is a made-up word. You should recognise that it ends with 'mania'. Mania means an excessive interest in something. People with tulipmania would do anything to get tulip bulbs.

11 Notice you are asked: What type of soils are not suitable for tulips? You have to eliminate soils that are suitable for tulips. Wet soils are unsuitable because they cause the bulbs to rot.

12 Because some tulip beds are masterpieces in design, it would suggest that tulip growers are creative gardeners. They create works of art.

Comprehension
13 A **14** B **15** D **16** *Growing tulips* A, B;
Comprehension A, D

EXPLANATIONS

13 The cartoon is called Comprehension because Jim doesn't understand (comprehend) his father's remarks. In fact, he only comprehends them in the light of his training experiences. He misunderstands.

14 The look on grandpa's face is wicked delight. Grandpa is probably being a bit irresponsible.

15 The bubbles are an illustrator's technique of indicating the thoughts Jim is having about his father's comments. It is a technique used in many graphic publications, including comics.

16 The *Growing tulips* text is intended to **encourage** the reader to take up tulip growing as well as **explain** how to go about it. The *Comprehension* cartoon is to **entertain** people. It also **explains** how some communications are misunderstood.

As if I would
17 written response **18** D **19** B **20** C **21** *As if I would* A, C; *Night of the Muttonbirds* A, B **22** A

EXPLANATIONS

17 Possible answer:
Sue rides her skateboard in the park. She is warned not to 'fall off those skateboards at the park!'

18 This is a main idea type of question because you have to understand what the whole poem is about. Try to imagine Sue's parents. They are protective. They don't want anything to happen to her (much to Sue's dismay). They keep telling what to do or what not to do.

19 Notice you are asked: What doesn't worry Sue's parents? You have to eliminate the things that worry Sue's parents. Sue's parents are not worried about Sue getting lost.

20 This is a judgement (evaluation) type of question because you have to work out how the parents feel. Read the whole poem

through. What are the warnings Sue's parents offer? The warnings are unnecessary advice—Sue implies that she understands completely. 'As if I would!' she thinks.

21 The poem *As if I would* is intended to **engage** the reader with an amusing poem as well as show the **attitude** of certain situations some families have. The *Night of the Muttonbirds* text is a **fictional recount**. The full narrative is meant to **engage** the reader and provide enjoyment.

22 Sue's parents worry that Sue will stay all day at her friend's (mate's) place. Her dad says 'Now don't stay there all day!'

Extract: Night of the Mutton Birds
23 D **24** 1B, 2A, 3D, 4C **25** A **26** B
27 3, 1, 5, 4, 2 **28** A

EXPLANATIONS

23 Matthew is preparing for school. His school clothes are laid out neatly on a chair. He starts to get dressed—then decides to do it later when he has to.

24 You read clothes were on a chair, a (hot) kettle was on the stove, shells were on top of the chest of drawers, and full jam jars were on the kitchen table.

25 This is an inferring type of question because you have to 'read between the lines' when you read the passage. You have to use your knowledge of word meanings as they are applied to the passage. Matthew is feeling reluctance, which means he is feeling a lack of enthusiasm for what he has to do—get ready for school.

26 You have to read the whole passage to get an overall impression. You have to use your knowledge of word meanings as they are applied to the passage. It is a busy household. The woodstove never went out. 'In it, his mother cooked all the meals; the roasts and the stew, the cakes and the scones.' A lot happens in the house.

27 This is a sequencing type of question. By reading the text carefully you can identify the correct order of events.

28 For some questions you will have to combine the facts that you read in the text with your own knowledge and observations. Sighing as used in the passage means about to boil. It is a soft sound made before the water really begins to bubble.

CD balloon hovercraft

29 A **30** D **31** C **32** written response **33** C **34** D

EXPLANATIONS

29 An adhesive is a sticking agent (glue). You are not told directly but there is a clue in the first step (What to do): glue the pop-top lid to the CD.

30 For some questions, you will have to combine the facts that you read in the text with your own knowledge and observations: Terrain in the passage refers to surfaces with different textures. Normally terrain would mean an area of land as seen for its surface physical features, especially when used for military purposes.

31 For some questions you will have to combine the facts that you read in the text with your own knowledge and observations: a gentle push would start the CD hovercraft gliding before the balloon ran out of air.

32 Possible answer:

It is suggested that a CD balloon hovercraft be tested on a flat surface because a flat surface will allow the air to escape evenly.

33 For some questions you will have to combine the facts that you read in the text with your own knowledge and observations: the CD hovercraft won't work if the pop-top is closed because the air cannot escape.

34 For some questions you will have to combine the facts that you read in the text with your own knowledge and observations: The hovercraft would be useful in a science experiment on friction. When the CD is not in contact with the surface it 'slides' smoothly over the surface. The amount of friction is reduced.

Interview with Brian McWilliam

35 B **36** Young **37** B **38** C **39** A

EXPLANATIONS

35 One of Brian's other interests is flying radio-controlled model planes.

36 Brian was a keen member of a photography club in the town of Young.

37 This is a straightforward fact-finding type of question. Brian states early in the interview that he enjoys making scenery and scale buildings to add to his track layout.

38 Brian paints his model trains, not to make them look like new, but to make them look like real working trains.

39 There are a number of options for someone interested in model trains as a hobby. One of Brian's suggestions is to get advice from people who have model trains.

LITERACY – CONVENTIONS OF LANGUAGE
Pages 118–121

1 D **2** C **3** B **4** they **5** C **6** B **7** is **8** C **9** A
10 D **11** C **12** B **13** A **14** D **15** A **16** C **17** C
18 A, B **19** B **20** Four, noisy, ripe, plum **21** C
22 B **23** C, D **24** B **25** A **26** heard **27** unable
28 butcher **29** prompt **30** valiant **31** athletics
32 envelope **33** saddened **34** quarter
35 pencil **36** business **37** plain **38** trousers
39 casual **40** near **41** clippings **42** aside
43 dozens **44** possible **45** hungry **46** for
47 kilometres **48** border **49** underwater
50 telegraph

EXPLANATIONS

1 *Drive* is an irregular verb. Most verbs in English form their past tense by adding 'ed', e.g. she *played*. There are a number of irregular verbs when this doesn't happen. When the past participle of *drive* is formed we say *was driven*. 'Droven' is not a word.

2 This is a grammar question. *However* is a conjunction that is used to show a contrast with something said previously.

3 This is a grammar question. The words not required are *the question*. The phrase is redundant. *Ask* means 'to say a question to

get an answer'. Meaning is not lost by omitting *the question*.

4 This is a grammar question. Pronouns are words that stand in the place of nouns. *They* stands for *both girls*.

5 This is a grammar question. *Either* is a conjunction that is used before the first of two given alternatives. The second alternative is introduced by *or* (an *either—or* combination).

6 This is a punctuation question. The apostrophe is an apostrophe of possession— *Peter's old bus pass. Inspectors* is a plural noun.

7 This is a grammar question. Singular nouns (dream) require singular verbs (is)—Bruno's dream is. *It* is a pronoun standing for *dream*.

8 This is a punctuation question. *Seek* with a question mark (?), followed by a closing speech mark, completes this question.

9 This is a grammar question. *Who* is a relative pronoun adding further information about *my brother*.

10 This is a grammar question. *Taking* is a verb from the word *take*. *Taken* is part of the past participle *was taken* and is not correct in this sentence.

11 This is a punctuation question. *I'm* is a contraction of *I am*. The apostrophe indicates that a letter (a) has been left out.

12 This is a grammar question. *Or* is a conjunction linking two alternatives.

13 This is a grammar question. *My* is a possessive pronoun (determiner) indicating something belonging to the speaker. A capital is required as *My* is the beginning of a new sentence following a full stop. *Me* should be used as the object in a sentence.

14 This is a punctuation question. This is an example of indirect speech (reported speech). The actual words spoken are not quoted. No speech marks are required.

15 This is a punctuation question. *It's* is a contraction for *it is*. The apostrophe indicates that a letter (i) has been left out. *Sharon's* is a possessive form indicating

Sharon's turn. Yours is a possessive pronoun and does not require an apostrophe.

16 This is a grammar question. *Better* is an adverb adding meaning to *felt*. It is not an adjective in this example. *More* used with *better* forms a double comparative which is incorrect. *Good* is used to describe a single situation. Remember the comparative adjectives: *good, better, best*.

17 This is a grammar question. The sentence is in past tense. Plural subjects (days) need plural verbs. Singular subjects (nouns) need singular verbs. In this case *were* must be used because there is more than one day. *Week* is an additional piece of information adding meaning to the subject. It is not the subject of the sentence.

18 This is a punctuation question. The words *Ms Peters* is additional information inserted into the sentence. Commas indicate pauses.

19 This is a punctuation question. The sentence starts with a capital letter (O). *Utility* is a common noun and does not need a capital letter. The words *Ted and Jan Tsang* is additional information inserted into the sentence. Commas indicate pauses.

20 This is a grammar question. Adjectives are describing words. *Four* and *noisy* describe the parrots, *ripe* describes the fruit and *plum* describes the type of tree.

21 This is a grammar question. Future tense must be used throughout this sentence (*will bring* and [*will*] *dry*). 'Brang' is not a word.

22 This is a punctuation question. Brackets are used to include additional information that may be useful. This could be helpful for the reader wanting more precise details. Bracketed information does not interrupt the flow of basic information.

23 This is a punctuation question. Speech marks go around direct (quoted) speech. Tanya has said two sentences: *'Look over here Janis'* and *'There's a crack in the glass.'* The information showing who spoke separates the two parts. A total of four speech marks are required.

24 This is a grammar question. *Stand* is the correct tense. *Stood* is past tense and is incorrect.

25 This is a grammar question. *Fleet* is a collective noun. Certain collective nouns tend to go with certain groups of things or people. *Fleet* is the most appropriate collective noun. The other options are less acceptable.

26 *Heard* and *herd* are homonyms—words that sound the same but which have different meanings. <u>*Heard*</u> is the past tense of <u>*hear*</u>. *Herd* refers to a group of animals.

27 *Unable* has the prefix 'un' on the word *able*. The syllable 'le' is a common word ending. It is important to be familiar with the correct spelling of words with similar endings, e.g. *cable*, *table*.

28 'Tch' is a common letter combination. Learn to recognise the family of words that have similar 'tch' spellings, e.g. *pitch*, *hatch*, *fetch*.

29 *Prompt* is an adjective. Take care to pronounce the word correctly and sound the final *t*.

30 Take care to pronounce the word correctly and sound the 'ant'. Learn to recognise the family of words that have similar 'ant' endings, e.g. *radiant*, *compliant*.

31 *Athletics* has three syllables not four, e.g. *ath–let–ics*.

32 Take care to pronounce the word correctly. It is *envelope*.

33 *Saddened* is *sad* with the suffixes 'en' and 'ed'. When adding a suffix beginning with a vowel to a short word ending in a single vowel and consonant you double the final consonant, e.g. *trod* → *trodden*, *flat* → *flatten*.

34 *Quart* has to do with four (4).

35 *Pencil* is a common school word you should remember.

36 *Business* is *busy* with the suffix 'ness'. Because *busy* ends with a single consonant and *y* you change the *y* to *i* then add the 'ness'.

37 *Plain* and *plane* are homonyms—words that sound the same but which have different meanings. *Plain* means 'not decorated'. *Plane* refers to surfaces.

38 Take care not to reverse the order of vowels. Note the 'er' ending, not 'or'.

39 Most double-syllable words that end with an *l* have a single *l*, e.g. *travel*, *level*, *hotel*.

40 The letter combinations 'ea' and 'ee' can represent the same sound, e.g. *sea*, *see*. Learn to recognise the 'ear' family of words, e.g. *fear*, *dear*, *clear*.

41 When adding a suffix beginning with a vowel to a short word ending in a single vowel and consonant you double the final consonant, e.g. *ship* → *shipping*, *drum* → *drumming*.

42 *Aside* has the prefix *a* on the word *side*.

43 Take care to pronounce the word correctly. It is *doz<u>en</u>s* not 'doz<u>on</u>s'.

44 Take care to pronounce the word correctly. It is *poss<u>ible</u>* not 'possable'. 'Ible' and 'able' are common word endings and you should remember when to use them.

45 *Hungry* has only two syllables. The name of the country *Hungary* has three.

46 *For* and *fore* (and *four*) are homonyms—words that sound the same but which have different meanings. *For* is a preposition. *Fore* is an adjective meaning 'in front'.

47 'Kilometers' is the American spelling and not accepted in Australia.

48 *Border* and *boarder* are homonyms—words that sound the same but which have different meanings. *Border* is an edge. A *boarder* is a person who pays rent.

49 *Underwater* is a compound word: *under* + *water*.

50 *Telegraph* is a combination of the prefix 'tele' and the word *graph*. The 'ph' in *graph* has an *f* sound.

NUMERACY　　　　　　　　　Pages 122–127

1 A **2** A **3** C **4** D **5** A **6** A **7** B and C **8** B **9** A
10 B and C **11** 267 **12** C **13** 1.50 **14** 21 **15** D
16 D **17** C **18** 6 **19** B **20** B **21** B **22** C **23** A
24 A **25** 4020.6 **26** 7605 **27** 3.25 **28** A, B and C
29 1103 **30** A **31** D **32** A, C and D **33** D **34** A
35 B **36** 2 **37** A **38** 75 **39** 16 **40** B **41** D **42** 5

EXPLANATIONS

1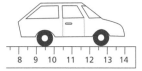

The toy car measures from 8 cm to 14 cm:
Length = 14 – 8
　　　　= 6
The toy car is 6 cm long.

2 From 12:30 to 1:30 is 1 hour, to 2:00 is 30
minutes and to 2:15 is another 15 minutes.
This makes a total of 1 hour 45 minutes.
The movie ran for 1 hour 45 minutes.

3 Mackay is north-east of Leigh Creek.

4

5 Jay's email was received

6 3405 = 3 × 1000 + 4 × 100 + 0 × 10 + 5 × 1
　　　　= 3 thousands + 4 hundreds + 5
This means 3405 is three thousand four
hundred and five.

7 17 × 9 = 17 × 10 – 17 × 1
　　　　= 17 × 10 – 17
17 × 9 = 20 × 9 – 3 × 9
　　　　= 20 × 9 – 27

8 As 50 ÷ 25 is 2, Cameron can buy 2 × 3 = 6
DVDs for $50.

9 By counting, there are 18 whole shaded
squares plus 4 half squares that are shaded.
Number = 18 + 4 halves
　　　　= 18 + 2
　　　　= 20
The area is 20 square units.

10 23 – 5 = 23 – 3 – 2
　　　　　= 20 – 2
　　　　　= 18
34 – 16 = 34 – 10 – 6
　　　　　= 24 – 6
　　　　　= 24 – 4 – 2
　　　　　= 20 – 2
　　　　　= 18
The pairs of numbers are 23 and 5, and, 34
and 16.

11 310 – 43 = 310 – 10 – 33
　　　　　　= 300 – 33
　　　　　　= 300 – 30 – 3
　　　　　　= 270 – 3
　　　　　　= 267

12 The order of popularity from least popular is
Mexican, Indian, Pizza, then Thai. This means
that Pizza is represented by column C.

13 Add the amounts　　　4.65
　　　　　　　　　　　+ 3.85
　　　　　　　　　　　―――
　　　　　　　　　　　　8.50

The total is $8.50.
Difference　= $10.00 – $8.50
　　　　　　= $2.00 – 50c
　　　　　　= $1.50

14 84 arranged in groups of 4 means
84 ÷ 4 = 21.

15 On the map, 2 units = 80 metres, which
means a scale of 1 unit = 40 metres.
Claudia and Shakira are 5 units apart.
This means distance = 40 × 5
　　　　　　　　　　 = 200
Claudia and Shakira are 200 m apart.

16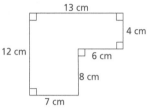

First we find the length of the missing side by subtraction: 12 − 8 = 4. This means the missing side is 4 cm. Now add all lengths:
Perimeter = 13 + 12 + 7 + 8 + 6 + 4
= 50
The perimeter is 50 cm.

17 Six out of the twelve discs are white.

This can be written as $\frac{6}{12} = \frac{1}{2}$.

18 The hexagonal prism has hexagons at its 2 ends and 6 rectangular faces. This means Mario used 6 rectangles to build the hexagonal prism.

19

Using the scale, the distance on the map from 5K classroom to the toilets appears to be 5 lots of the 10 metre lengths.

This means an estimate of the distance is 5 × 10 = 50 or 50 metres.

20

2	7	3
+ 6		8
9	3	1

The missing number must be 5 so that the sum looks like

$$\begin{array}{r} 2\,7\,3 \\ +\,{}_16{}_15\,8 \\ \hline 9\,3\,1 \end{array}$$

The missing number is 5.

21
$$\begin{array}{r} 503 \\ 5\overline{)2515} \end{array}$$

as 5 into 25 is 5;
and 5 into 1 is 0 with remainder 1
and 5 into 15 is 3
The answer is 503.

22 The temperature when Ravi arrived home was 32 degrees.
Increase = 32 − 18
The temperature increased by 14 degrees.

$$\begin{array}{r} {}^2\cancel{3}{}^12 \\ -\,1\,8 \\ \hline 1\,4 \end{array}$$

23 As $2^2 = 4$, $3^2 = 9$ and $4^2 = 16$,
$2^2 + 3^2 + 4^2 = 4 + 9 + 16$
$= 4 + 16 + 9$
$= 20 + 9$
$= 29$
Hung's answer was 29.

24 There are 2 diamonds in the 8 cards. This means the chance of a diamond is

2 out of 8 = $\frac{2}{8}$ = $\frac{1}{4}$ = 1 out of 4

25 4 thousands + 2 tens + 6 tenths
= 4 thousands + 0 hundreds + 2 tens + 0 ones + 6 tenths
= 4020.6
The answer is 4020.6

26 A four-digit odd number will have an odd digit in the last position. The largest possible number will have the other digits in descending order (going down).
The answer is 7605.

27 Total cost $0.55 + $1.20

$$\begin{array}{r} 0.55 \\ +\,1.20 \\ \hline 1.75 \end{array}$$

Change = $5.00 − $1.75

$$\begin{array}{r} 5.00 \\ -\,1.75 \\ \hline 3.25 \end{array}$$

Jacqueline receives $3.25 change.
The answer is $3.25

28 In A, B and C both letters cover exactly half the spinner.

29 Sum = 953 + 150

$$\begin{array}{r} 953 \\ + 150 \\ \hline 1103 \end{array}$$

The total is 1103.

30 Difference = 10.49 – 9.58

$$\begin{array}{r} 10.49 \\ -\ 9.58 \\ \hline 0.91 \end{array}$$

The difference in time is 0.91 seconds.

31 Change = $5.00 – $3.65

= $1.35

$$\begin{array}{r} {}^4\mathbf{5}.{}^9\mathbf{0}{}^1\mathbf{0} \\ -\ 3.\ 6\ 5 \\ \hline 1.\ 3\ 5 \end{array}$$

Su-Li receives $1.35 in change.

32 Numbers ending in 0 or 5 are multiples of 5.

33 Look for a pair of faces that we can see will be opposite when the cube is made.
4 and 10 will be opposite, so 4 + 10 = 14.
This means that opposite faces will add to 14.

34

$$\begin{array}{r} 345 \\ +\ ?7 \\ \hline 402 \end{array} \qquad \begin{array}{r} 3\ 4\ 5 \\ +_1\ {}_1 5\ 7 \\ \hline 4\ 0\ 2 \end{array}$$

As, Units column: 5 + 7 = 12
Tens column: 1 + 4 + ? = 10   ? = 5
Hundreds column: 1 + 3 = 4

35 The total length of rectangles R and S is 20 cm.
As rectangle P is 5 cm,
Length of rectangle Q = 20 – 5
= 15
Length of rectangle Q is 15 cm.

36 A factor will divide into the number with no remainder.
8 ÷ 4 = 2, with no remainder
22 ÷ 4 = 5, with remainder 2
18 ÷ 4 = 4, with remainder 2
28 ÷ 4 = 7, with no remainder
34 ÷ 4 = 8, with remainder 2
The answer is 2 numbers (8 and 28).

37 As 748 ÷ 10 = 74.8, the missing number is 10.

38 To multiply 30 by 2.5 you can double 30 to get 60 and then add half of 30. This means 60 + 15 = 75. It will take 75 minutes.

39 Start with the answer and work backwards using the opposite operations: 6 + 2 is 8 and then double 8 which gives 16.

40 60 degrees is less than a right angle. Angle D looks too small, so the answer is angle B.

41 Use the Sydney row and the Perth column. Sydney to Perth is 3910 km.

42 The difference is $300 – $200 = $100. As Marg saves $20 each week then we divide: 100 ÷ 20 = 5. This means Marg saves for 5 weeks.

SAMPLE TEST PAPER 2

LITERACY – WRITING   Page 128

Factual recount
Tick each correct point.
Read the student's work through once to get an overall view of their response.

Focus on general points
☐ Did it make sense?
☐ Did it flow?
☐ Did the events arouse any feeling?
☐ Did you want to read on? (Were the events interesting?)
☐ Was the handwriting readable?

Now focus on the detail. Read each of the following points and find out whether the student's work has these features.

Focus on content
☐ Did the opening sentence(s) introduce the subject of the recount?
☐ Was the setting established, i.e. when and where the action took place?
☐ Was the reader told when the action takes place?
☐ Was it apparent who the main characters(s) is/are?
☐ Have personal pronouns been used? (e.g. *he, her, him, them*)

☐ Were the events recorded in chronological (time) order?

☐ Was the recount in past tense?

☐ Did the writing include some personal comments on the events? (e.g. *surprised, thrilled*)

☐ Did descriptions make reference to any of the senses? (e.g. *wet rocks, salty air*)

☐ Were interesting details included?

☐ Did the conclusion have a satisfactory summing-up comment?

Focus on structure, vocabulary, grammar, spelling, punctuation

☐ Was there a variation in sentence length and beginnings?

☐ Was there a new paragraph started for changes in time, place or action?

☐ Were subheadings used? (optional)

☐ Were adjectives used to improve descriptions? (e.g. <u>smelly</u> bait)

☐ Were adverbs used to make 'actions' more interesting? (e.g. yelled <u>loudly</u>)

☐ Were adverbs used for time changes? (e.g. *later, soon, then*)

☐ Were capital letters where they should have been?

☐ Was punctuation correct?

☐ Was the spelling of words correct?

Marker's suggestions (optional)

LITERACY – READING   Pages 129–135

The Rats of Wolfe Island

1 D **2** A **3** B **4** documents **5** 5, 2, 1, 4, 3 **6** A

EXPLANATIONS

1 This is a general fact-finding type of question because you can find the fact in the passage. You then have to apply the information you have found. The bus was supposed to arrive half an hour after Eddie (narrator) asked his question. It arrived three-quarters of an hour later. It was a quarter of an hour late.

2 You have to use your knowledge of word meanings as they are applied to the passage. In the latter part of the passage Kingy is described as being introspective—he was a little less outgoing. He was subdued (quiet and restrained).

3 This is a general fact-finding type of question because you can find the fact in the passage. The sight of the village was a surprise to Eddie because he (they) came across it very suddenly.

4 You read that as Kingy and Eddie walked down the track to the village Kingy was 'swinging his precious documents'.

5 This is a sequencing type of question. By reading the text carefully you can identify the correct order of events.

6 You have to read the whole passage right through to get an overall picture of what is happening. Eddie and Kingy are making their way to the village. A suitable title for the passage would be Village Visit. Do not be distracted by unimportant details.

The Smile

7 C **8** D **9** B **10** A **11** C

EXPLANATIONS

7 This is a general fact-finding type of question. You have to read through the whole poem. A smile is passed from person to person.

8 This is an inferring type of question because you have to 'read between the lines' when you read the poem. Each stanza tells the reader to smile openly; that is, share the smile. Don't conceal it.

9 This is a general fact-finding type of question because you can find the fact in the poem. The poet is first seen smiling at a corner. 'When someone smiled at me today/ I started smiling too./ I passed around the corner/ and someone saw my grin.'

10 This is an inferring type of question because you have to 'read between the lines' when you read part of the whole poem. A smile can be like an epidemic. Everyone will be affected.

11 You have to work out what feeling the poet is conveying in the poem. Since people are sharing smiles it is a feeling of friendliness.

Names for parts of a house
12 B **13** D **14** 4 **15** A **16** *The Smile* A, B;
House diagram C, D

EXPLANATIONS

12 As a reader, you often have to interpret graphics (such things as pictures, photos and posters). The value of this labelled diagram would help eliminate confusion when discussing parts of a house. It would be of little value to professional builders.

13 As a reader, you often have to interpret graphics (such things as pictures, photos and posters). The 'hooked' arrow is the illustrator's way of directing the viewer's attention to the eave which is under the roof overhang.

14 As a reader, you often have to interpret graphics (such things as pictures, photos and posters). This is a general fact-finding type of question because you can find the fact in the diagram. You then have to apply the information you have found. Determine what part of the house is a shutter. There are four shutters shown (two on the right window and two on the left window).

15 As a reader, you often have to interpret graphics (such things as pictures, photos and posters). This is a general fact-finding type of question because you can find the fact in the diagram. You then have to apply the information you have found. A fascia is a flat board used to cover the ends of the roof.

16 *The Smile* is a poem that **encourages** a *change of behaviour*. It also uses figurative language (like the flu). The *House diagram* is to **inform** through the use of graphics. It educates and portrays in a visual way.

Delicious chicken dragon sandwich
17 C **18** dragon herb **19** A **20** B **21** C **22** A

EXPLANATIONS

17 The writer suggests that most chicken sandwiches are not very interesting (they have no oomph).

18 This is a general fact-finding type of question. You can find the fact in the passage. You then have to apply the information you have found. Another name for tarragon is dragon herb. It is explained in the second paragraph.

19 This is a sequencing, fact-finding type of question because you have to work out the order in which things happen in the recipe. The lettuce leaves are included in the dish after the chicken mixture has been spread on the bread. 'Spread the chicken mixture onto four slices of bread. Add the lettuce leaves ...'

20 Only one chicken is required. One roast chicken will serve four.

21 This is a general fact-finding type of question because you can find the fact in the passage. The final ingredient (For four serves you will need) is: salt to taste.

22 This is a general fact-finding type of question because you can find the fact in the passage. The last sentence suggests that the sandwich be served with a glass of juice.

Living rocks
23 the sun **24** A **25** D **26** C **27** C **28** D

EXPLANATIONS

23 This is a general fact-finding type of question because you can find the fact in the passage. Stromatolites get their energy from the sun. 'Stromatolites are formed when micro-organisms photosynthesise—the same process green plants use to take energy from the sunlight.'

24 Read the whole passage. You have to eliminate the choices that are incorrect. Millions of years ago there was no ozone layer.

25 This is a general fact-finding type of question because you can find the fact in the passage. Stromatolites are found in shallow water.

26 This is a general fact-finding type of question. In the first paragraph it states that Lake Clifton is important because it has the largest stromatolite reef in the southern hemisphere.

27 This is a general fact-finding type of question. You can find the fact in the passage. The calcium comes from fresh underground water.

28 This is a judgement (evaluation) type of question because you have to work out how the author has written the passage. Eliminate those choices that are not applicable. Geologists (people who study rocks and landforms) would be interested in going to Lake Clifton because the formations there are rather unusual and uncommon occurrences.

Letter to council
29 written response **30** C **31** B **32** D
33 *Living rocks* A, C; *Letter to Council* B, C

EXPLANATIONS
29 Possible answer:

Ms Turner is objecting strongly to the road to the boatshed. She states very clearly in the opening paragraph: 'I am writing to express my disapproval at the plans to construct a new council road … to allow a boat-hiring shed to be built'.

30 The Blue Bay Council is responsible for building 'a new council road'.

31 This is an inferring type of question because you have to 'read between the lines' when you read the passage. You have to use your knowledge of word meanings as used in the passage. Pocket refers to a small area of land. Ms Turner refers to the area as a small tract of wilderness.

32 Ms Turner is most concerned about the bats. The bats are a rare variety. Bats are very territorial and if they are forced out, the colony will die out.

33 *Living rocks* is a factual text about an unusual phenomenon. It would **fascinate** and **inform** readers. The *Letter to Council* is to **persuade** Council to act in a certain way. It provides **information** to back up the request.

Feeling good poster
34 porridge and fruit **35** A **36** D **37** written response **38** B **39** C

EXPLANATIONS
34 As a reader, you often have to interpret posters. This is a general fact-finding type of question because you can find the fact in the poster. Porridge and fruit make a good healthy breakfast, particularly in winter.

35 As a reader, you often have to interpret posters. This is a general fact-finding type of question. You can find the fact in the poster. It is beside the fourth smiley face. Vegetables go well in curries.

36 As a reader, you often have to interpret posters. This is a judgement type of question. For some questions you will have to combine the facts that you read in the poster with your own knowledge and observations. Eliminate the choices that are less likely. A good place for a poster like this would be in a health food store.

37 Possible answer:

To stay healthy, people should eat more vegetables and fruit.

38 As a reader, you often have to interpret posters. The poster is trying persuade the reader to eat healthy foods that will help them to feel good.

39 This is an inferring type of question because you have to interpret a symbol when you study the poster. For some questions you will have to combine the facts that you read in the poster with your own knowledge and observations. Red usually means danger, or beware! The foods in the 'Sometimes Food' can lead to poor health.

LITERACY – CONVENTIONS OF LANGUAGE
Pages 136–139

1 A **2** Neither **3** A **4** C **5** A **6** C, D **7** D **8** A
9 B **10** D **11** D **12** C **13** A **14** B **15** later,
quickly, quietly **16** B **17** A **18** B, C **19** D
20 A, E **21** B **22** smallest **23** B **24** C **25** C
26 Wednesday **27** strawberry **28** blackboard
29 thought **30** dinosaurs **31** hopeful **32** lollies
33 welcome **34** lettuce **35** mosquito **36** postage
37 private **38** label **39** postcode **40** flying
41 annually **42** breezes **43** alive **44** Local
45 popular **46** giant **47** complete **48** where
49 dangerous **50** until

EXPLANATIONS

1 *Sell* is an irregular verb. Most verbs in English form their past tense by adding 'ed', e.g. she *played*. There are a number of irregular verbs when this doesn't happen. We say *sold* instead of 'selled'. 'Solled' is not a word.

2 *Neither—nor* is a paired conjunction. This conjunction is used to connect two balanced clauses, phrases or words. It is a set format used for negatives.

3 This is a grammar question. If a person has their hand made into a fist then it must be closed. The word *closed* is unnecessary. No meaning is lost by omitting *closed*.

4 This is a grammar question. Plural subjects (teachers) need plural verbs. Singular subjects (nouns) need singular verbs. In this case *take* must be used because there is more than one teacher.

5 This is a grammar question. *He* is a personal pronoun. Pronouns are words that substitute for or replace nouns. *He* is a substitute for the proper noun *John*. Without pronouns we would have to keep repeating the noun.

6 This is a punctuation question. The full stops go after *up* and *something*. Jill has asked a question then made a statement. A full stop completes the first part of the text and the end of Jill's statement.

7 This is a grammar question. *Slowly* is an adverb indicating how the dog should walk. *Slow* is an adjective.

8 This is a grammar question. *On* is a preposition indicating a physical contact with a surface, e.g. *on a field*. In everyday speech certain prepositions regularly tend to go with certain verbs.

9 This is a grammar question. Plural subjects (players) need plural verbs. Singular subjects (nouns) need singular verbs. In this case *are* must be used because there are eight players. Don't be distracted by *team* as it simply qualifies the subject (eight players).

10 This is a punctuation/grammar question. *Players* is the first word in a new sentence following a full stop and so it takes a capital letter. The plural noun *players* is followed by the plural verb *wear*.

11 This is a punctuation question. *A* is an indefinite article. It is correct to say *A cloth strip* because it is not a specific piece of cloth. *An* is incorrect because the following word does not begin with a vowel sound.

12 This is a punctuation question. *Tag* is the last word in a statement and so is followed by a full stop and does not begin with a capital letter.

13 This is a grammar question. *Who* is a pronoun used when referring to people. *Which* is usually used when referring to objects. *What* is incorrect.

14 This is a punctuation question. This is an example of indirect or reported speech. The actual words spoken are not recorded. No speech marks are required.

15 This is a grammar question. Adverbs modify other words, expressing manner, place, time or degree. Most end with the suffix *ly* but not all (*later*).

16 This is a grammar/punctuation question. A command is a form of an order. Someone is told what to do. Commands end with full stops.

17 This is a grammar question. Plural subjects need plural verbs. *Red and green* are the names of <u>two</u> colours. In this case *are* must be used because there are two colours joined by *and*.

18 This is a punctuation question. Commas are used to separate items in a series. *And* is used to separate the last two items. No comma is required after *yellow*.

19 This is a punctuation question. Both *aren't* and *it's* are contractions. The apostrophe indicates that a letter has been omitted. *Aren't* is a contraction of *are not*. *It's* is a contraction of *it is*.

20 This is a grammar question. *Sheep* and *deer* can be both singular and plural.

21 This is a grammar question. The correct sentence is: *Tina had a head start in her race.* Adjectives are used to describe people, places or things. *Head* in this sentence describes the position Tina had at the start of the race.

22 This is a grammar question. *Smallest* is a comparative adjective. Comparative adjectives that end with 'est' are used to show a comparison between more than two objects (puppies). 'Er' is used for comparisons between two objects.

23 This is a punctuation question. The sentence indicates that there is only one baby. The possessive form is *baby's*. *Aren't* is a contraction of *are not*. The apostrophe indicates that a letter has been omitted.

24 This is a grammar question. The bottle has been smashed the *last time* the grass has been mown, which indicates the action took place some time before Natalie went for her ball.

25 This is a grammar question. *Into* is a preposition indicating an action that results in the eagle entering an environment that encloses or surrounds him: *into the valley*. In everyday speech certain prepositions regularly tend to go with certain verbs.

26 *Wednes<u>d</u>ay* has a silent *d*.

27 *Strawberry* is a compound word: *straw + berry*. *Berry* and *bury* are homonyms—words that sound the same but which have different meanings. *Berry* is a small fruit. *Bury* refers to digging.

28 *Blackboard* is a compound word: *black + board*. *Board* and 'bord' sound the same. Learn to recognise other 'oard' family words, e.g. *hoard, abroad, outboard*.

29 It is easy to omit the final letter in some 'ough' words. If you pronounce the word correctly you can hear the final *t* sound.

30 The letter combination 'au' has an 'or' sound. The letters 'aur' form a common ending for creatures of the dinosaur era, e.g. *brontosaurus, tyrannosaur*.

31 When *full* is used as a suffix it is spelt with a single *l*, e.g. *wasteful, careful, useful*.

32 One *lolly*, many *lollies*. Learn to recognise and remember other two-syllable 'lly' family words, e.g. *belly, jolly, rally*.

33 *Welcome* is an old compound word: *well + come*. There is no silent *b* on *come* and an *l* has been dropped from *well*.

34 *Lettuce* is a common food word. It is a word that must be remembered. Take care to pronounce the word carefully.

35 This word is not spelt as it sounds. It is a word that must be remembered.

36 *Postage* is *post* with the suffix 'age'. 'Age' is a common suffix. Learn to recognise and remember the family of 'age' words, e.g. *drainage, cartage, hostage*.

37 Think of *private* as two syllables: *pri–vate*. Take care to pronounce the word carefully. Learn to recognise and remember the family of 'ate' words, e.g. *locate, ornate, sedate*.

38 The syllable 'el' is a common word ending. It is important to be familiar with the correct spelling of words with similar endings, e.g. *bagel, barrel, chapel*.

39 *Postcode* is a compound word: *post + code*. The letter combinations 'ode' and 'oad' can represent the same sound, e.g. *road, rode*. Learn to recognise the 'ode' family of words, e.g. *node, abode, mode*.

40 *Flying* is *fly* with the suffix 'ing'. The *y* follows two consonants and is not dropped (or changed to an *i*). Examples of words with a similar spelling are *bullying, crying* and *drying*.

41 *Annually* is *annual* with the suffix 'ly'. The double *l* (ll) is required.

42 The letter combinations 'ea' and 'ee' can represent the same sound, e.g. *see, sea*. Learn to recognise the 'eeze' family of words, e.g. *freeze, sneeze, tweezers*.

43 *Alive* is the prefix *a* followed by *live*. The double *l* (ll) is <u>not</u> required. *A* is a common prefix, e.g. *amiss, awake, abide*.

44 Most double-syllable words that end with an *l* have a single *l*, e.g. *gravel, level, rebel*. *Locale* refers to a place where something happens and is incorrect.

45 Take care to pronounce the word carefully. Many words ending in 'ar' are adjectives. The suffix 'er' often refers to people in occupations or activities, e.g. *keeper, player, builder*.

46 *J* and *g* can make the same sound at the beginning of a word, e.g. *jug, gentle*. The letter *g* is used to spell two sounds as in *giraffe* and *gas*. For most common words you need to remember the correct spelling.

47 The letter combinations 'eat' and 'ete' can represent the same sound, e.g. *feet, feat*. Learn to recognise some of the words ending in 'ete', e.g. *delete, secrete, deplete*.

48 *Where* is an adverb referring to a place. *Were* is a verb and the past tense of *are*.

49 *Dangerous* is *danger* with the suffix 'ous'. It has three syllables: *dang–er–ous*. Take care to pronounce the word correctly.

50 *Until* is an old word: *un + till*. The final *l* has been dropped from *till*. You need to remember the correct spelling.

NUMERACY	**Pages 140–145**

1 C **2** 1224 **3** A and D **4** A **5** D **6** B **7** 69 **8** C
9 9 **10** 17 **11** 277 **12** C **13** D **14** B **15** C
16 B and C **17** C **18** D **19** C **20** B **21** C **22** B
23 B **24** 80 **25** C and E **26** 22 **27** 4.3 **28** D **29** C
30 B **31** D **32** 12 **33** A **34** 14 **35** A, B and C
36 32 **37** 0.35 m, 3095 mm, 320 cm, 3800 mm
38 A, B and D **39** 585 **40** 50 **41** 30 **42** 540

EXPLANATIONS

1
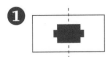

2 204×6

$$\begin{array}{r} 204 \\ \times\ \ \ 6 \\ \hline 1224 \end{array}$$

The answer is 1224.

3 $18 + 7 = 18 + 2 + 5$
$\qquad = 20 + 5$
$\qquad = 25$
$6 + 19 = 6 + 10 + 9$
$\qquad = 16 + 9$
$\qquad = 16 + 4 + 5$
$\qquad = 25$
The two pairs are 18 and 7, and, 6 and 19.

4 Counting the sections for each colour:
red: 3 times;   blue: 2 times;
green: 2 times;   yellow: 1 time
This means the colour with the smallest chance is yellow.

5

6 The youngest cousin is the person who was born most recently. The order from youngest is Jarryd (1993), Nicole (1992), Jessica (1990), and so on. The second youngest is Nicole.

7 The number line is in marked in 3s.
The missing number is 69.

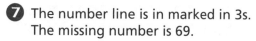

42 45 48 51 54 57 60 63 66 [?] 72 75 78 81

8 Add 25 minutes on to 5:45.
From 5:45 plus 15 minutes is 6:00 and
another 10 minutes is 6:10.
The correct time is 6:10.

9   ?7
    − 45
    ———
     52

Starting with the units, 7 − 5 = 2
Now, the tens: 'what number' − 4 = 5.
The missing number is 9, as 9 − 4 = 5
The answer is 9.

10 Difference = 35 − 18 = 17. The weight of the
block is 17 grams.

11 385 + 11 = 396
Missing number = 673 − 396
$$= 673 − 400 + 4$$
$$= 273 + 4$$
$$= 277$$

12 One whole is $\frac{5}{5}$.

This means 5 hearts = 1 whole.

13 If the height of a stack of 3 cubes is 12 cm
then 1 cube is 4 cm high. As 5 × 4 = 20, the
stack of cubes will be 20 cm high.

14 Number of bags = 64 ÷ 5 = 12 with a
remainder of 4. Sam can fill a maximum of
12 bags (and then she can eat the rest
herself).

15 The distance from the School to the Chemist
is a little further than the distance from the
Post Office to the Hospital. This means the
distance will be a little more than 200 metres.
Considering the choices, the best estimate is
250 metres.

16 Total goals = 3 + 5 + 1 + 1 + 7 + 3 + 6 = 26.
Also, in Games 2, 5 and 6 there were at least
4 goals scored.

17 Simon's height is half-way between 80 cm
and 140 cm. We need to find the average of
80 and 140:

$$\text{Average} = \frac{80 + 140}{2}$$
$$= \frac{220}{2}$$
$$= 110$$

This means Simon is 110 cm high.

18 In 6M, 5 symbols = 10 students.
In 5T, $1\frac{1}{2}$ symbols = 3 students
This means 7 more students in 6M had
mobile phones than in 5T.

19 Connor's train leaves at 3:43.
The time 20 minutes before
3:43 is 3:23 because
43 − 20 = 23.
Connor arrived at the railway
station at 3:23.

20 6 out of the 24 squares are shaded.

This can be written as a fraction: $\frac{6}{24} = \frac{1}{4}$

[Remember, $\frac{6}{24} = \frac{6 \times 1}{6 \times 4} = \frac{\cancel{6} \times 1}{\cancel{6} \times 4} = \frac{1}{4}$]

21 Add the numbers in the column of Australia:
Total = 12 + 18
$$= 12 + 8 + 10$$
$$= 20 + 10$$
$$= 30$$
30 parents were born in Australia.

22 The mass in the bowl is 350 g,
and 1 kg = 1000 g
Mass remaining = 1000 − 350
$$= 650$$

$$\begin{array}{r} 1\,{}^9\cancel{0}\,{}^1 0\ 0 \\ -\ \ 3\ 5\ 0 \\ \hline 6\ 5\ 0 \end{array}$$

650 grams remain in the packet.

23 The answer to the left side of the equal sign
is 30. The missing number × 6 is 30. This
means the missing number is 5.

24 There are 100 cm in 1 metre. As 100 ÷ 5 = 20,
Fiona can cut 20 pieces of string for every
metre cut from the ball. As there is 4 metres
on the ball she can cut 20 × 4 = 80 pieces in
total.

25 4.75 = 4 wholes + 7 tenths + 5 hundredths
   = 4 + 0.7 + 0.05
4.75 = 4.70 + 0.05
This means the two answers are 4 + 0.7 + 0.05
and 4.7 + 0.05.

26 Days in 4 weeks = 7 × 4 = 28. As Henry is 28
days old and Gus is 6 days old the difference
is 22 days.

27 Distance from Pines Picnic Area to Moirs
Lookout is 0.8 km.
Total distance = 3.5 + 0.8 = 4.3.
Chris walked 4.3 km.

28 The original large square is divided into 16
very small squares. By counting, there are 5
very small squares shaded. This means
five-sixteenths of the large square is shaded.

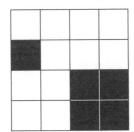

29 Discs are placed on multiples of 3.
The 16th disc will be placed on 16 × 3.

$$\begin{array}{r} 16 \\ \times_1 3 \\ \hline 48 \end{array}$$

The 16th disc is placed on 48.

30 On the map, Jamison to Broughton is 4 units.
If 4 units = 20 km, then 1 unit = 5 km.
As 30 km = 6 units, we now look on the map
for 2 towns that are 6 units apart.
Werona and Petrel are 6 units apart, and so
are 30 km apart.

31 The section for green will be
3 times the size of blue; and,
the section for red will be
twice the size of blue.

32 The 8 cm-side of the small box is placed
along the 8 cm-side of the large box.
As 20 ÷ 5 = 4 then 4 boxes can fit along the
bottom of the large box.
As 18 ÷ 6 = 3 then 3 boxes can be placed up
the side of the large box.
Now 4 × 3 = 12 means 12 small boxes can fit
in the large box.

33 The fold line is like the line of
reflection of the letter R.
The correct square is:

34 Use crosses to represent the other people in
the line.
x x x x M x x x x x x x J x x
This means there are 14 people in the line.

35 The correct answer can be found by
subtracting (used in A and B) and adding
(used in C).

36 Price reduction = $\frac{1}{3} \div 48$
   = 48 ÷ 3
   = 16
New price = 48 − 16
   = 32
Grace will pay $32.

37 Firstly, 320 cm = 3.2 m, 3095 mm = 3.095 m,
3800 mm = 3.8 m and 0.35 m. This means
the order is 0.35 m, 3095 mm, 320 cm,
3800 mm.

38 Probability ranges from 0 to 1. This means
possible probabilities are $\frac{1}{3}$, 0.25 and $\frac{3}{8}$.

39 As 10% is one-tenth we can find one-tenth
of $650 by dividing by 10. This gives $65.
The sale price is $650 minus $65 which is
$585.

40 You can start with the answer 45 and work
backwards using opposite operations. This
means the missing number is 45 + 16 − 11
which is 50.

41 1 white disc = 2 black discs. This means we can say 4 black discs = 24 so 1 black disc = 6. This means 1 white disc = 12.

Value of 2 white and 1 black
= 12 × 2 + 6 = 30

42

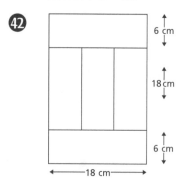

A small rectangle has a length equalling 3 times its width, which means a length of 18 cm. The area of each small rectangle is 18 × 6 = 108 square centimetres. As there are 5 rectangles and 108 × 5 = 540, the area of the large rectangle is 540 square centimetres.

SPELLING WORDS FOR REAL TESTS

To the teacher or parent

First read and say the word slowly and clearly. Then read the sentence with the word in it. Then repeat the word again.

Give the student time to write their answer. If the student is not sure, then ask them to guess. It is okay to skip a word if it is not known.

Spelling words for Real Test Week 1

Word	Example
1. addresses	We wrote addresses next to all the names.
2. fabric	Your shirt is made from a soft fabric.
3. brushes	My father brushes his shoes each morning.
4. escaping	After escaping from the pen the pig crossed the road.
5. carpenter	The carpenter is working in the kitchen.
6. shoulder	David hurt his shoulder when he was tackled.

Spelling words for Real Test Week 2

Word	Example
1. discover	What did you discover in your bag?
2. allowed	You are not allowed to walk on the grass!
3. wonder	I sometimes wonder why I go to training.
4. elastic	Year 3 students were playing with elastic bands.
5. assembly	The school assembly was shorter today.
6. garage	Dad parked his car in the neighbour's garage.

Spelling words for Real Test Week 3

Word	Example
1. attach	Can you attach that new tag to your bag?
2. conflict	There was some sort of conflict on the sports oval.
3. hospital	Andy spent a week in hospital after the accident.
4. various	There were various reasons for staying at home.
5. drowsy	Mary felt drowsy after the long hike.
6. vowel	The first letter of the alphabet is a vowel.

Spelling words for Real Test Week 4

Word	Example
1. achieve	Did you achieve the top score for maths?
2. knapsack	A solid knapsack is essential for camping.
3. blanket	Emma was huddled under a warm blanket.
4. single	Not a single day passes without a complaint.
5. gloated	Did you see how Pat gloated after winning the prize!
6. whirlpool	The kayak was caught in a whirlpool near the rapids.

To the teacher or parent

First read and say the word slowly and clearly. Then read the sentence with the word in it. Then repeat the word again.

Give the student time to write their answer. If the student is not sure, then ask them to guess. It is okay to skip a word if it is not known.

Spelling words for Sample Test 1

Word		Example
26.	heard	We heard the bell when we were a block from school.
27.	unable	Jessie was unable to find her ticket.
28.	butcher	The butcher has no steak after five o'clock.
29.	prompt	A prompt answer meant Simon won the quiz.
30.	valiant	Our team made a valiant effort but Cowra was too strong!
31.	athletics	What is the world's greatest athletics contest?
32.	envelope	Put the card in the envelope then post it.
33.	saddened	I am saddened by your bad luck.
34.	quarter	The cook put a quarter of a chilli in the curry!
35.	pencil	You'll need a sharp pencil for the test.
36.	business	Dad has a business suit for office work.
37.	plain	Under his coat Dad wears a plain shirt.
38.	trousers	White trousers are not very sensible for gardening!
39.	casual	We can wear casual shoes to school on dress-up days.
40.	near	Near the playground was a walking track.

Spelling words for Sample Test 2

Word		Example
26.	Wednesday	On Wednesday we have sport and music.
27.	strawberry	I wanted a strawberry with my cream tart.
28.	blackboard	The blackboard was removed from the classroom.
29.	thought	Dad thought about the puzzle then shook his head.
30.	dinosaurs	The project on dinosaurs is due next week!
31.	hopeful	The team was hopeful of a win.
32.	lollies	Did you share the lollies with your sister?
33.	welcome	The coach said that new players were welcome.
34.	lettuce	Dad put too much lettuce in the mixed salad!
35.	mosquito	It's not yet summer and I can hear a mosquito near my ear!
36.	postage	Postage on the parcel was more than the present cost.
37.	private	The bank will keep our personal details private.
38.	label	I couldn't read the label on the parcel. It had faded.
39.	postcode	Add your postcode to your return address.
40.	flying	I love flying through the air in an aeroplane.

Notes

Notes